#SAD!

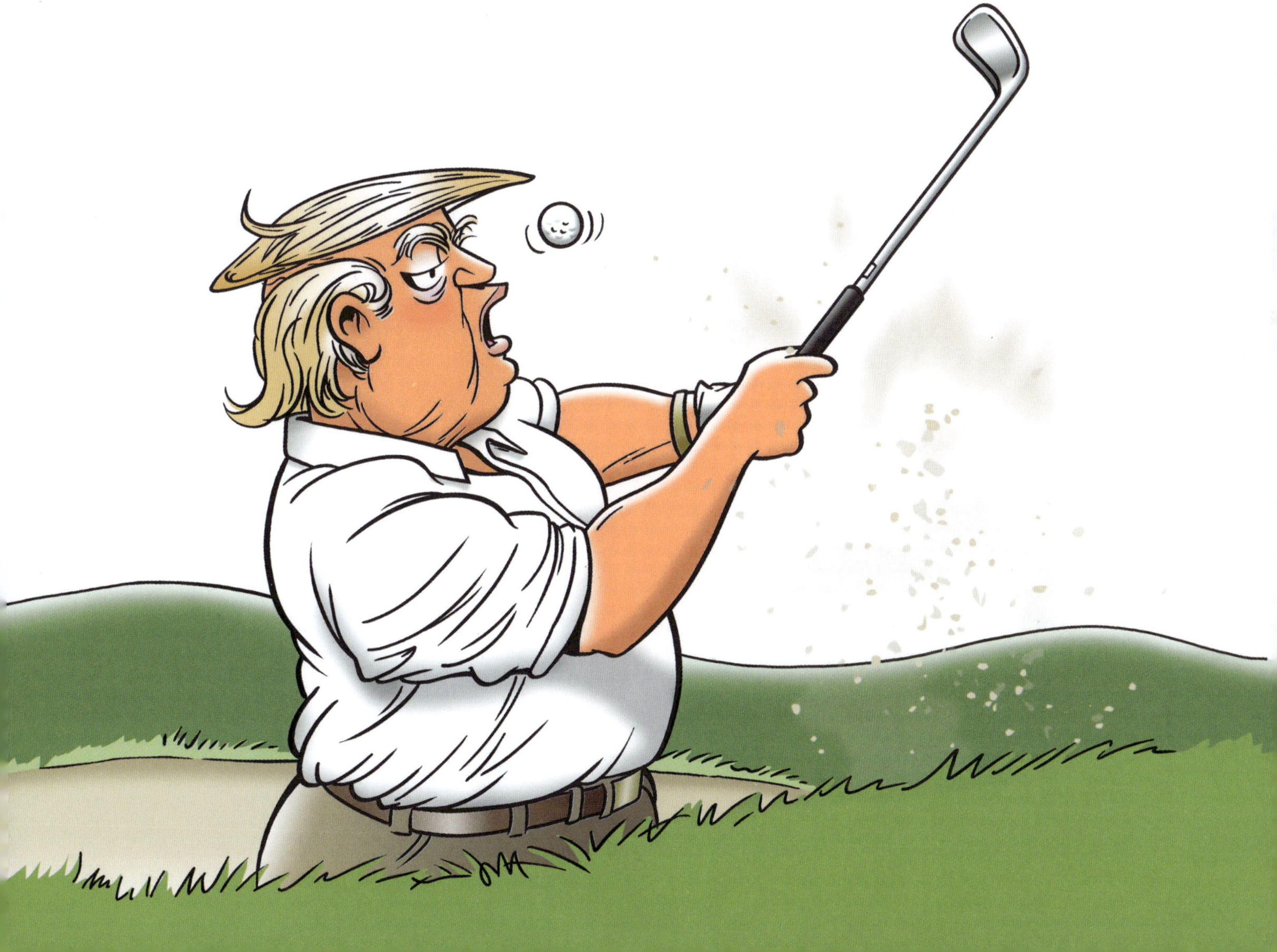

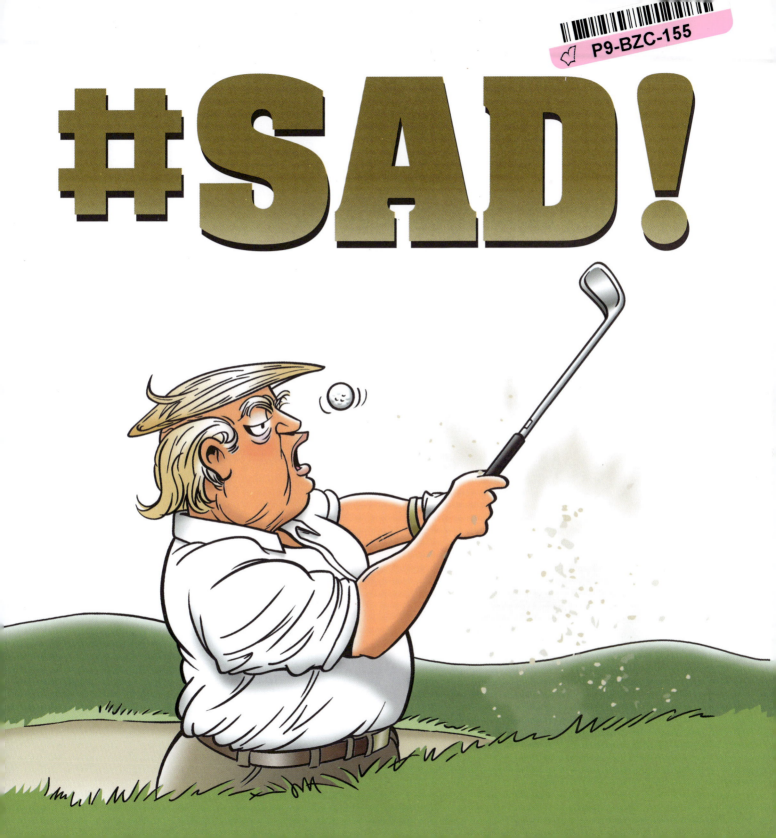

Recent Collections

Virtual Doonesbury
Planet Doonesbury
Buck Wild Doonesbury
Duke 2000: Whatever It Takes
The Revolt of the English Majors
Peace Out, Dawg!
Got War?
Talk to the Hand
Heckuva Job, Bushie!
Welcome to the Nerd Farm!
Tee Time in Berzerkistan
Red Rascal's War
Squared Away
The Weed Whisperer
Yuge!: 30 Years of Doonesbury on Trump

Anthologies

The Doonesbury Chronicles
Doonesbury's Greatest Hits
The People's Doonesbury
Doonesbury Dossier: The Reagan Years
Doonesbury Deluxe: Selected Glances Askance
Recycled Doonesbury: Second Thoughts on a Gilded Age
The Portable Doonesbury
The Bundled Doonesbury
40: A Doonesbury Retrospective

Special Collections

Action Figure!: The Life and Times of Doonesbury's Uncle Duke
Dude: The Big Book of Zonker
Flashbacks: Twenty-Five Years of Doonesbury
The Sandbox: Dispatches from Troops in Iraq and Afghanistan
The War in Quotes
"My Shorts R Bunching. Thoughts?": The Tweets of Roland Hedley

Wounded Warrior Series

The Long Road Home: One Step at a Time
The War Within: One More Step at a Time
Signature Wound: Rocking TBI
Mel's Story: Surviving Military Sexual Assault

~~Mar 2020~~

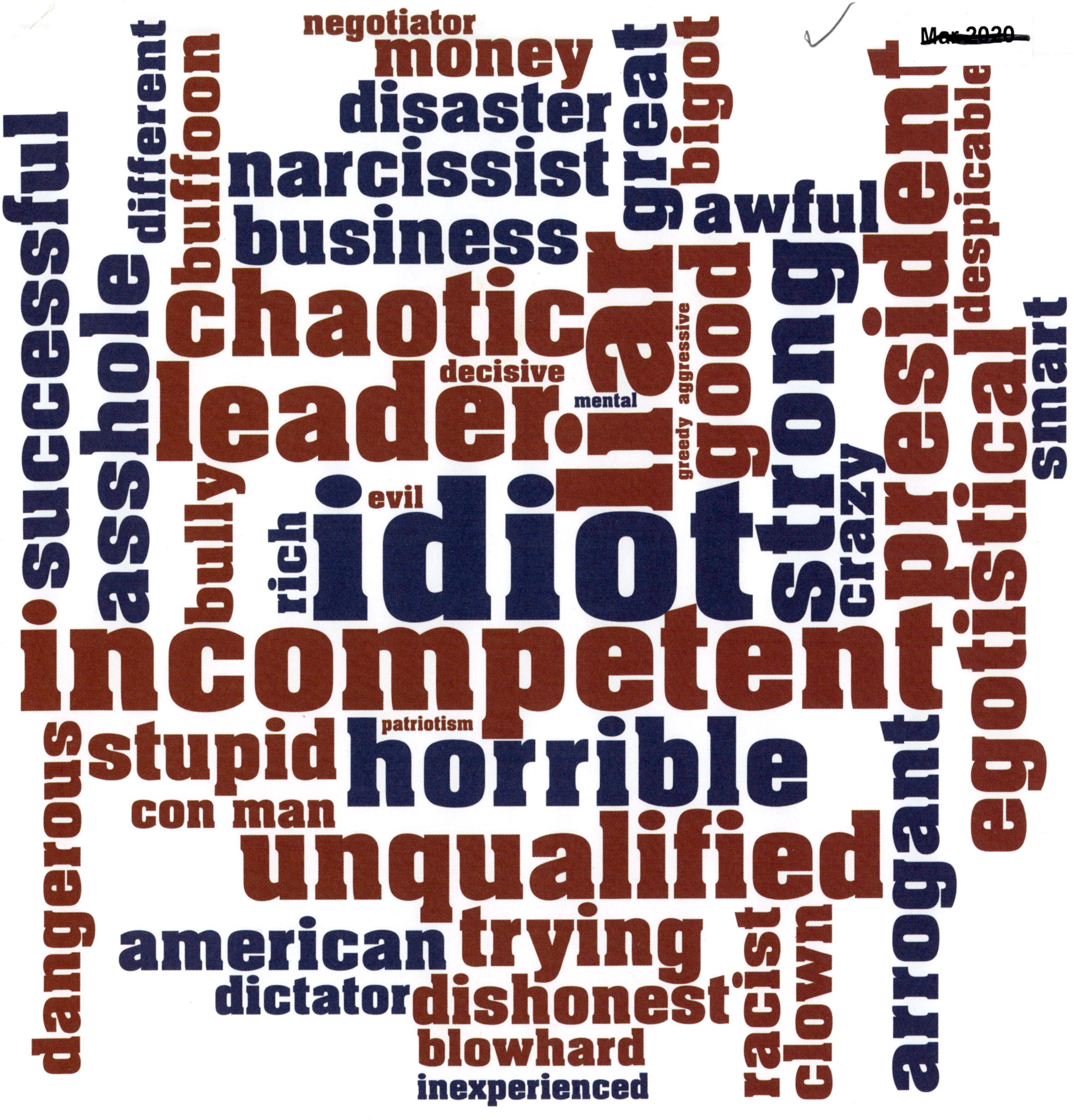
negotiator
money
disaster
narcissist
business
awful
different
buffoon
great
bigot
successful
asshole
chaotic
liar
good
strong
president
despicable
egotistical
smart
decisive
mental
aggressive
greedy
leader
evil
bully
rich
idiot
crazy
incompetent
patriotism
dangerous
stupid
horrible
arrogant
con man
unqualified
american
trying
racist
clown
dictator
dishonest
blowhard
inexperienced

Poll (U.S.): "What is the one word you would use to describe President Trump?"

#SAD!

DOONESBURY IN THE TIME OF TRUMP

A DOONESBURY BOOK
by G. B. TRUDEAU

Andrews McMeel
PUBLISHING®

DOONESBURY is distributed internationally by Andrews McMeel Syndication.

#SAD!: Doonesbury in the Time of Trump copyright © 2018 by G.B. Trudeau.

Andrews McMeel Publishing
a division of Andrews McMeel Universal
1130 Walnut Street, Kansas City, Missouri 64106

www.andrewsmcmeel.com

18 19 20 21 22 SDB 10 9 8 7 6 5 4 3 2 1

ISBN: 978-1-4494-8997-7

Library of Congress Control Number: 2018930850

DOONESBURY may be viewed on the Internet at
www.doonesbury.com and www.GoComics.com.

ATTENTION: SCHOOLS AND BUSINESSES

Andrews McMeel books are available at quantity discounts with bulk purchase for educational, business,
or sales promotional use. For information, please e-mail the Andrews McMeel Publishing
Special Sales Department: specialsales@amuniversal.com.

PREFACE

"I walk, I this, I that." —*Donald Trump*

A friend of mine, alarmed by the surfeit of Trump-inspired satire, has written to inquire: With the political landscape awash in anti-administration snark, is a single mind being changed? I write back to disillusion him: That's not the goal. It never has been.

If satire has a mission statement, it's surely a variant of humorist Finley Dunne's famous prescription for advocacy journalism: to afflict the comfortable and comfort the afflicted. On this first point, it's well known how sensitive the president is to ridicule; for evidence, consult the back of this book or any of the dozens of toxic Trump tweets about "third-rate" comedians or impressionists. And it's now accepted wisdom that the humiliation he suffered at the hands of Obama at a Washington dinner may have been the defining moment when his presidential ambitions truly crystallized. So let's check that box: Mission accomplished. Satire definitely gets under his skin.

As to providing a salve for the afflicted, the nation's wise guys must be doing something right. Late-night comedy, with its relentless focus on all things Trump, has been soaring in the ratings. Countless monologues, sketches, and cartoons are built around his daily bumblings and petty cruelties. If the president is determined to fill our every waking moment with revulsion and outrage, our solace is to see it all mercilessly mocked in a kind of therapeutic reset before bedtime.

But no, satire rarely changes minds. That's purely aspirational—me in a wishful mood. Indeed, there is some evidence that the current carnival of scorn may only harden the views of Trump's followers, ever poised to feel patronized by a smug cultural elite. But just because two-fifths of the country are still in the thrall of a humungous con "like no one's ever seen before," doesn't mean that the rest of us—appalled, disenfranchised, writhing in embarrassment for our country—should forgo the comfort of laughter. At this benighted moment, it's all we have.

Garry Trudeau
April 13, 2018

"That was some weird shit."

—George W. Bush, on Trump's inaugural speech

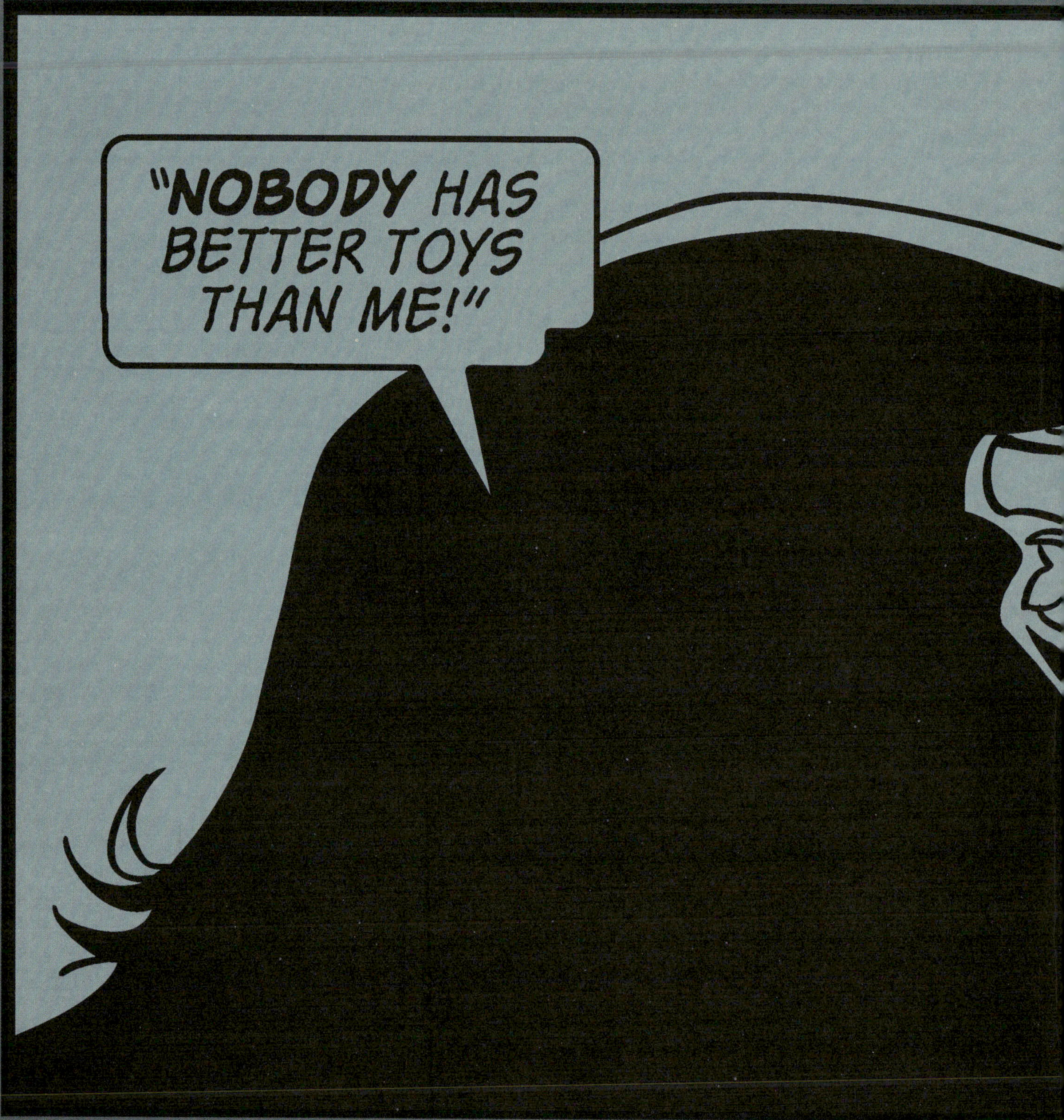
"NOBODY HAS BETTER TOYS THAN ME!"

PART I

The Gathering Shitstorm

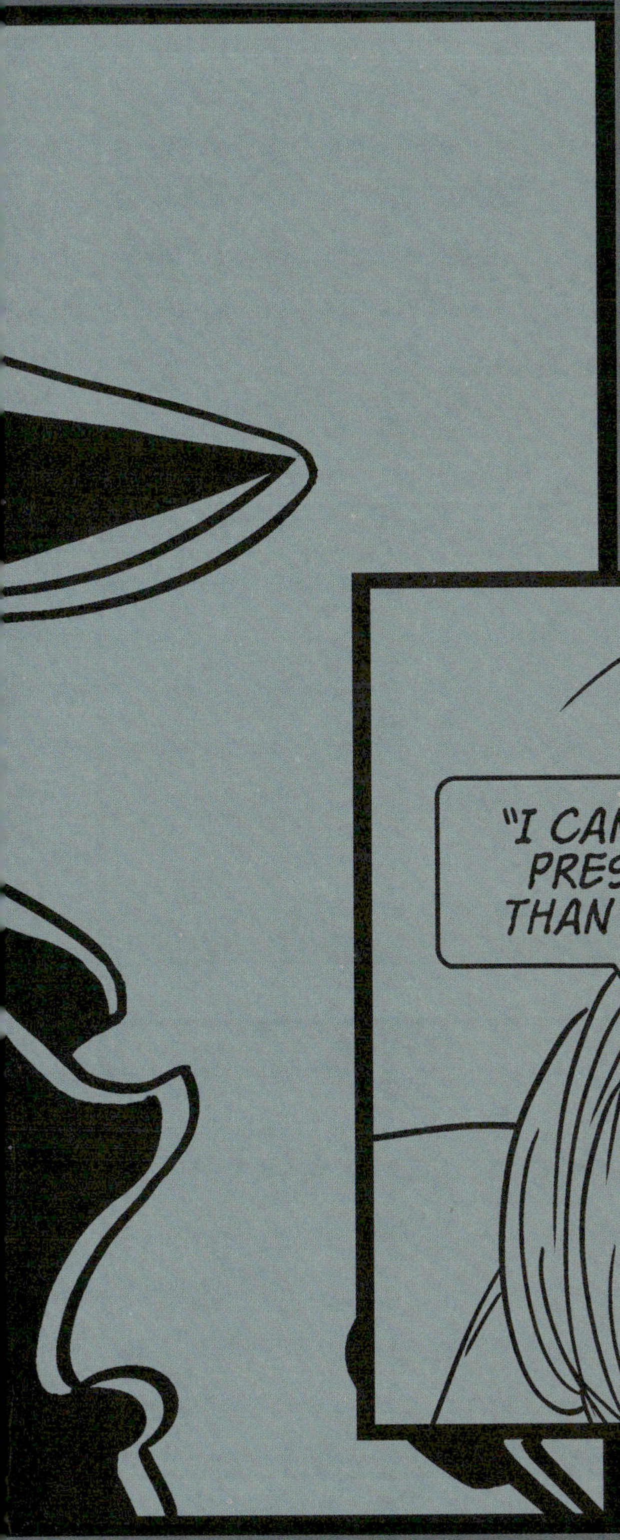

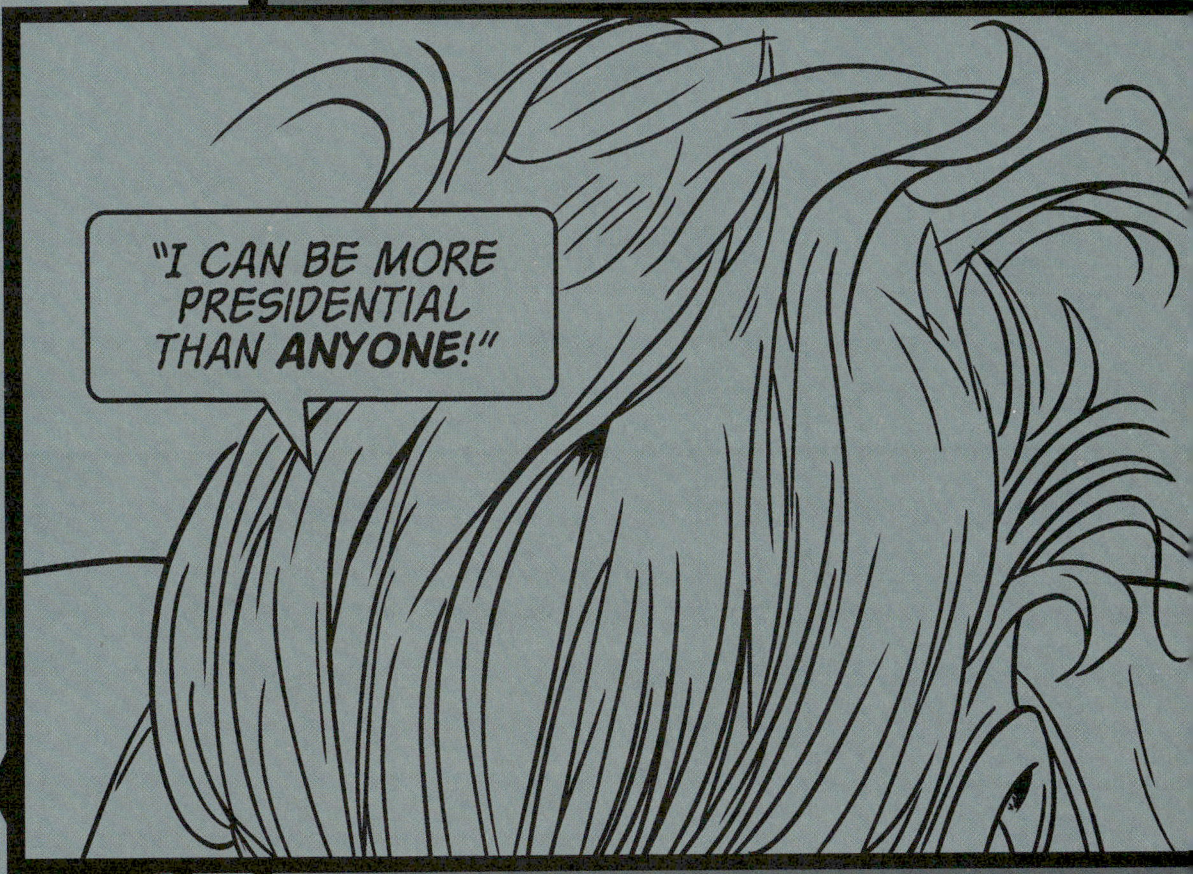
"I CAN BE MORE PRESIDENTIAL THAN ANYONE!"

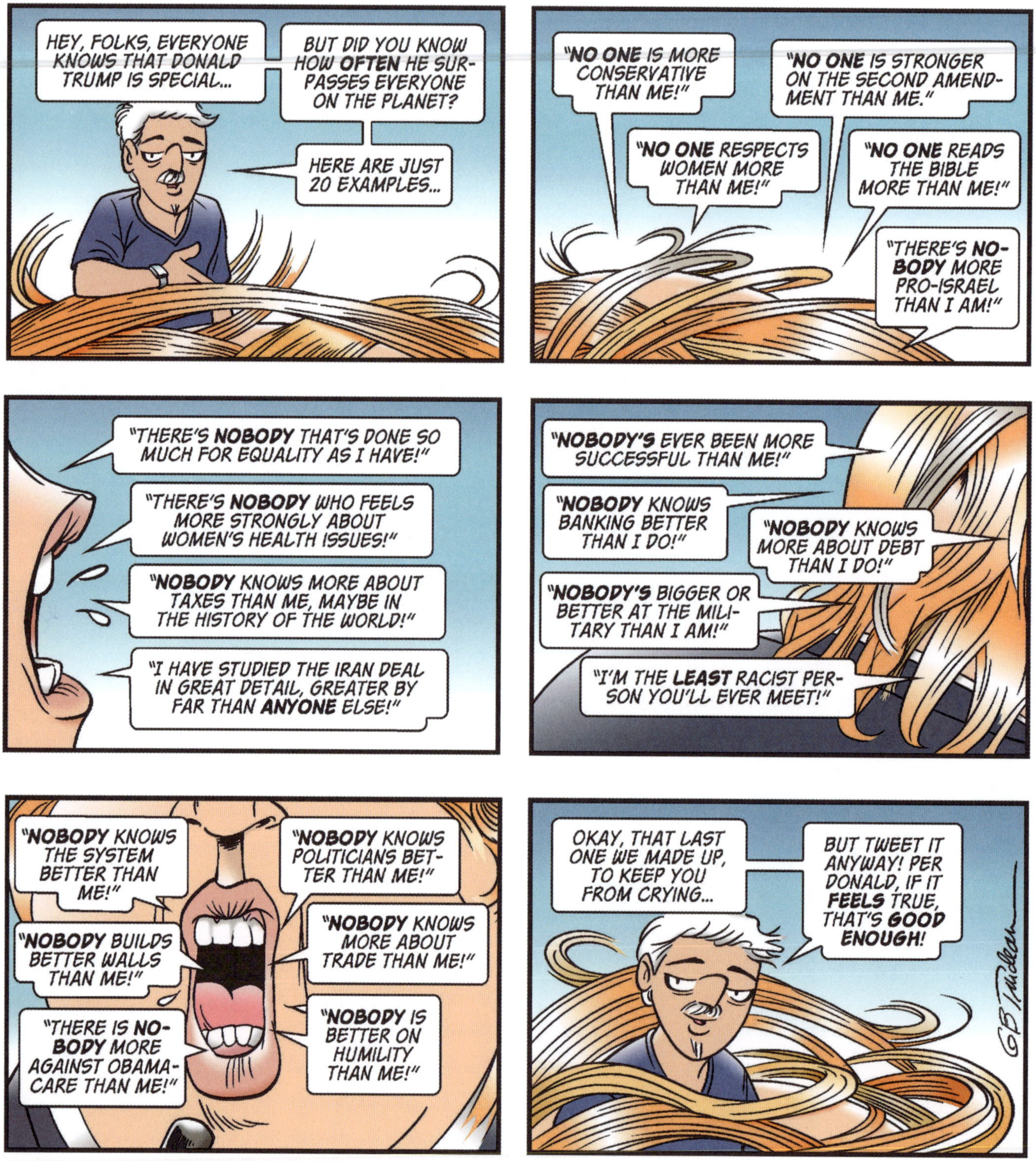
HEY, FOLKS, EVERYONE KNOWS THAT DONALD TRUMP IS SPECIAL...
BUT DID YOU KNOW HOW OFTEN HE SURPASSES EVERYONE ON THE PLANET?
HERE ARE JUST 20 EXAMPLES...
"NO ONE IS MORE CONSERVATIVE THAN ME!"
"NO ONE IS STRONGER ON THE SECOND AMENDMENT THAN ME."
"NO ONE RESPECTS WOMEN MORE THAN ME!"
"NO ONE READS THE BIBLE MORE THAN ME!"
"THERE'S NOBODY MORE PRO-ISRAEL THAN I AM!"
"THERE'S NOBODY THAT'S DONE SO MUCH FOR EQUALITY AS I HAVE!"
"THERE'S NOBODY WHO FEELS MORE STRONGLY ABOUT WOMEN'S HEALTH ISSUES!"
"NOBODY KNOWS MORE ABOUT TAXES THAN ME, MAYBE IN THE HISTORY OF THE WORLD!"
"I HAVE STUDIED THE IRAN DEAL IN GREAT DETAIL, GREATER BY FAR THAN ANYONE ELSE!"
"NOBODY'S EVER BEEN MORE SUCCESSFUL THAN ME!"
"NOBODY KNOWS BANKING BETTER THAN I DO!"
"NOBODY KNOWS MORE ABOUT DEBT THAN I DO!"
"NOBODY'S BIGGER OR BETTER AT THE MILITARY THAN I AM!"
"I'M THE LEAST RACIST PERSON YOU'LL EVER MEET!"
"NOBODY KNOWS THE SYSTEM BETTER THAN ME!"
"NOBODY KNOWS POLITICIANS BETTER THAN ME!"
"NOBODY BUILDS BETTER WALLS THAN ME!"
"NOBODY KNOWS MORE ABOUT TRADE THAN ME!"
"THERE IS NOBODY MORE AGAINST OBAMACARE THAN ME!"
"NOBODY IS BETTER ON HUMILITY THAN ME!"
OKAY, THAT LAST ONE WE MADE UP, TO KEEP YOU FROM CRYING...
BUT TWEET IT ANYWAY! PER DONALD, IF IT FEELS TRUE, THAT'S GOOD ENOUGH!

June 19, 2016

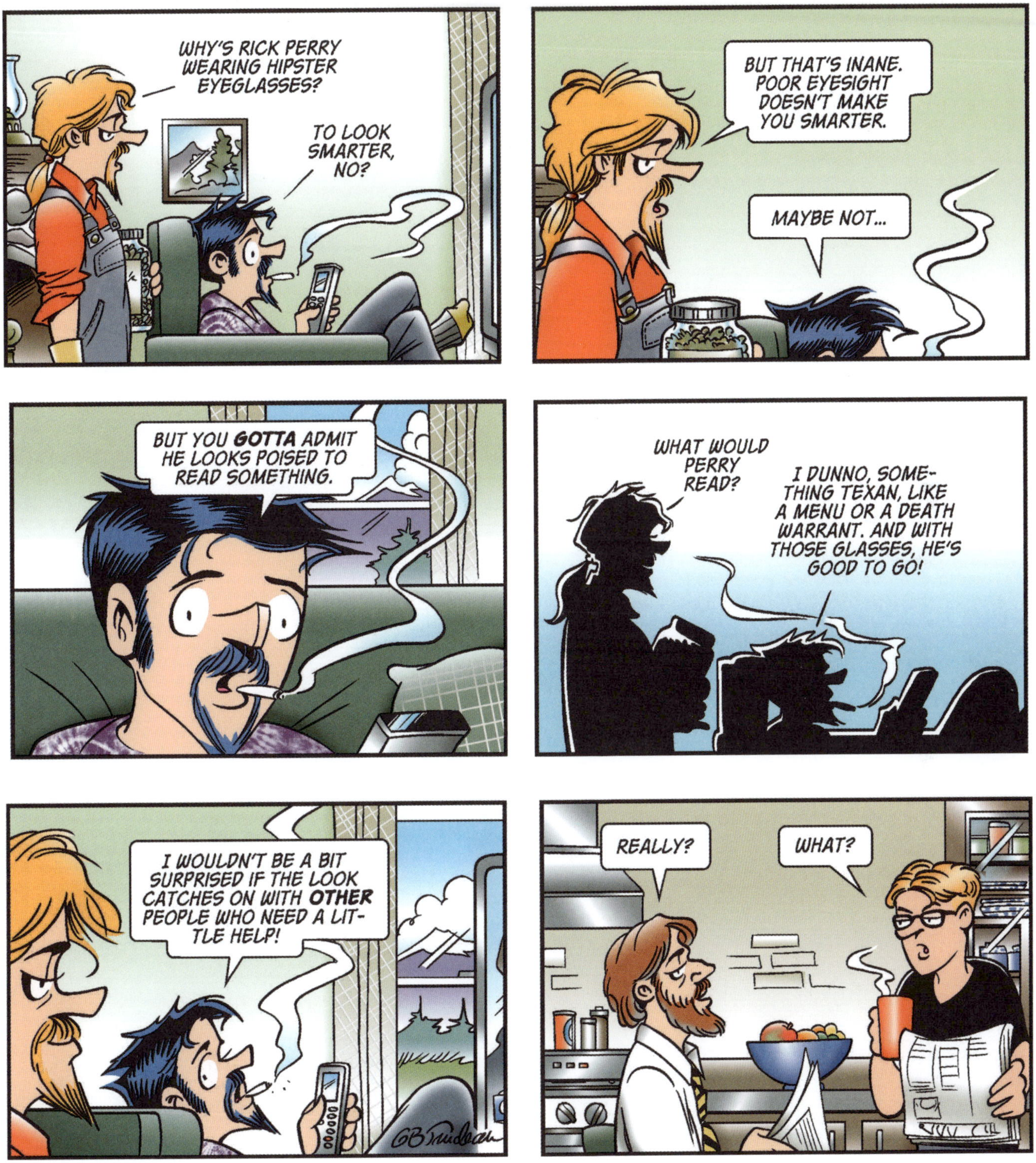
WHY'S RICK PERRY WEARING HIPSTER EYEGLASSES?
TO LOOK SMARTER, NO?
BUT THAT'S INANE. POOR EYESIGHT DOESN'T MAKE YOU SMARTER.
MAYBE NOT...
BUT YOU GOTTA ADMIT HE LOOKS POISED TO READ SOMETHING.
WHAT WOULD PERRY READ?
I DUNNO, SOME-THING TEXAN, LIKE A MENU OR A DEATH WARRANT. AND WITH THOSE GLASSES, HE'S GOOD TO GO!
I WOULDN'T BE A BIT SURPRISED IF THE LOOK CATCHES ON WITH OTHER PEOPLE WHO NEED A LIT-TLE HELP!
GB Trudeau
REALLY?
WHAT?

July 12, 2015

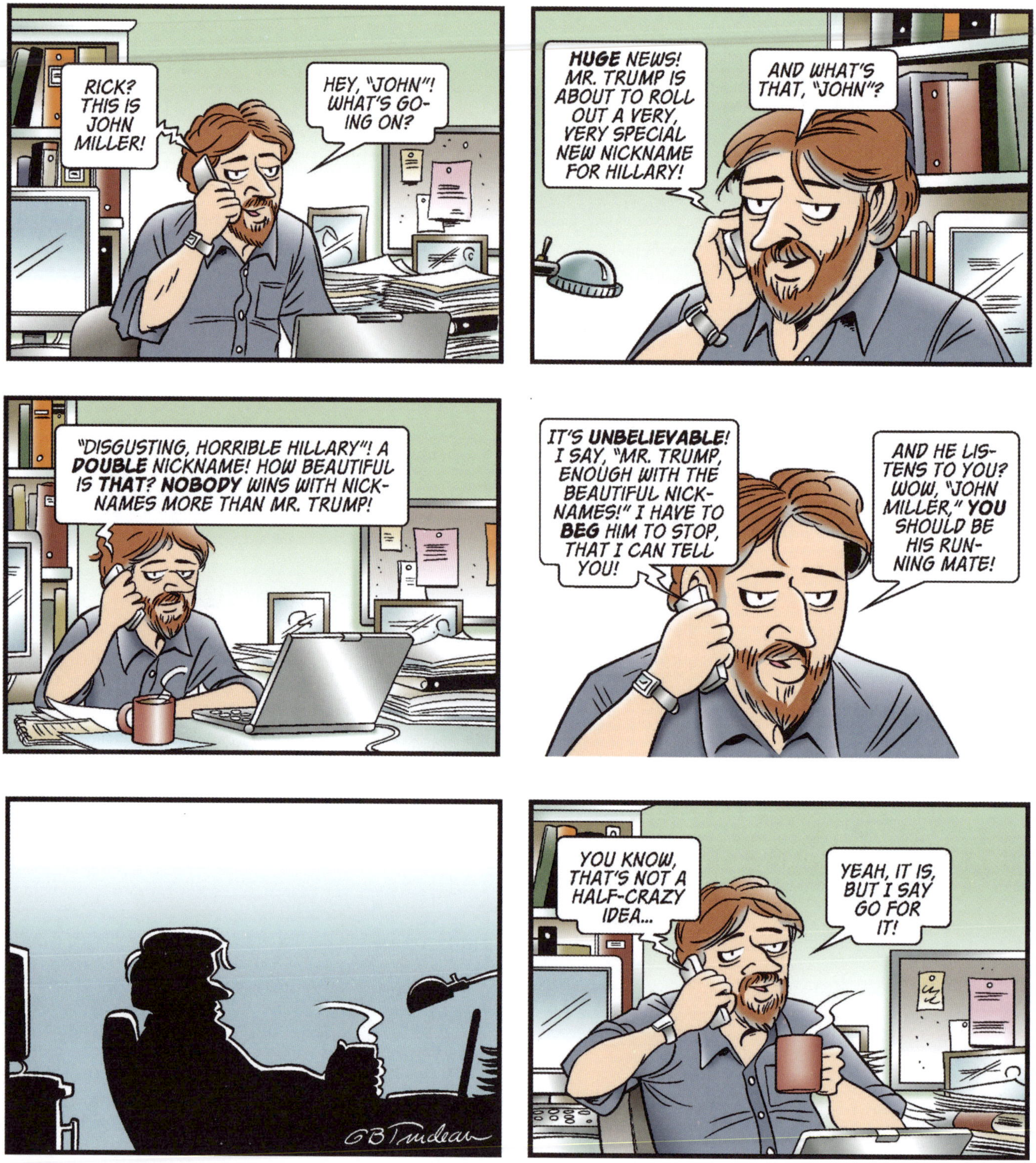
RICK? THIS IS JOHN MILLER!
HEY, "JOHN"! WHAT'S GO-ING ON?
HUGE NEWS! MR. TRUMP IS ABOUT TO ROLL OUT A VERY, VERY SPECIAL NEW NICKNAME FOR HILLARY!
AND WHAT'S THAT, "JOHN"?
"DISGUSTING, HORRIBLE HILLARY"! A DOUBLE NICKNAME! HOW BEAUTIFUL IS THAT? NOBODY WINS WITH NICK-NAMES MORE THAN MR. TRUMP!
IT'S UNBELIEVABLE! I SAY, "MR. TRUMP, ENOUGH WITH THE BEAUTIFUL NICK-NAMES!" I HAVE TO BEG HIM TO STOP, THAT I CAN TELL YOU!
AND HE LIS-TENS TO YOU? WOW, "JOHN MILLER," YOU SHOULD BE HIS RUN-NING MATE!
GBTrudeau
YOU KNOW, THAT'S NOT A HALF-CRAZY IDEA...
YEAH, IT IS, BUT I SAY GO FOR IT!

June 26, 2016

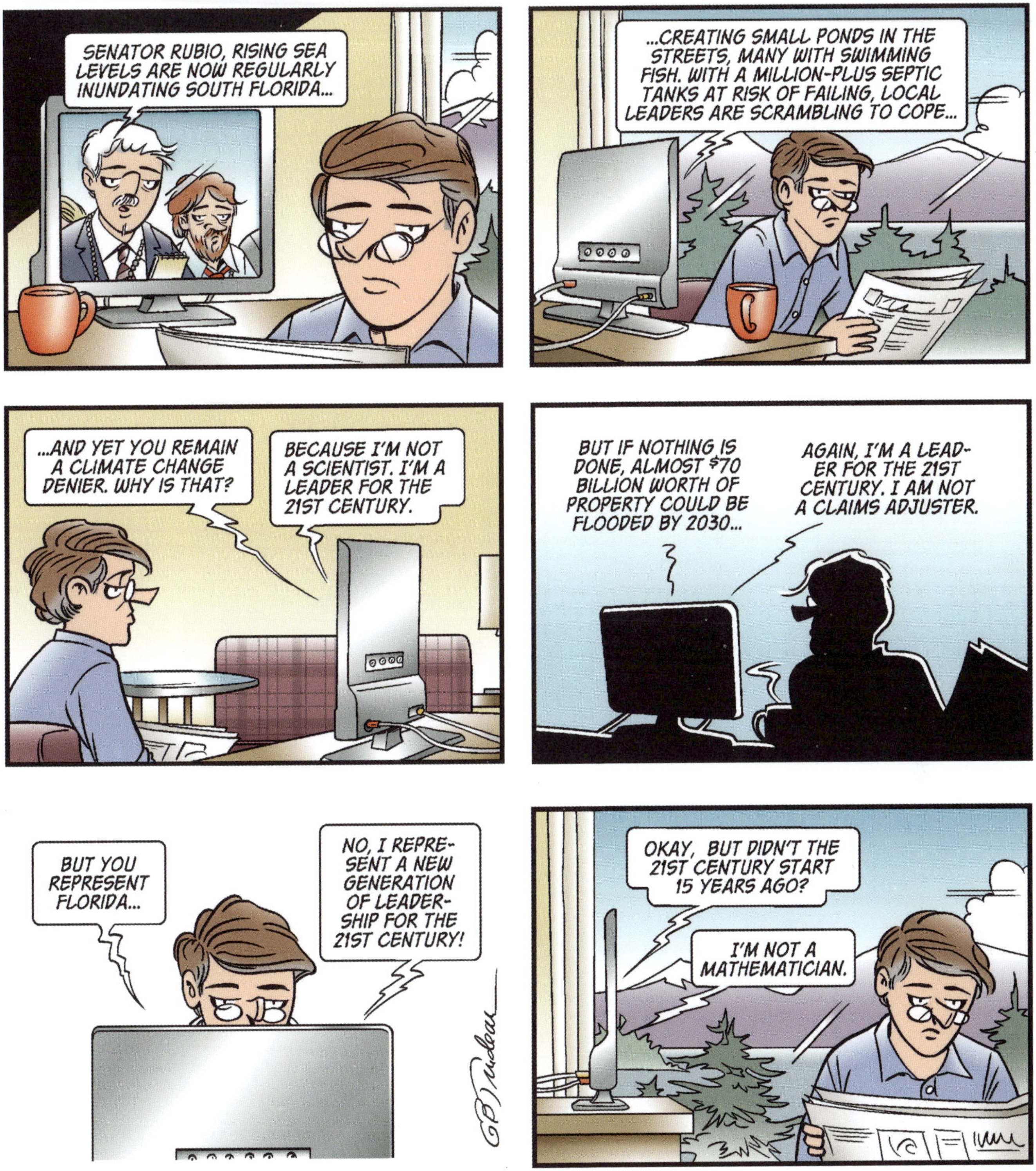
SENATOR RUBIO, RISING SEA LEVELS ARE NOW REGULARLY INUNDATING SOUTH FLORIDA...
...CREATING SMALL PONDS IN THE STREETS, MANY WITH SWIMMING FISH. WITH A MILLION-PLUS SEPTIC TANKS AT RISK OF FAILING, LOCAL LEADERS ARE SCRAMBLING TO COPE...
...AND YET YOU REMAIN A CLIMATE CHANGE DENIER. WHY IS THAT?
BECAUSE I'M NOT A SCIENTIST. I'M A LEADER FOR THE 21ST CENTURY.
BUT IF NOTHING IS DONE, ALMOST $70 BILLION WORTH OF PROPERTY COULD BE FLOODED BY 2030...
AGAIN, I'M A LEADER FOR THE 21ST CENTURY. I AM NOT A CLAIMS ADJUSTER.
BUT YOU REPRESENT FLORIDA...
NO, I REPRESENT A NEW GENERATION OF LEADERSHIP FOR THE 21ST CENTURY!
OKAY, BUT DIDN'T THE 21ST CENTURY START 15 YEARS AGO?
I'M NOT A MATHEMATICIAN.
GBTrudeau

March 27, 2016

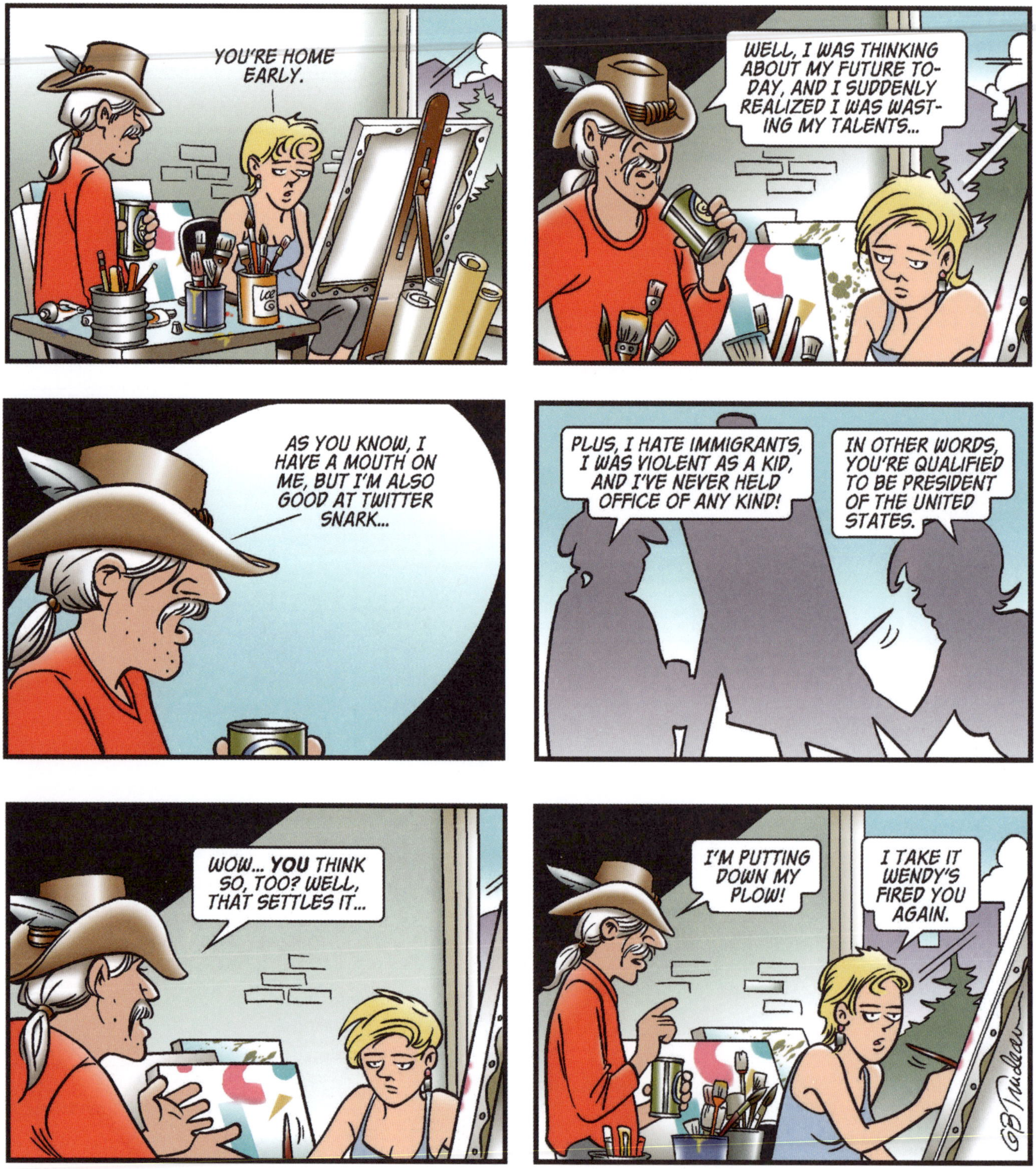
YOU'RE HOME EARLY.
WELL, I WAS THINKING ABOUT MY FUTURE TO-DAY, AND I SUDDENLY REALIZED I WAS WASTING MY TALENTS...
AS YOU KNOW, I HAVE A MOUTH ON ME, BUT I'M ALSO GOOD AT TWITTER SNARK...
PLUS, I HATE IMMIGRANTS, I WAS VIOLENT AS A KID, AND I'VE NEVER HELD OFFICE OF ANY KIND!
IN OTHER WORDS, YOU'RE QUALIFIED TO BE PRESIDENT OF THE UNITED STATES.
WOW... **YOU** THINK SO, TOO? WELL, THAT SETTLES IT...
I'M PUTTING DOWN MY PLOW!
I TAKE IT WENDY'S FIRED YOU AGAIN.
GBTrudeau

December 13, 2015

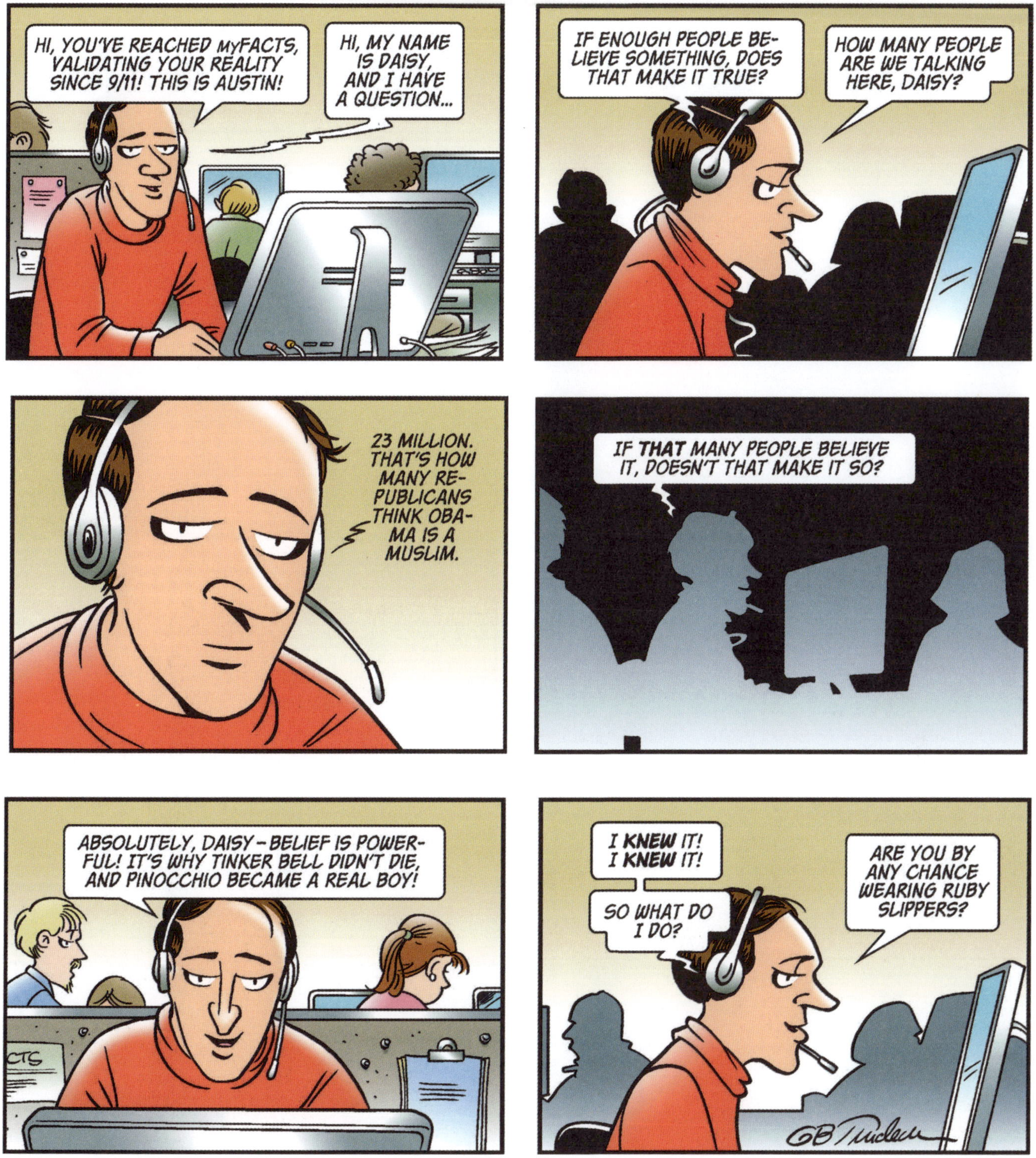
HI, YOU'VE REACHED MyFACTS, VALIDATING YOUR REALITY SINCE 9/11! THIS IS AUSTIN!
HI, MY NAME IS DAISY, AND I HAVE A QUESTION...
IF ENOUGH PEOPLE BELIEVE SOMETHING, DOES THAT MAKE IT TRUE?
HOW MANY PEOPLE ARE WE TALKING HERE, DAISY?
23 MILLION. THAT'S HOW MANY REPUBLICANS THINK OBAMA IS A MUSLIM.
IF THAT MANY PEOPLE BELIEVE IT, DOESN'T THAT MAKE IT SO?
ABSOLUTELY, DAISY – BELIEF IS POWERFUL! IT'S WHY TINKER BELL DIDN'T DIE, AND PINOCCHIO BECAME A REAL BOY!
I KNEW IT! I KNEW IT!
SO WHAT DO I DO?
ARE YOU BY ANY CHANCE WEARING RUBY SLIPPERS?
GB Trudeau

November 15, 2015

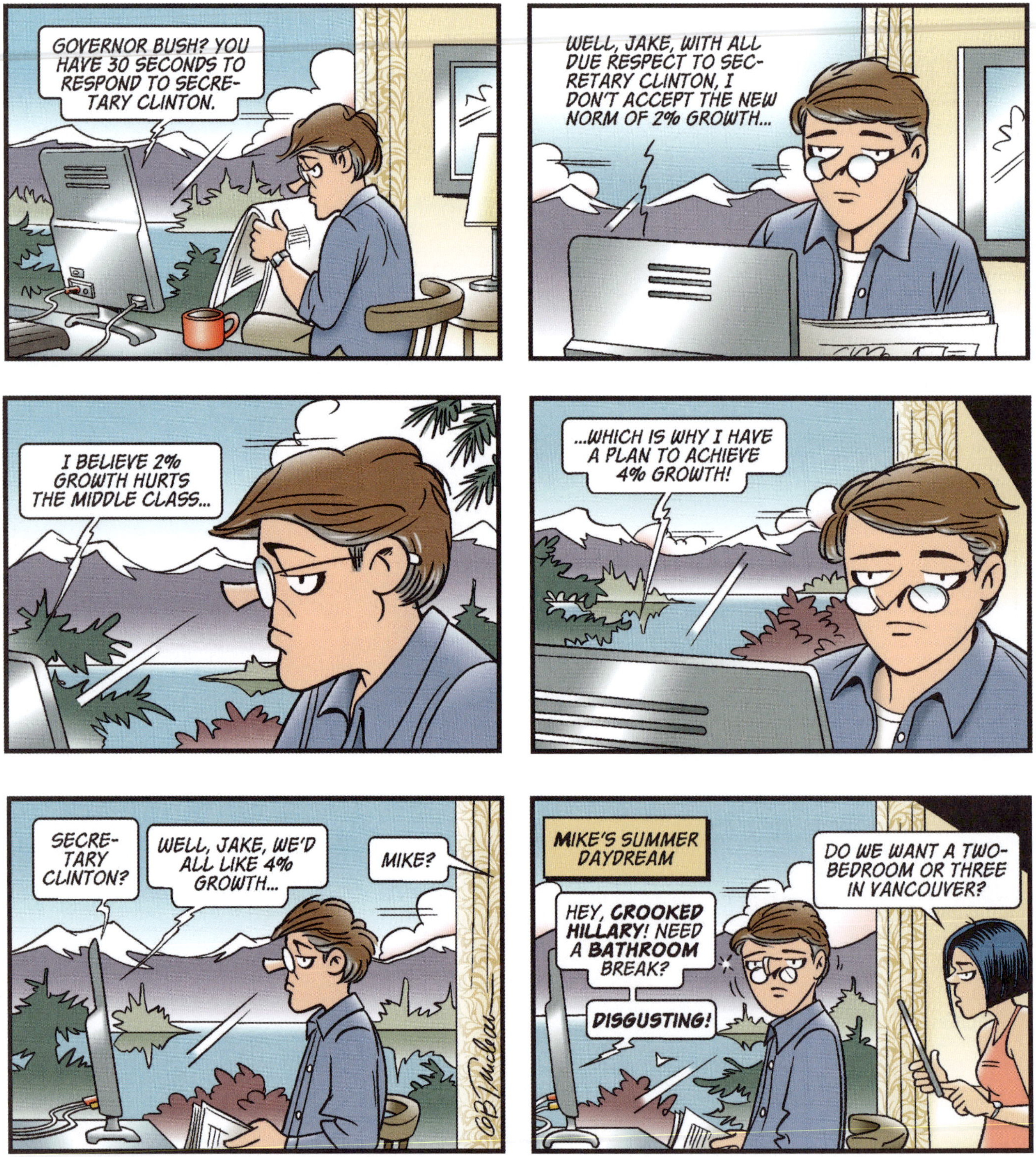
GOVERNOR BUSH? YOU HAVE 30 SECONDS TO RESPOND TO SECRETARY CLINTON.
WELL, JAKE, WITH ALL DUE RESPECT TO SECRETARY CLINTON, I DON'T ACCEPT THE NEW NORM OF 2% GROWTH...
I BELIEVE 2% GROWTH HURTS THE MIDDLE CLASS...
...WHICH IS WHY I HAVE A PLAN TO ACHIEVE 4% GROWTH!
SECRETARY CLINTON?
WELL, JAKE, WE'D ALL LIKE 4% GROWTH...
MIKE?
MIKE'S SUMMER DAYDREAM
HEY, **CROOKED HILLARY**! NEED A **BATHROOM** BREAK?
DISGUSTING!
DO WE WANT A TWO-BEDROOM OR THREE IN VANCOUVER?

August 28, 2016

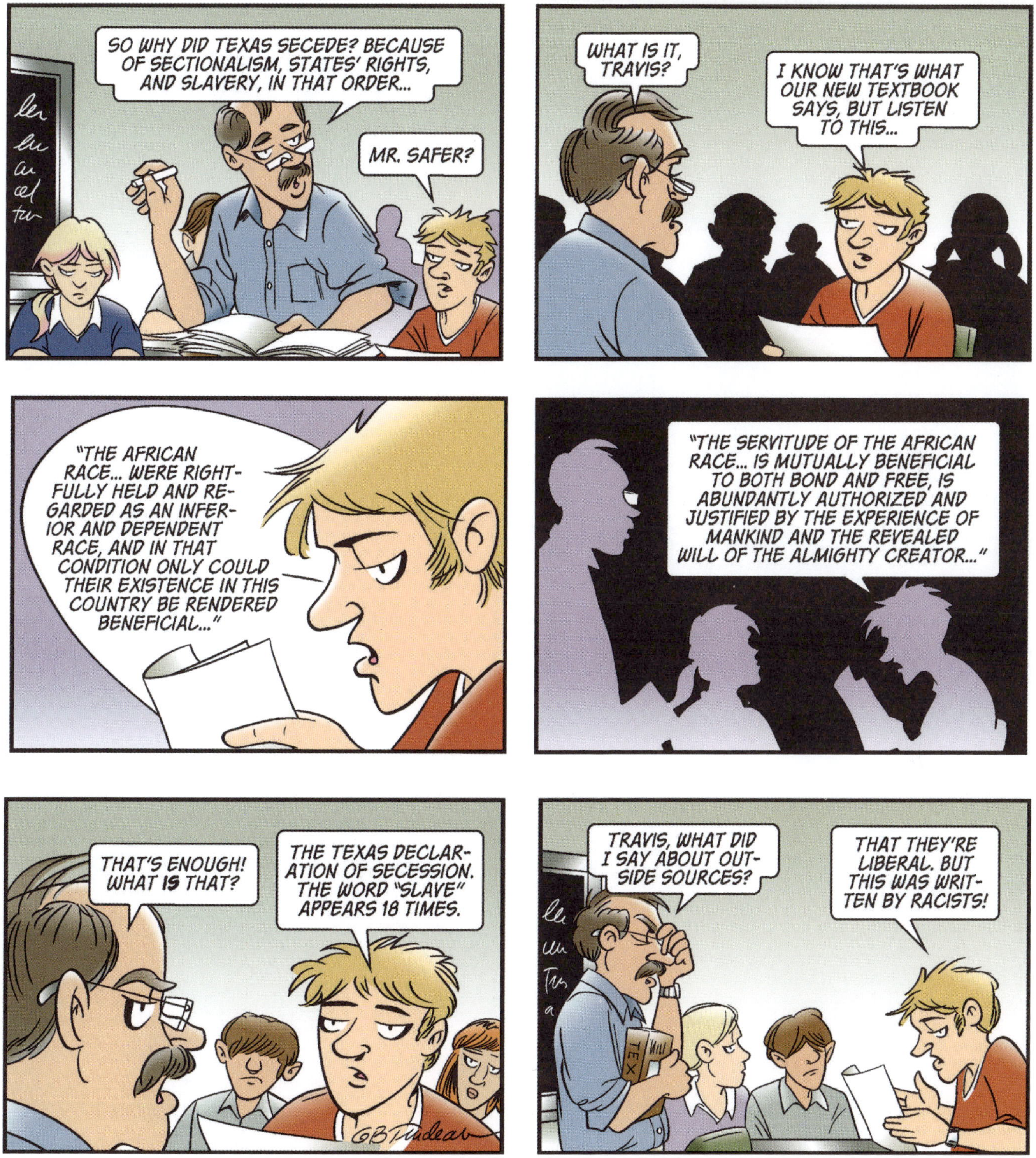
SO WHY DID TEXAS SECEDE? BECAUSE OF SECTIONALISM, STATES' RIGHTS, AND SLAVERY, IN THAT ORDER...
MR. SAFER?
WHAT IS IT, TRAVIS?
I KNOW THAT'S WHAT OUR NEW TEXTBOOK SAYS, BUT LISTEN TO THIS...
"THE AFRICAN RACE... WERE RIGHTFULLY HELD AND REGARDED AS AN INFERIOR AND DEPENDENT RACE, AND IN THAT CONDITION ONLY COULD THEIR EXISTENCE IN THIS COUNTRY BE RENDERED BENEFICIAL..."
"THE SERVITUDE OF THE AFRICAN RACE... IS MUTUALLY BENEFICIAL TO BOTH BOND AND FREE, IS ABUNDANTLY AUTHORIZED AND JUSTIFIED BY THE EXPERIENCE OF MANKIND AND THE REVEALED WILL OF THE ALMIGHTY CREATOR..."
THAT'S ENOUGH! WHAT IS THAT?
THE TEXAS DECLARATION OF SECESSION. THE WORD "SLAVE" APPEARS 18 TIMES.
GBTrudeau
TRAVIS, WHAT DID I SAY ABOUT OUTSIDE SOURCES?
THAT THEY'RE LIBERAL. BUT THIS WAS WRITTEN BY RACISTS!

August 16, 2015

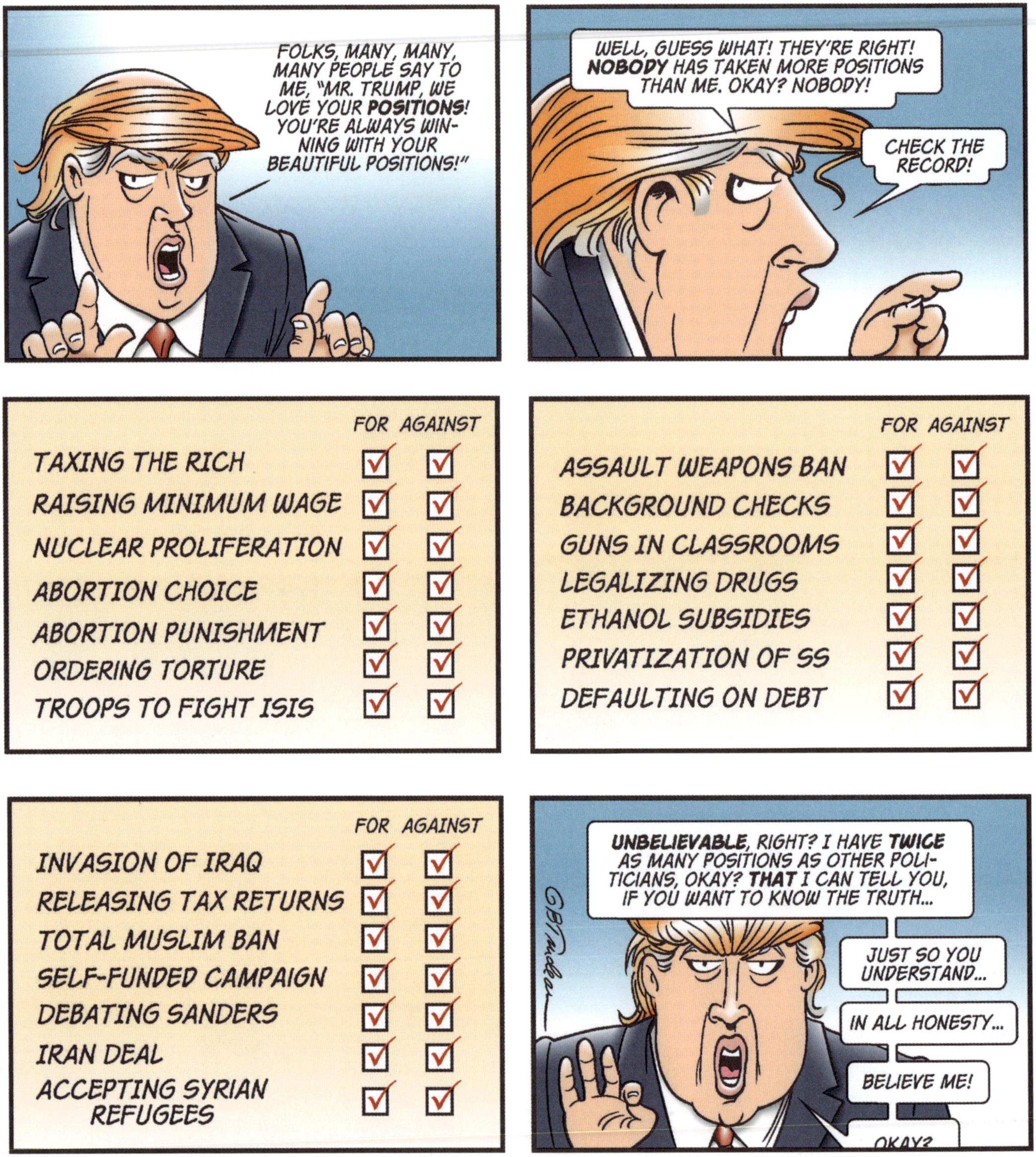
FOLKS, MANY, MANY, MANY PEOPLE SAY TO ME, "MR. TRUMP, WE LOVE YOUR **POSITIONS**! YOU'RE ALWAYS WINNING WITH YOUR BEAUTIFUL POSITIONS!"
WELL, GUESS WHAT! THEY'RE RIGHT! **NOBODY** HAS TAKEN MORE POSITIONS THAN ME. OKAY? NOBODY!
CHECK THE RECORD!
FOR AGAINST
TAXING THE RICH
RAISING MINIMUM WAGE
NUCLEAR PROLIFERATION
ABORTION CHOICE
ABORTION PUNISHMENT
ORDERING TORTURE
TROOPS TO FIGHT ISIS
FOR AGAINST
ASSAULT WEAPONS BAN
BACKGROUND CHECKS
GUNS IN CLASSROOMS
LEGALIZING DRUGS
ETHANOL SUBSIDIES
PRIVATIZATION OF SS
DEFAULTING ON DEBT
FOR AGAINST
INVASION OF IRAQ
RELEASING TAX RETURNS
TOTAL MUSLIM BAN
SELF-FUNDED CAMPAIGN
DEBATING SANDERS
IRAN DEAL
ACCEPTING SYRIAN REFUGEES
UNBELIEVABLE, RIGHT? I HAVE **TWICE** AS MANY POSITIONS AS OTHER POLITICIANS, OKAY? **THAT** I CAN TELL YOU, IF YOU WANT TO KNOW THE TRUTH...
JUST SO YOU UNDERSTAND...
IN ALL HONESTY...
BELIEVE ME!
OKAY?

July 10, 2016

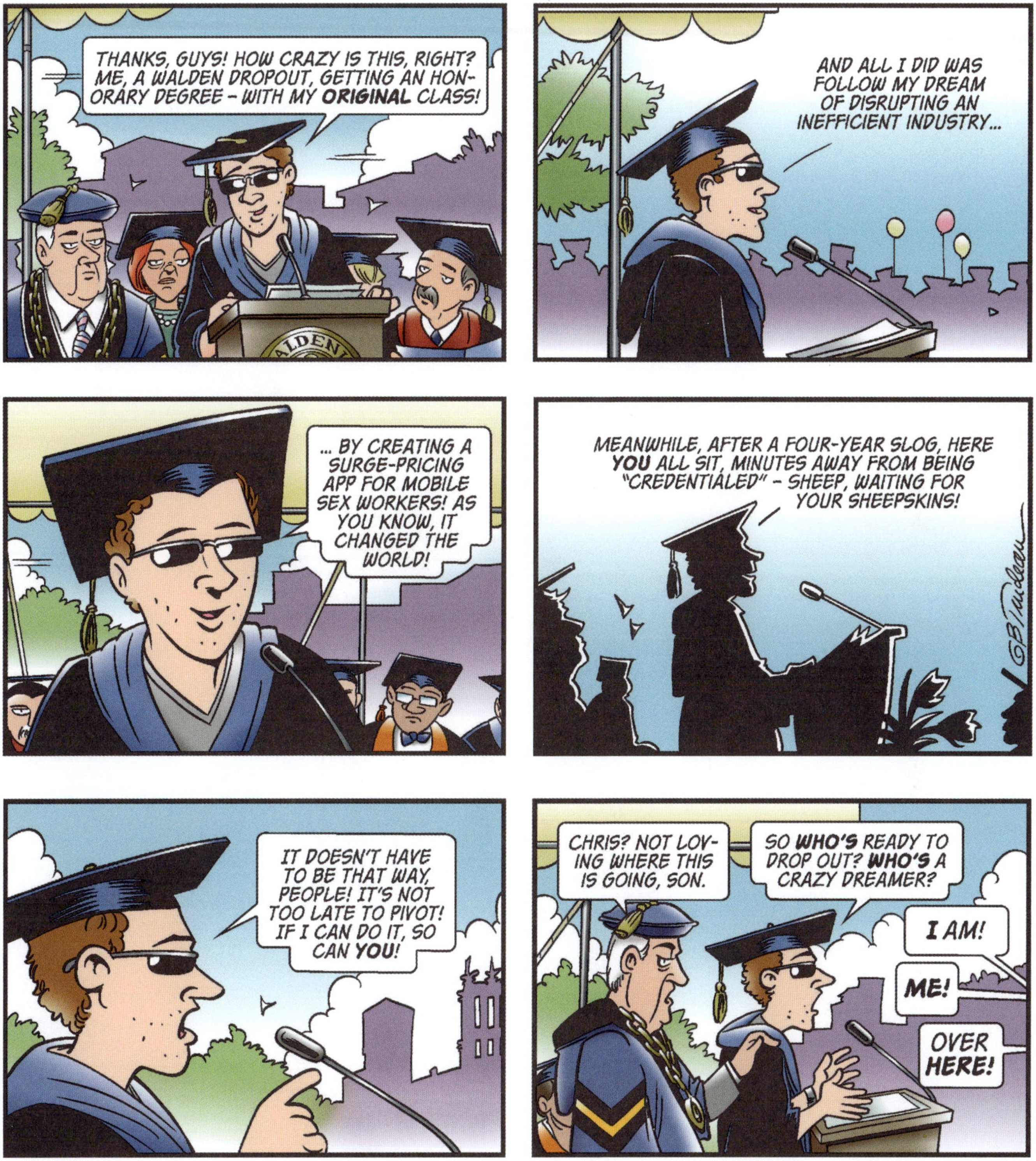
THANKS, GUYS! HOW CRAZY IS THIS, RIGHT? ME, A WALDEN DROPOUT, GETTING AN HONORARY DEGREE – WITH MY **ORIGINAL** CLASS!
WALDEN
AND ALL I DID WAS FOLLOW MY DREAM OF DISRUPTING AN INEFFICIENT INDUSTRY...
... BY CREATING A SURGE-PRICING APP FOR MOBILE SEX WORKERS! AS YOU KNOW, IT CHANGED THE WORLD!
MEANWHILE, AFTER A FOUR-YEAR SLOG, HERE **YOU** ALL SIT, MINUTES AWAY FROM BEING "CREDENTIALED" – SHEEP, WAITING FOR YOUR SHEEPSKINS!
©BTrudeau
IT DOESN'T HAVE TO BE THAT WAY, PEOPLE! IT'S NOT TOO LATE TO PIVOT! IF I CAN DO IT, SO CAN **YOU**!
CHRIS? NOT LOVING WHERE THIS IS GOING, SON.
SO **WHO'S** READY TO DROP OUT? **WHO'S** A CRAZY DREAMER?
I AM!
ME!
OVER HERE!

June 12, 2016

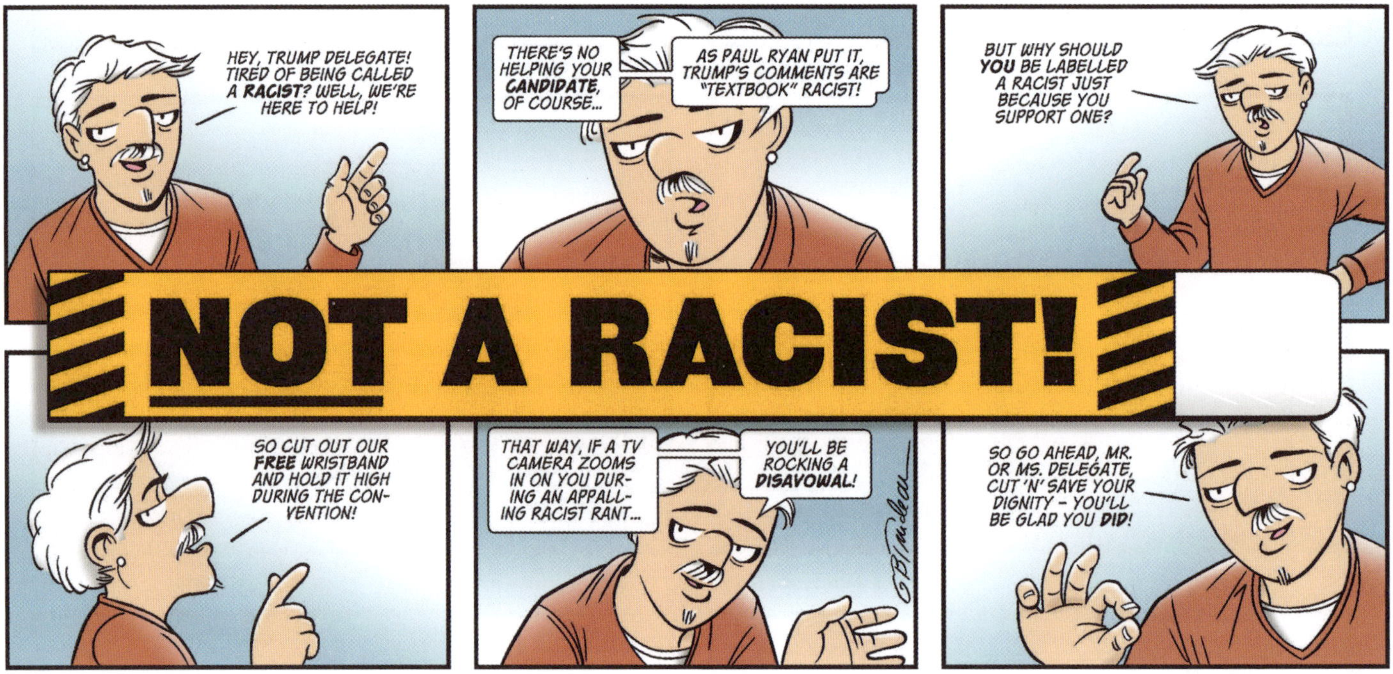
HEY, TRUMP DELEGATE! TIRED OF BEING CALLED A RACIST? WELL, WE'RE HERE TO HELP!
THERE'S NO HELPING YOUR CANDIDATE, OF COURSE...
AS PAUL RYAN PUT IT, TRUMP'S COMMENTS ARE "TEXTBOOK" RACIST!
BUT WHY SHOULD YOU BE LABELLED A RACIST JUST BECAUSE YOU SUPPORT ONE?
NOT A RACIST!
SO CUT OUT OUR FREE WRISTBAND AND HOLD IT HIGH DURING THE CON-VENTION!
THAT WAY, IF A TV CAMERA ZOOMS IN ON YOU DUR-ING AN APPALL-ING RACIST RANT...
YOU'LL BE ROCKING A DISAVOWAL!
SO GO AHEAD, MR. OR MS. DELEGATE, CUT 'N' SAVE YOUR DIGNITY - YOU'LL BE GLAD YOU DID!

July 17, 2016

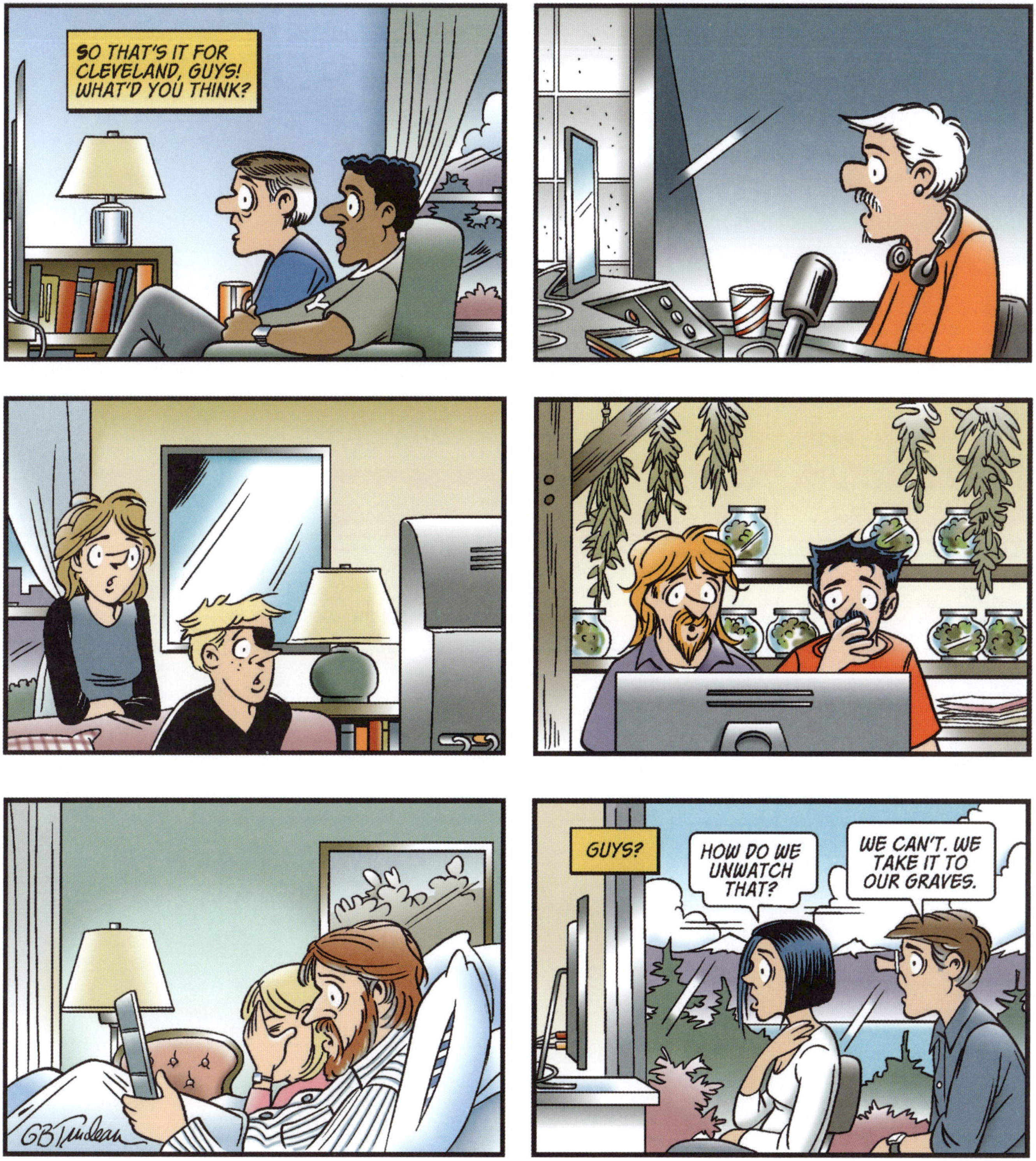
SO THAT'S IT FOR CLEVELAND, GUYS! WHAT'D YOU THINK?
GUYS?
HOW DO WE UNWATCH THAT?
WE CAN'T. WE TAKE IT TO OUR GRAVES.
GBTrudeau

July 24, 2016

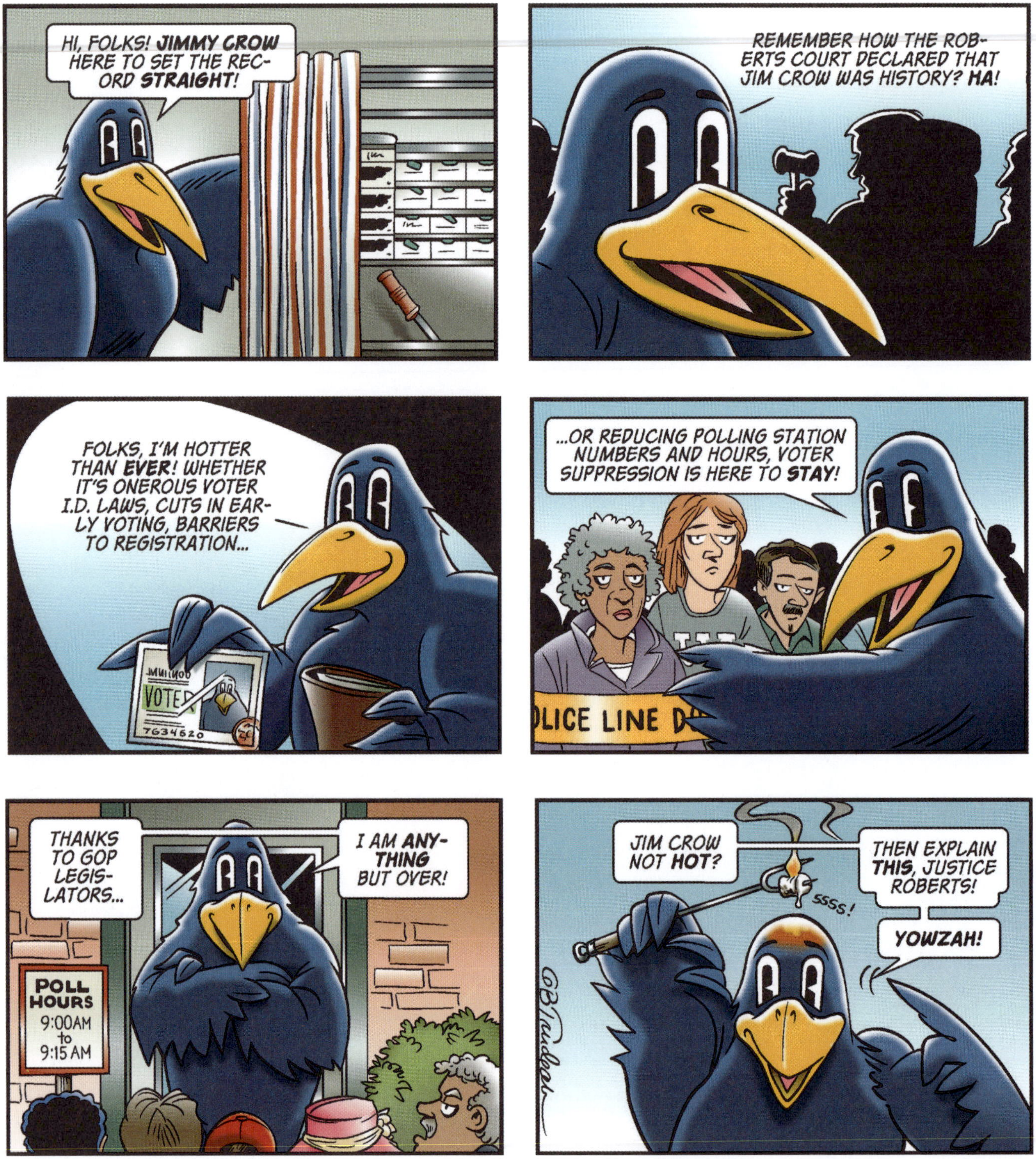
HI, FOLKS! **JIMMY CROW** HERE TO SET THE REC-ORD **STRAIGHT**!
REMEMBER HOW THE ROB-ERTS COURT DECLARED THAT JIM CROW WAS HISTORY? **HA**!
FOLKS, I'M HOTTER THAN **EVER**! WHETHER IT'S ONEROUS VOTER I.D. LAWS, CUTS IN EAR-LY VOTING, BARRIERS TO REGISTRATION...
7634620
...OR REDUCING POLLING STATION NUMBERS AND HOURS, VOTER SUPPRESSION IS HERE TO **STAY**!
THANKS TO GOP LEGIS-LATORS...
I AM **ANY-THING** BUT OVER!
POLL HOURS
9:00AM to 9:15AM
JIM CROW NOT **HOT**?
THEN EXPLAIN **THIS**, JUSTICE ROBERTS!
SSSS!
YOWZAH!

July 19, 2015

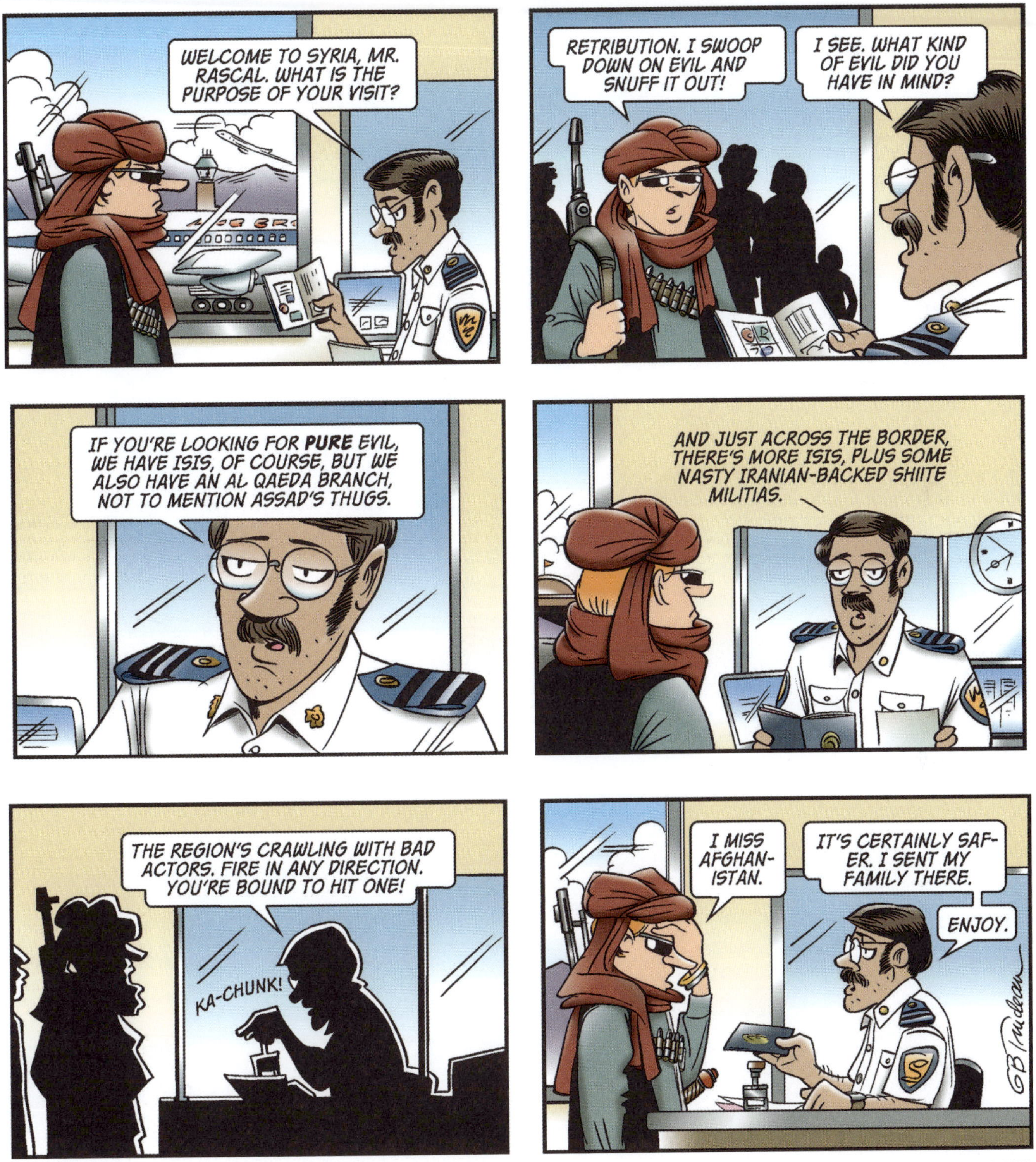
WELCOME TO SYRIA, MR. RASCAL. WHAT IS THE PURPOSE OF YOUR VISIT?
RETRIBUTION. I SWOOP DOWN ON EVIL AND SNUFF IT OUT!
I SEE. WHAT KIND OF EVIL DID YOU HAVE IN MIND?
IF YOU'RE LOOKING FOR PURE EVIL, WE HAVE ISIS, OF COURSE, BUT WE ALSO HAVE AN AL QAEDA BRANCH, NOT TO MENTION ASSAD'S THUGS.
AND JUST ACROSS THE BORDER, THERE'S MORE ISIS, PLUS SOME NASTY IRANIAN-BACKED SHIITE MILITIAS.
THE REGION'S CRAWLING WITH BAD ACTORS. FIRE IN ANY DIRECTION. YOU'RE BOUND TO HIT ONE!
KA-CHUNK!
I MISS AFGHAN-ISTAN.
IT'S CERTAINLY SAF-ER. I SENT MY FAMILY THERE.
ENJOY.
GB Trudeau

August 9, 2015

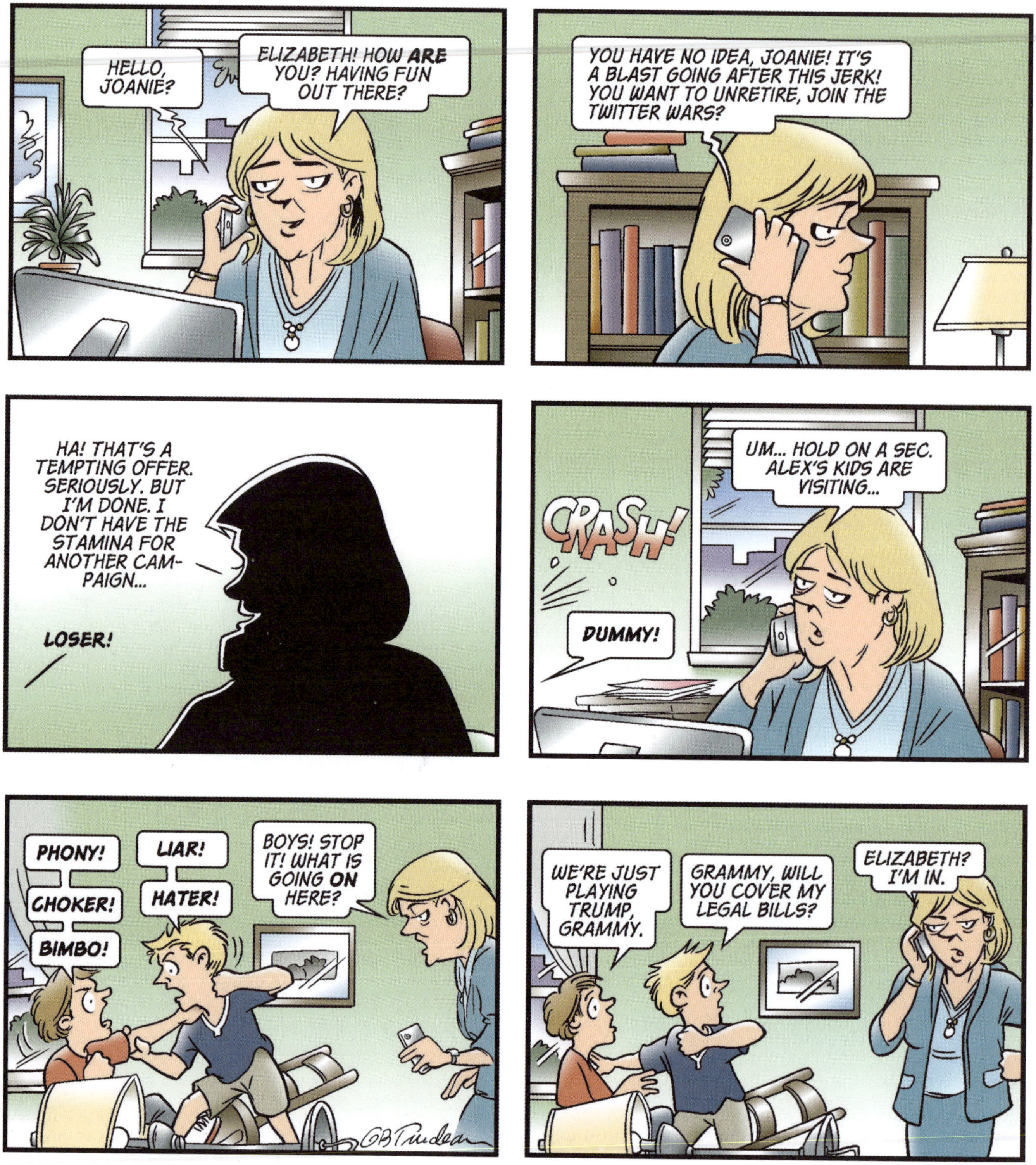
HELLO, JOANIE?
ELIZABETH! HOW ARE YOU? HAVING FUN OUT THERE?
YOU HAVE NO IDEA, JOANIE! IT'S A BLAST GOING AFTER THIS JERK! YOU WANT TO UNRETIRE, JOIN THE TWITTER WARS?
HA! THAT'S A TEMPTING OFFER. SERIOUSLY. BUT I'M DONE. I DON'T HAVE THE STAMINA FOR ANOTHER CAMPAIGN...
LOSER!
CRASH!
UM... HOLD ON A SEC. ALEX'S KIDS ARE VISITING...
DUMMY!
PHONY!
CHOKER!
BIMBO!
LIAR!
HATER!
BOYS! STOP IT! WHAT IS GOING ON HERE?
WE'RE JUST PLAYING TRUMP, GRAMMY.
GRAMMY, WILL YOU COVER MY LEGAL BILLS?
ELIZABETH? I'M IN.

July 31, 2016

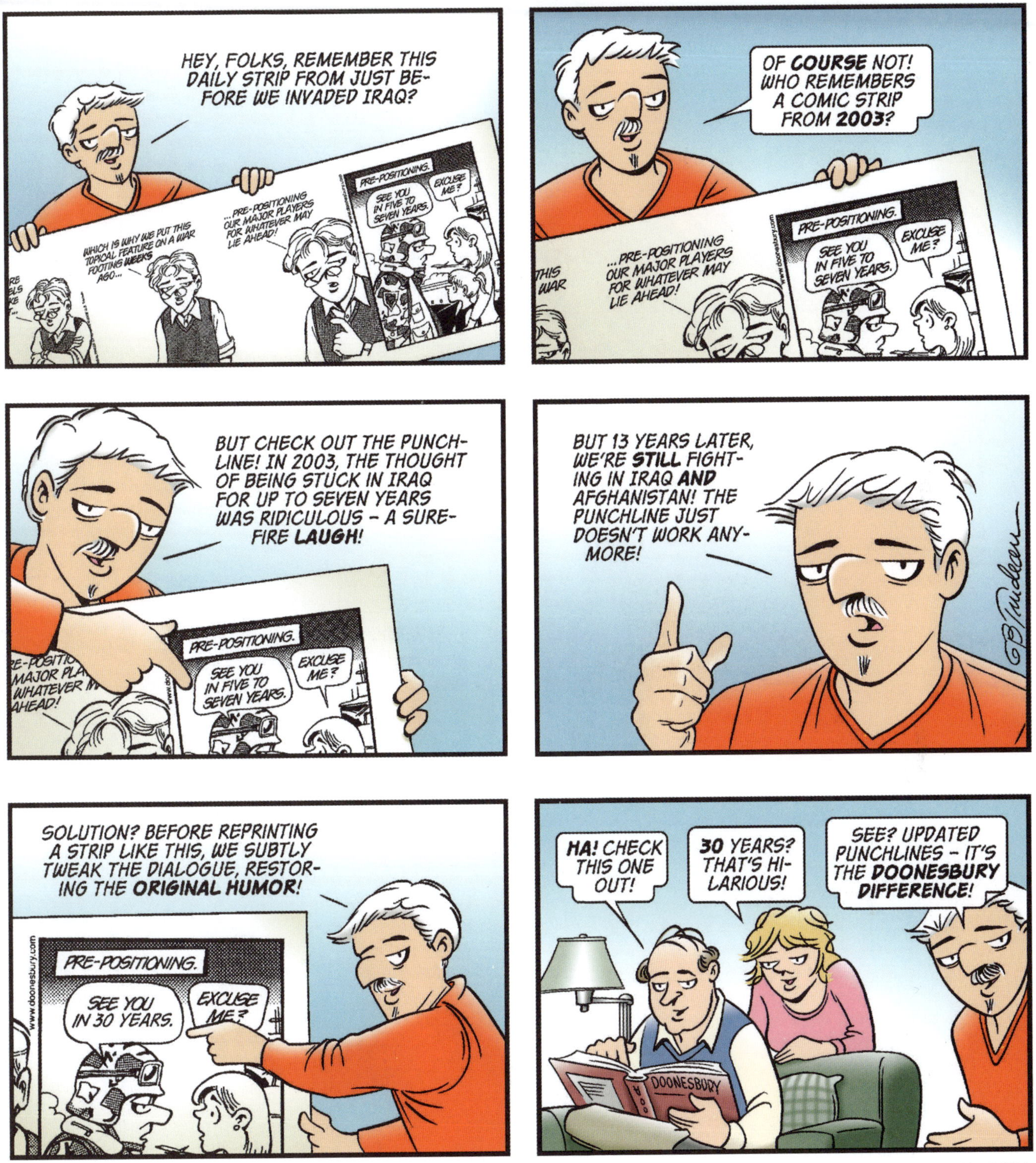
HEY, FOLKS, REMEMBER THIS DAILY STRIP FROM JUST BEFORE WE INVADED IRAQ?
WHICH IS WHY WE PUT THIS TOPICAL FEATURE ON A WAR FOOTING WEEKS AGO...
...PRE-POSITIONING OUR MAJOR PLAYERS FOR WHATEVER MAY LIE AHEAD!
PRE-POSITIONING.
SEE YOU IN FIVE TO SEVEN YEARS.
EXCUSE ME?
OF COURSE NOT! WHO REMEMBERS A COMIC STRIP FROM 2003?
BUT CHECK OUT THE PUNCHLINE! IN 2003, THE THOUGHT OF BEING STUCK IN IRAQ FOR UP TO SEVEN YEARS WAS RIDICULOUS – A SURE-FIRE LAUGH!
BUT 13 YEARS LATER, WE'RE STILL FIGHTING IN IRAQ AND AFGHANISTAN! THE PUNCHLINE JUST DOESN'T WORK ANYMORE!
GBTrudeau
SOLUTION? BEFORE REPRINTING A STRIP LIKE THIS, WE SUBTLY TWEAK THE DIALOGUE, RESTORING THE ORIGINAL HUMOR!
www.doonesbury.com
PRE-POSITIONING.
SEE YOU IN 30 YEARS.
EXCUSE ME?
HA! CHECK THIS ONE OUT!
30 YEARS? THAT'S HILARIOUS!
SEE? UPDATED PUNCHLINES – IT'S THE DOONESBURY DIFFERENCE!
DOONESBURY

May 1, 2016

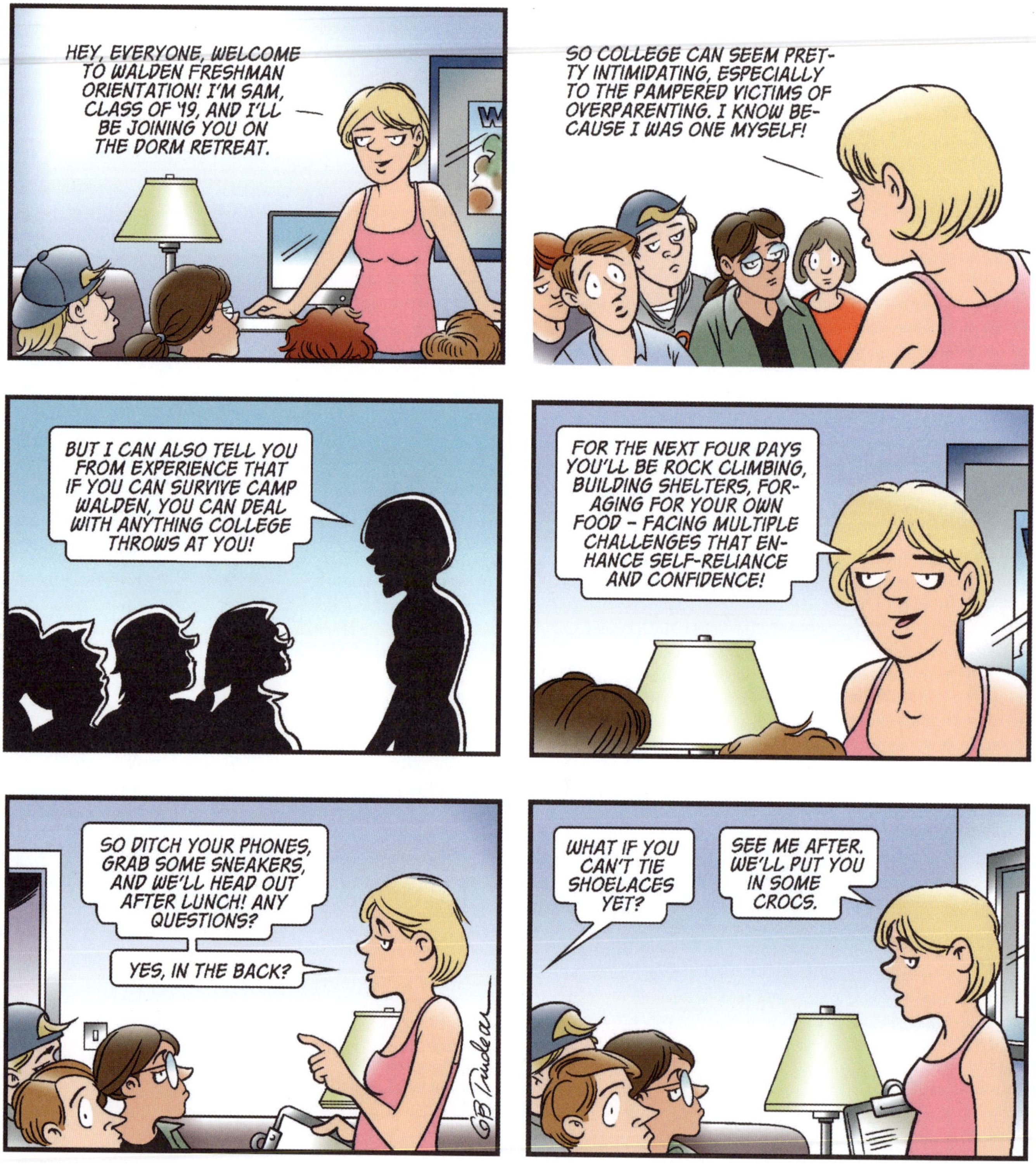

HEY, EVERYONE, WELCOME TO WALDEN FRESHMAN ORIENTATION! I'M SAM, CLASS OF '19, AND I'LL BE JOINING YOU ON THE DORM RETREAT.
SO COLLEGE CAN SEEM PRETTY INTIMIDATING, ESPECIALLY TO THE PAMPERED VICTIMS OF OVERPARENTING. I KNOW BECAUSE I WAS ONE MYSELF!
BUT I CAN ALSO TELL YOU FROM EXPERIENCE THAT IF YOU CAN SURVIVE CAMP WALDEN, YOU CAN DEAL WITH ANYTHING COLLEGE THROWS AT YOU!
FOR THE NEXT FOUR DAYS YOU'LL BE ROCK CLIMBING, BUILDING SHELTERS, FORAGING FOR YOUR OWN FOOD - FACING MULTIPLE CHALLENGES THAT ENHANCE SELF-RELIANCE AND CONFIDENCE!
SO DITCH YOUR PHONES, GRAB SOME SNEAKERS, AND WE'LL HEAD OUT AFTER LUNCH! ANY QUESTIONS?
YES, IN THE BACK?
WHAT IF YOU CAN'T TIE SHOELACES YET?
SEE ME AFTER. WE'LL PUT YOU IN SOME CROCS.

August 21, 2016

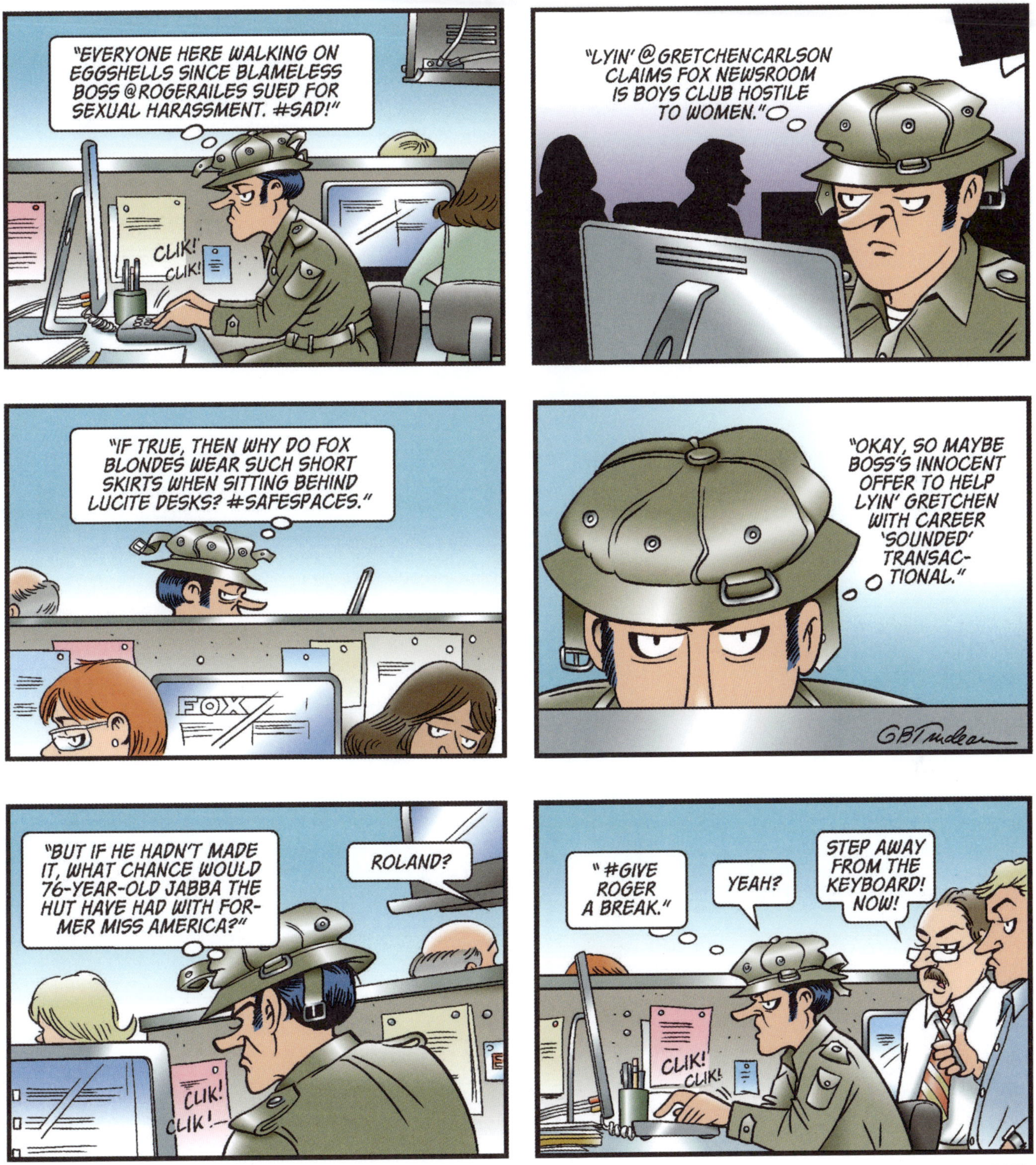
"EVERYONE HERE WALKING ON EGGSHELLS SINCE BLAMELESS BOSS @ROGERAILES SUED FOR SEXUAL HARASSMENT. #SAD!"
CLIK! CLIK!
"LYIN' @GRETCHENCARLSON CLAIMS FOX NEWSROOM IS BOYS CLUB HOSTILE TO WOMEN."
"IF TRUE, THEN WHY DO FOX BLONDES WEAR SUCH SHORT SKIRTS WHEN SITTING BEHIND LUCITE DESKS? #SAFESPACES."
FOX
"OKAY, SO MAYBE BOSS'S INNOCENT OFFER TO HELP LYIN' GRETCHEN WITH CAREER 'SOUNDED' TRANSAC-TIONAL."
GBTrudeau
"BUT IF HE HADN'T MADE IT, WHAT CHANCE WOULD 76-YEAR-OLD JABBA THE HUT HAVE HAD WITH FOR-MER MISS AMERICA?"
ROLAND?
CLIK! CLIK!
"#GIVE ROGER A BREAK."
YEAH?
STEP AWAY FROM THE KEYBOARD! NOW!
CLIK! CLIK!

August 7, 2016

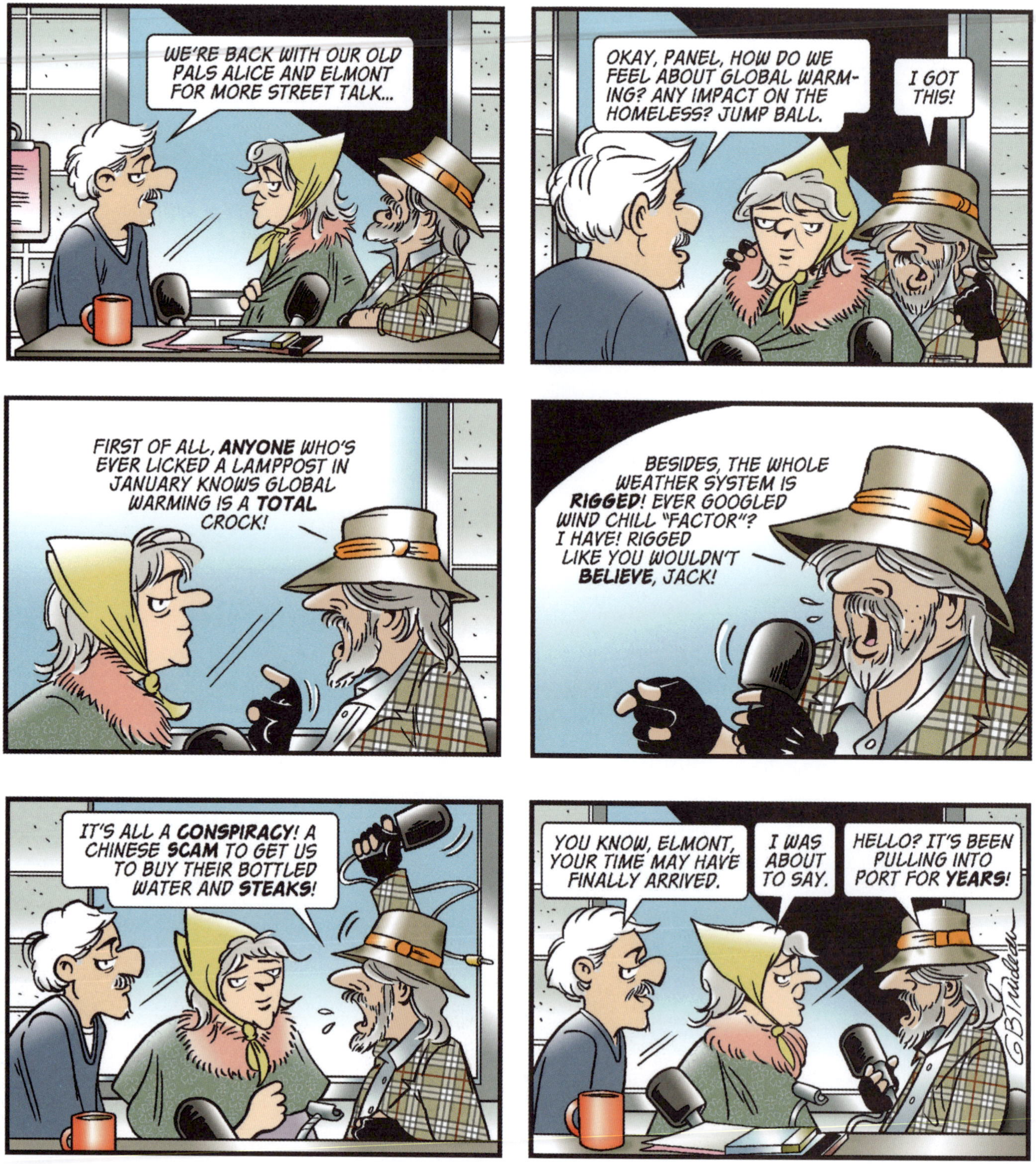
WE'RE BACK WITH OUR OLD PALS ALICE AND ELMONT FOR MORE STREET TALK...
OKAY, PANEL, HOW DO WE FEEL ABOUT GLOBAL WARMING? ANY IMPACT ON THE HOMELESS? JUMP BALL.
I GOT THIS!
FIRST OF ALL, ANYONE WHO'S EVER LICKED A LAMPPOST IN JANUARY KNOWS GLOBAL WARMING IS A TOTAL CROCK!
BESIDES, THE WHOLE WEATHER SYSTEM IS RIGGED! EVER GOOGLED WIND CHILL "FACTOR"? I HAVE! RIGGED LIKE YOU WOULDN'T BELIEVE, JACK!
IT'S ALL A CONSPIRACY! A CHINESE SCAM TO GET US TO BUY THEIR BOTTLED WATER AND STEAKS!
YOU KNOW, ELMONT, YOUR TIME MAY HAVE FINALLY ARRIVED.
I WAS ABOUT TO SAY.
HELLO? IT'S BEEN PULLING INTO PORT FOR YEARS!
GBTrudeau

August 14, 2016

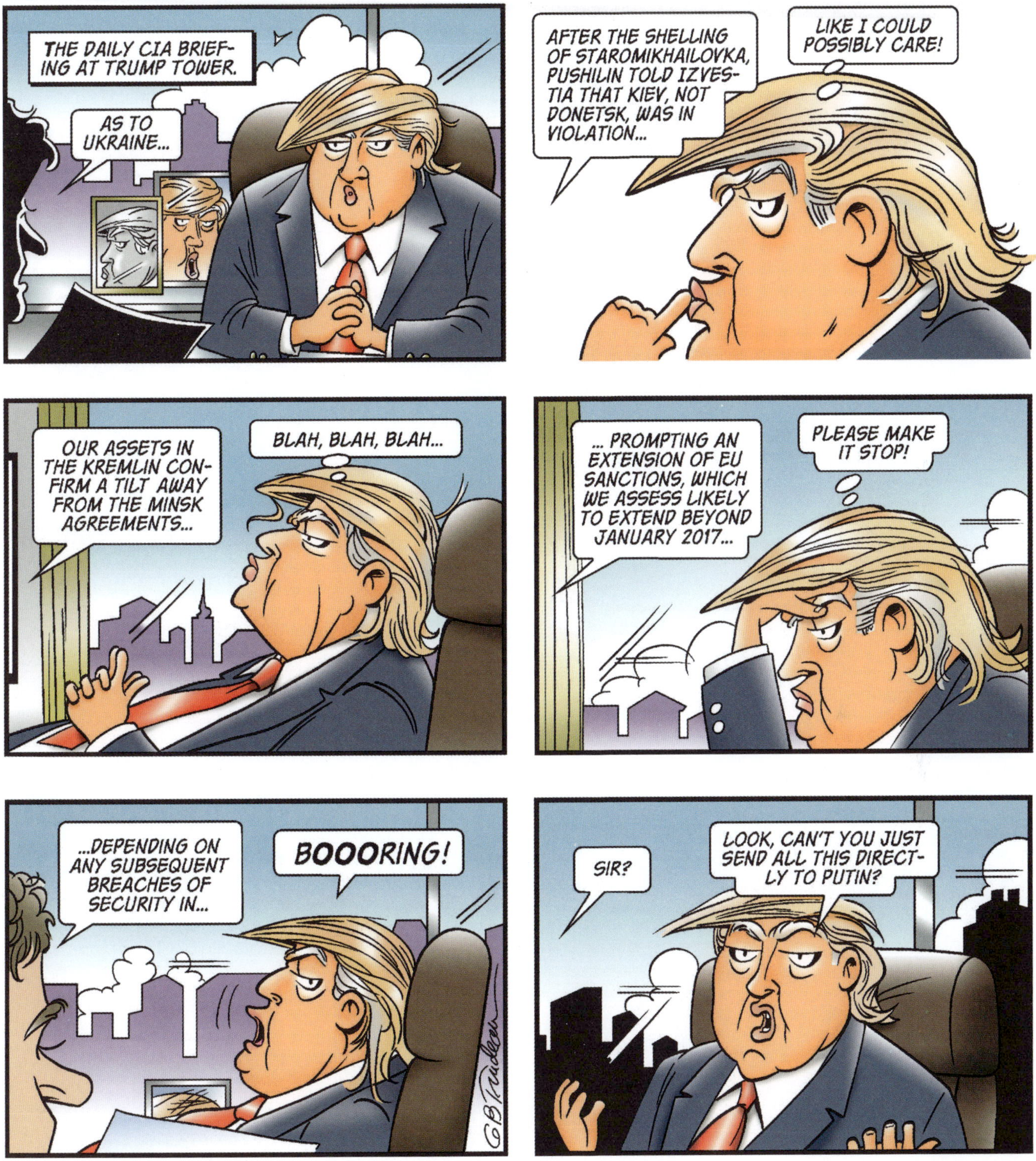
THE DAILY CIA BRIEFING AT TRUMP TOWER.
AS TO UKRAINE...
AFTER THE SHELLING OF STAROMIKHAILOVKA, PUSHILIN TOLD IZVESTIA THAT KIEV, NOT DONETSK, WAS IN VIOLATION...
LIKE I COULD POSSIBLY CARE!
OUR ASSETS IN THE KREMLIN CONFIRM A TILT AWAY FROM THE MINSK AGREEMENTS...
BLAH, BLAH, BLAH...
... PROMPTING AN EXTENSION OF EU SANCTIONS, WHICH WE ASSESS LIKELY TO EXTEND BEYOND JANUARY 2017...
PLEASE MAKE IT STOP!
...DEPENDING ON ANY SUBSEQUENT BREACHES OF SECURITY IN...
BOOORING!
GB Trudeau
SIR?
LOOK, CAN'T YOU JUST SEND ALL THIS DIRECTLY TO PUTIN?

September 11, 2016

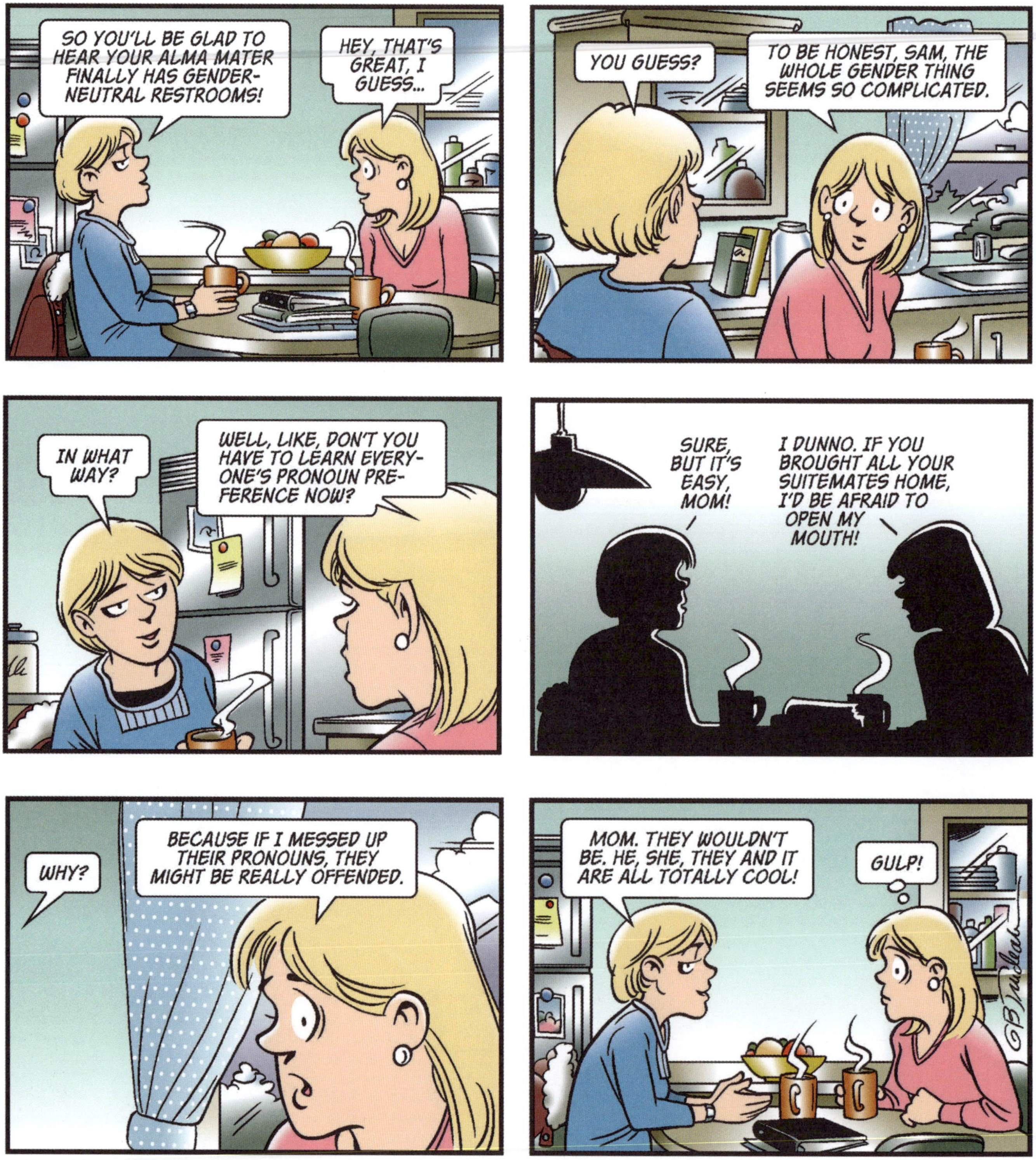
SO YOU'LL BE GLAD TO HEAR YOUR ALMA MATER FINALLY HAS GENDER-NEUTRAL RESTROOMS!
HEY, THAT'S GREAT, I GUESS...
YOU GUESS?
TO BE HONEST, SAM, THE WHOLE GENDER THING SEEMS SO COMPLICATED.
IN WHAT WAY?
WELL, LIKE, DON'T YOU HAVE TO LEARN EVERY-ONE'S PRONOUN PRE-FERENCE NOW?
SURE, BUT IT'S EASY, MOM!
I DUNNO. IF YOU BROUGHT ALL YOUR SUITEMATES HOME, I'D BE AFRAID TO OPEN MY MOUTH!
WHY?
BECAUSE IF I MESSED UP THEIR PRONOUNS, THEY MIGHT BE REALLY OFFENDED.
MOM. THEY WOULDN'T BE. HE, SHE, THEY AND IT ARE ALL TOTALLY COOL!
GULP!
©B Trudeau

December 20, 2015

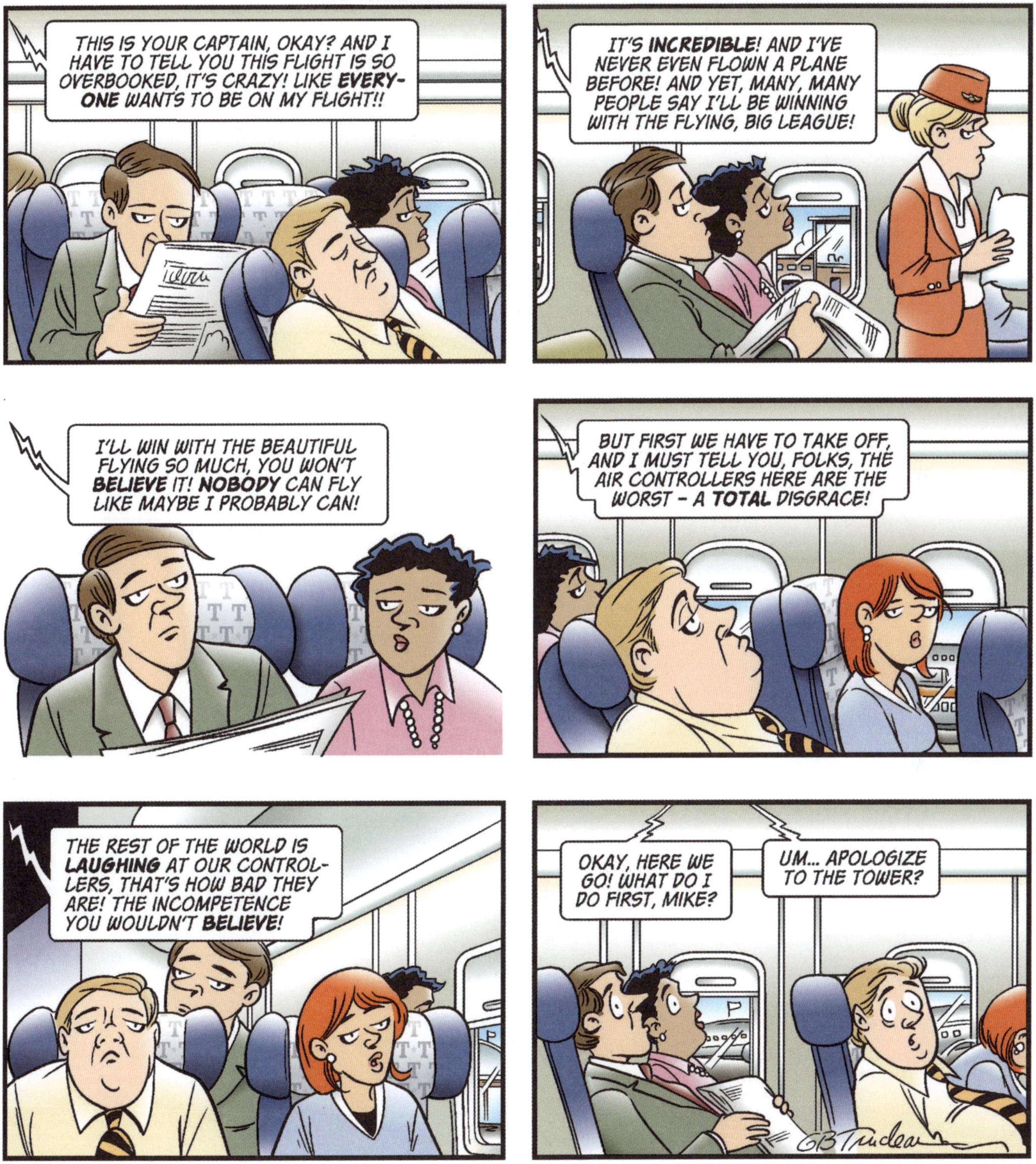
THIS IS YOUR CAPTAIN, OKAY? AND I HAVE TO TELL YOU THIS FLIGHT IS SO OVERBOOKED, IT'S CRAZY! LIKE **EVERYONE** WANTS TO BE ON MY FLIGHT!!
IT'S **INCREDIBLE**! AND I'VE NEVER EVEN FLOWN A PLANE BEFORE! AND YET, MANY, MANY PEOPLE SAY I'LL BE WINNING WITH THE FLYING, BIG LEAGUE!
I'LL WIN WITH THE BEAUTIFUL FLYING SO MUCH, YOU WON'T **BELIEVE** IT! **NOBODY** CAN FLY LIKE MAYBE I PROBABLY CAN!
BUT FIRST WE HAVE TO TAKE OFF, AND I MUST TELL YOU, FOLKS, THE AIR CONTROLLERS HERE ARE THE WORST – A **TOTAL** DISGRACE!
THE REST OF THE WORLD IS **LAUGHING** AT OUR CONTROLLERS, THAT'S HOW BAD THEY ARE! THE INCOMPETENCE YOU WOULDN'T **BELIEVE**!
OKAY, HERE WE GO! WHAT DO I DO FIRST, MIKE?
UM... APOLOGIZE TO THE TOWER?
GBTrudeau

September 18, 2016

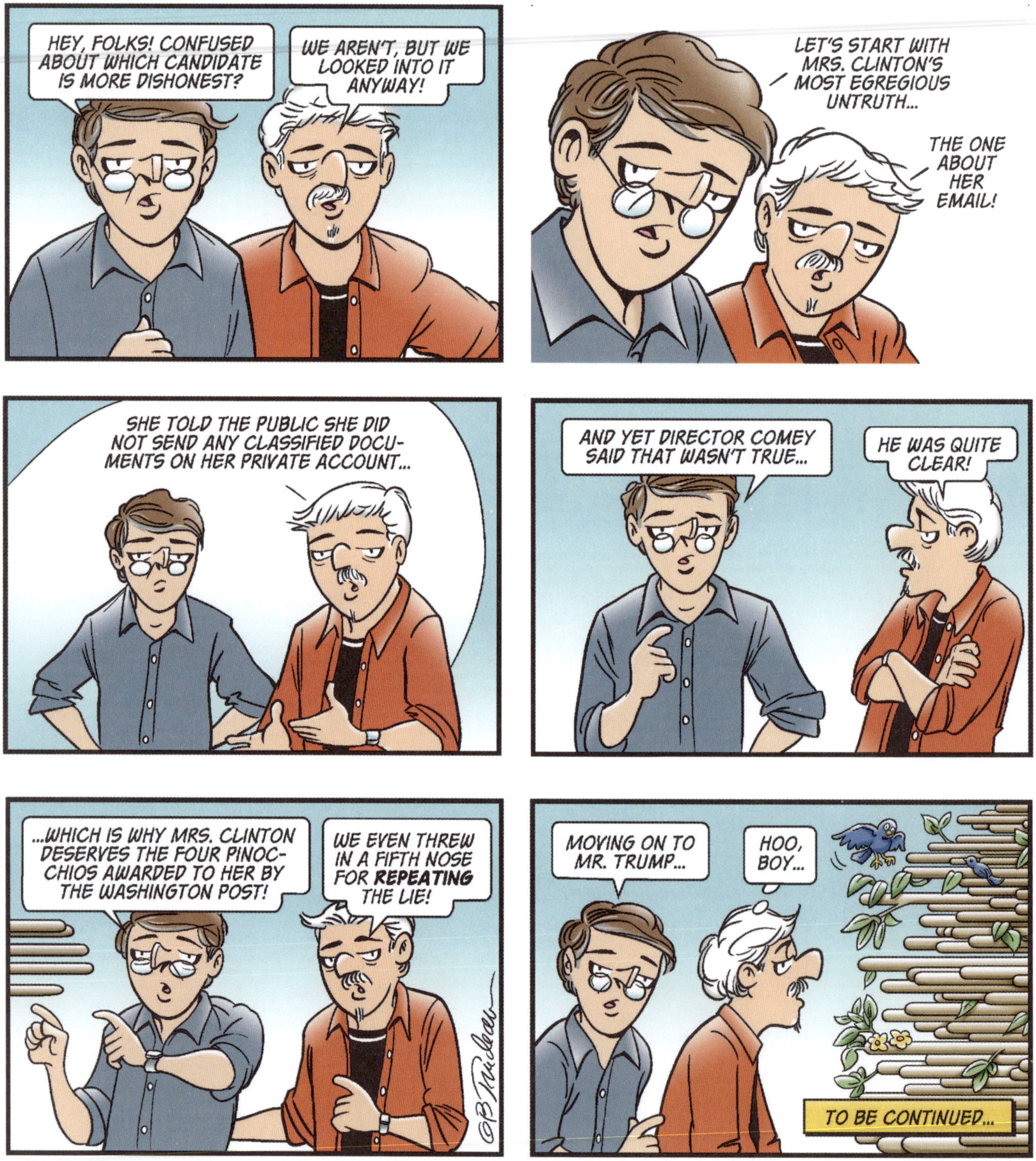
HEY, FOLKS! CONFUSED ABOUT WHICH CANDIDATE IS MORE DISHONEST?
WE AREN'T, BUT WE LOOKED INTO IT ANYWAY!
LET'S START WITH MRS. CLINTON'S MOST EGREGIOUS UNTRUTH...
THE ONE ABOUT HER EMAIL!
SHE TOLD THE PUBLIC SHE DID NOT SEND ANY CLASSIFIED DOCUMENTS ON HER PRIVATE ACCOUNT...
AND YET DIRECTOR COMEY SAID THAT WASN'T TRUE...
HE WAS QUITE CLEAR!
...WHICH IS WHY MRS. CLINTON DESERVES THE FOUR PINOCCHIOS AWARDED TO HER BY THE WASHINGTON POST!
WE EVEN THREW IN A FIFTH NOSE FOR **REPEATING** THE LIE!
©B Trudeau
MOVING ON TO MR. TRUMP...
HOO, BOY...
TO BE CONTINUED...

September 25, 2016

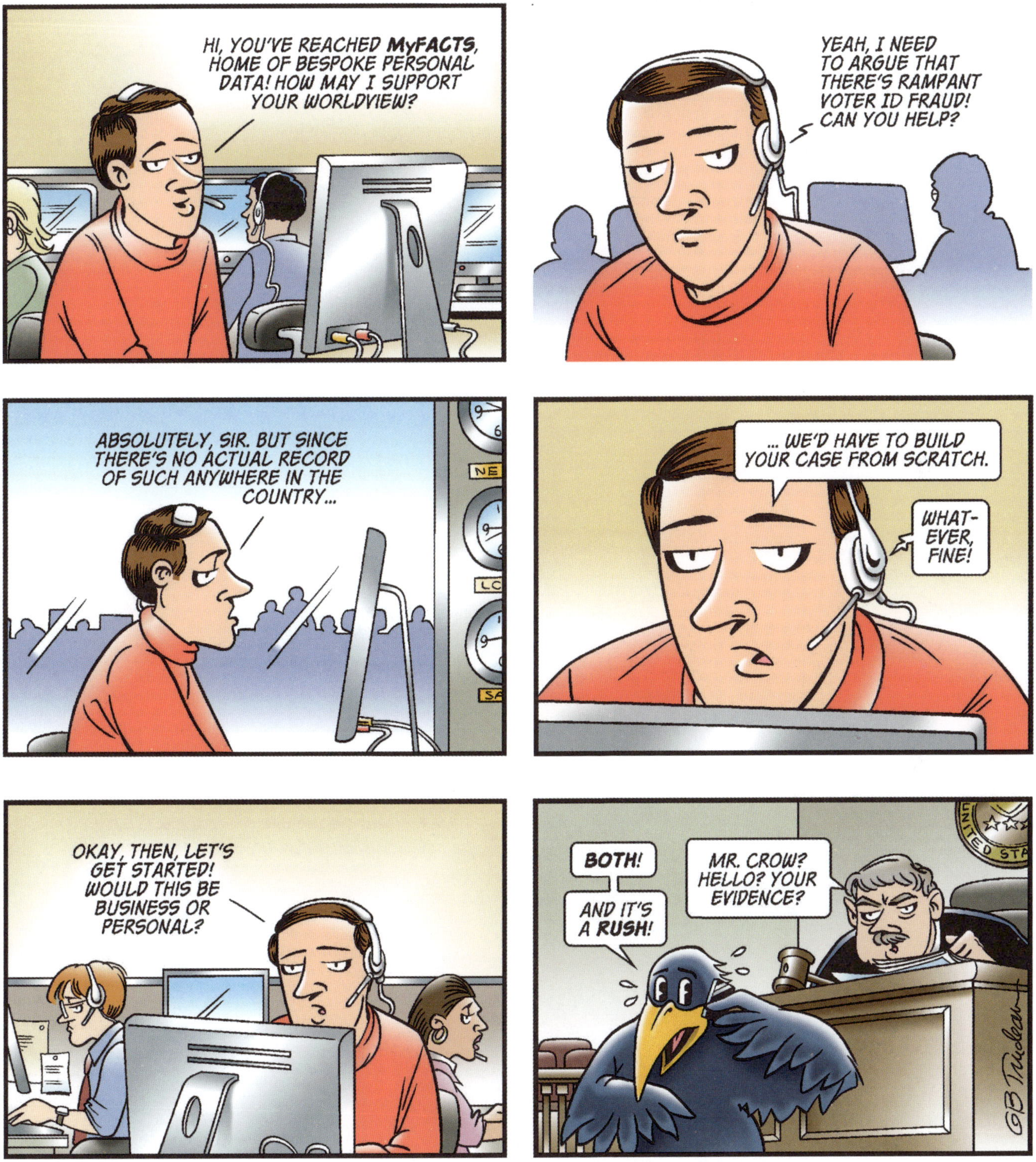
HI, YOU'VE REACHED MyFACTS, HOME OF BESPOKE PERSONAL DATA! HOW MAY I SUPPORT YOUR WORLDVIEW?
YEAH, I NEED TO ARGUE THAT THERE'S RAMPANT VOTER ID FRAUD! CAN YOU HELP?
ABSOLUTELY, SIR. BUT SINCE THERE'S NO ACTUAL RECORD OF SUCH ANYWHERE IN THE COUNTRY...
... WE'D HAVE TO BUILD YOUR CASE FROM SCRATCH.
WHAT-EVER, FINE!
OKAY, THEN, LET'S GET STARTED! WOULD THIS BE BUSINESS OR PERSONAL?
BOTH!
AND IT'S A RUSH!
MR. CROW? HELLO? YOUR EVIDENCE?
GB Trudeau

October 2, 2016

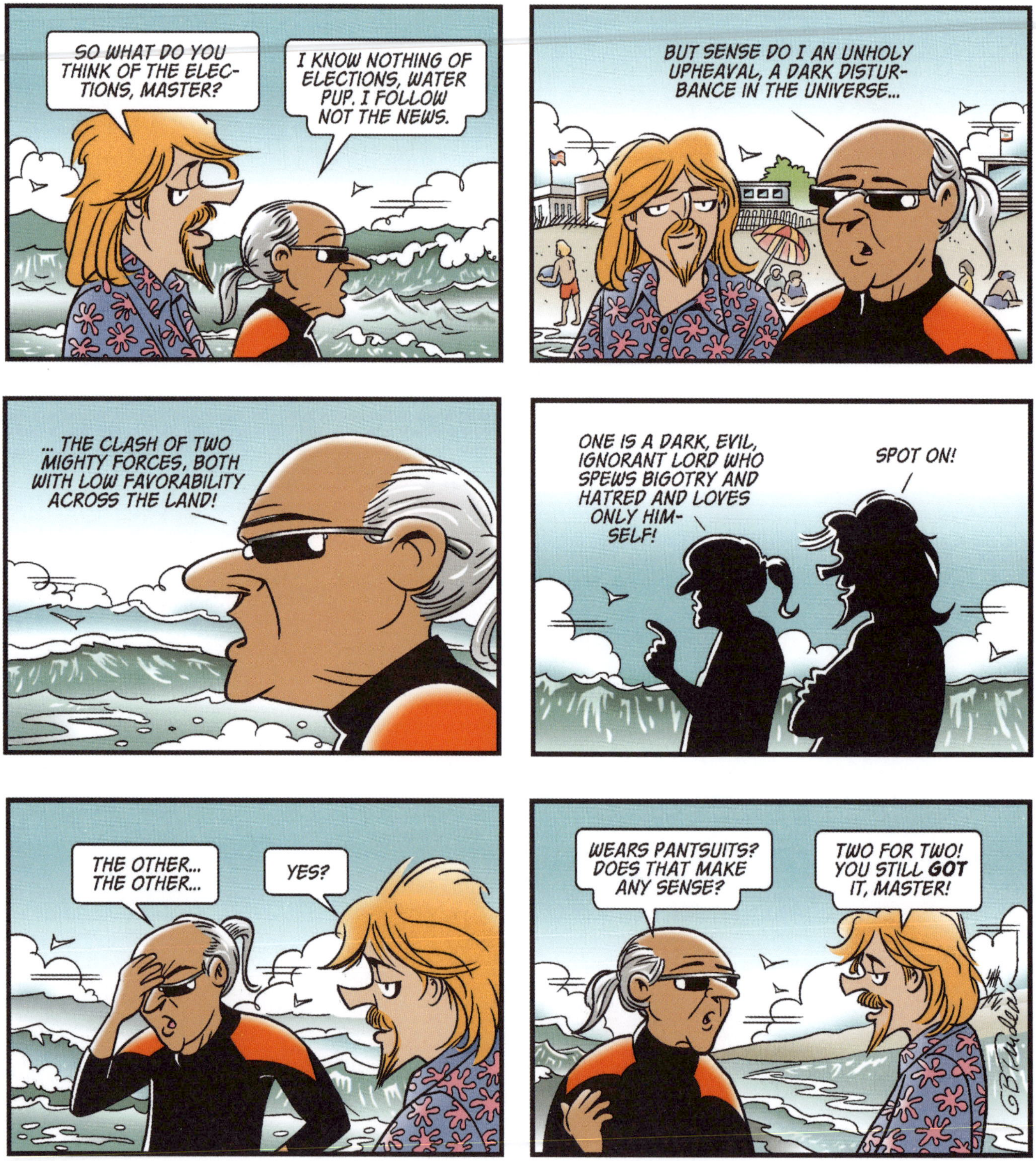
SO WHAT DO YOU THINK OF THE ELECTIONS, MASTER?
I KNOW NOTHING OF ELECTIONS, WATER PUP. I FOLLOW NOT THE NEWS.
BUT SENSE DO I AN UNHOLY UPHEAVAL, A DARK DISTURBANCE IN THE UNIVERSE...
... THE CLASH OF TWO MIGHTY FORCES, BOTH WITH LOW FAVORABILITY ACROSS THE LAND!
ONE IS A DARK, EVIL, IGNORANT LORD WHO SPEWS BIGOTRY AND HATRED AND LOVES ONLY HIMSELF!
SPOT ON!
THE OTHER... THE OTHER...
YES?
WEARS PANTSUITS? DOES THAT MAKE ANY SENSE?
TWO FOR TWO! YOU STILL **GOT** IT, MASTER!
GBTrudeau

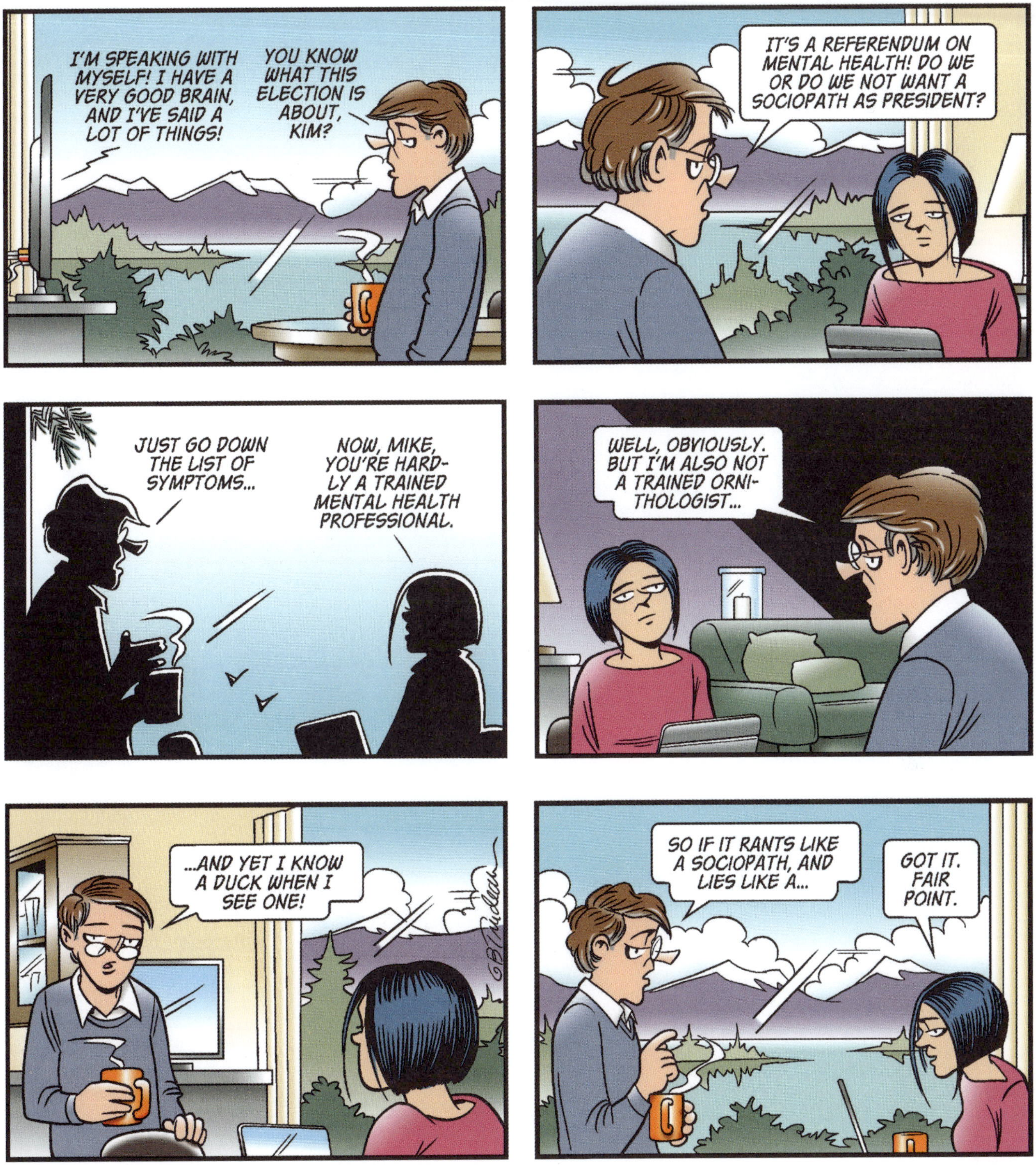
I'M SPEAKING WITH MYSELF! I HAVE A VERY GOOD BRAIN, AND I'VE SAID A LOT OF THINGS!
YOU KNOW WHAT THIS ELECTION IS ABOUT, KIM?
IT'S A REFERENDUM ON MENTAL HEALTH! DO WE OR DO WE NOT WANT A SOCIOPATH AS PRESIDENT?
JUST GO DOWN THE LIST OF SYMPTOMS...
NOW, MIKE, YOU'RE HARDLY A TRAINED MENTAL HEALTH PROFESSIONAL.
WELL, OBVIOUSLY. BUT I'M ALSO NOT A TRAINED ORNITHOLOGIST...
...AND YET I KNOW A DUCK WHEN I SEE ONE!
SO IF IT RANTS LIKE A SOCIOPATH, AND LIES LIKE A...
GOT IT. FAIR POINT.

October 23, 2016

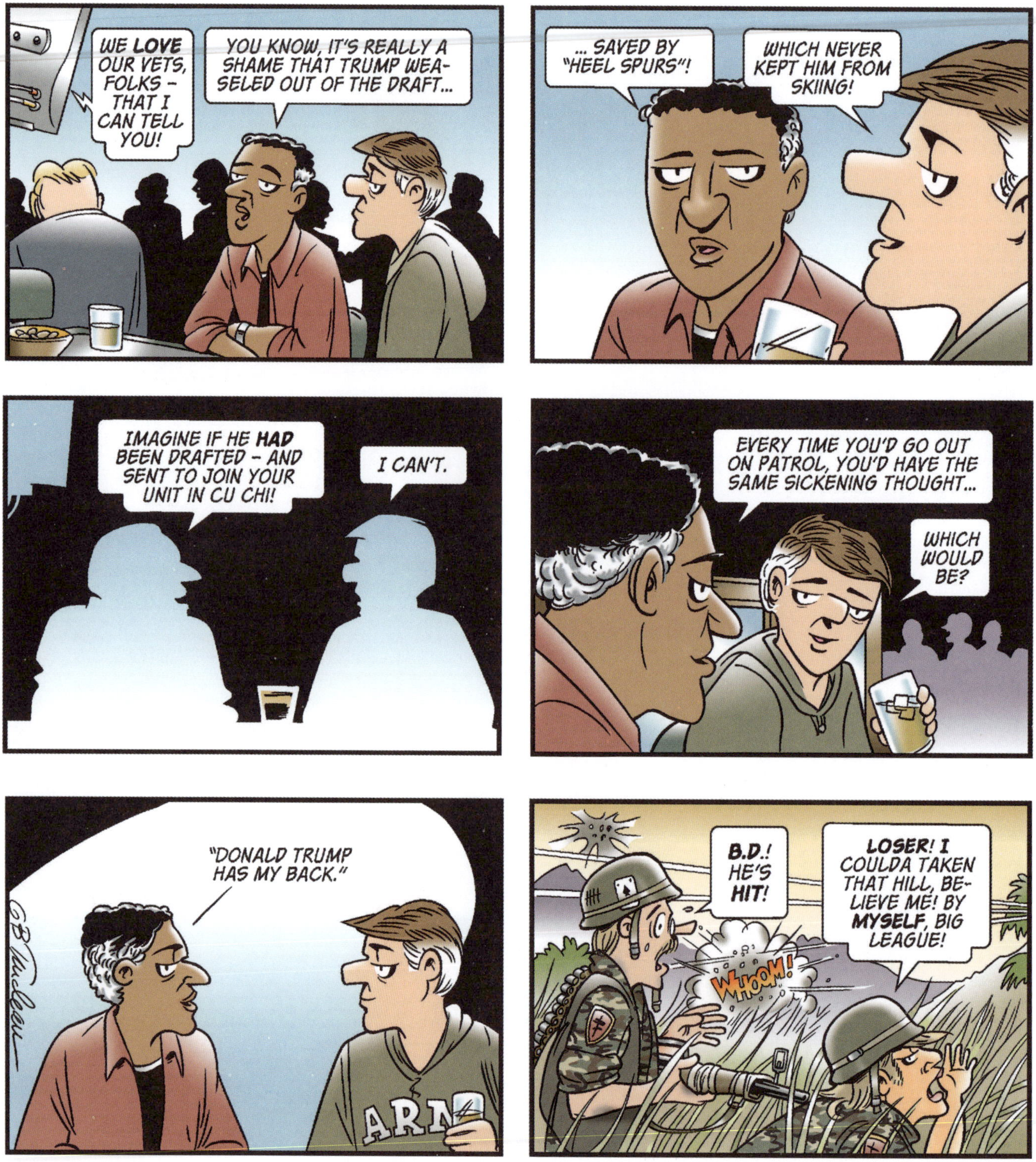
WE LOVE OUR VETS, FOLKS – THAT I CAN TELL YOU!
YOU KNOW, IT'S REALLY A SHAME THAT TRUMP WEASELED OUT OF THE DRAFT...
... SAVED BY "HEEL SPURS"!
WHICH NEVER KEPT HIM FROM SKIING!
IMAGINE IF HE HAD BEEN DRAFTED – AND SENT TO JOIN YOUR UNIT IN CU CHI!
I CAN'T.
EVERY TIME YOU'D GO OUT ON PATROL, YOU'D HAVE THE SAME SICKENING THOUGHT...
WHICH WOULD BE?
"DONALD TRUMP HAS MY BACK."
B.D.! HE'S HIT!
LOSER! I COULDA TAKEN THAT HILL, BELIEVE ME! BY MYSELF, BIG LEAGUE!
WHOOM!

October 30, 2016

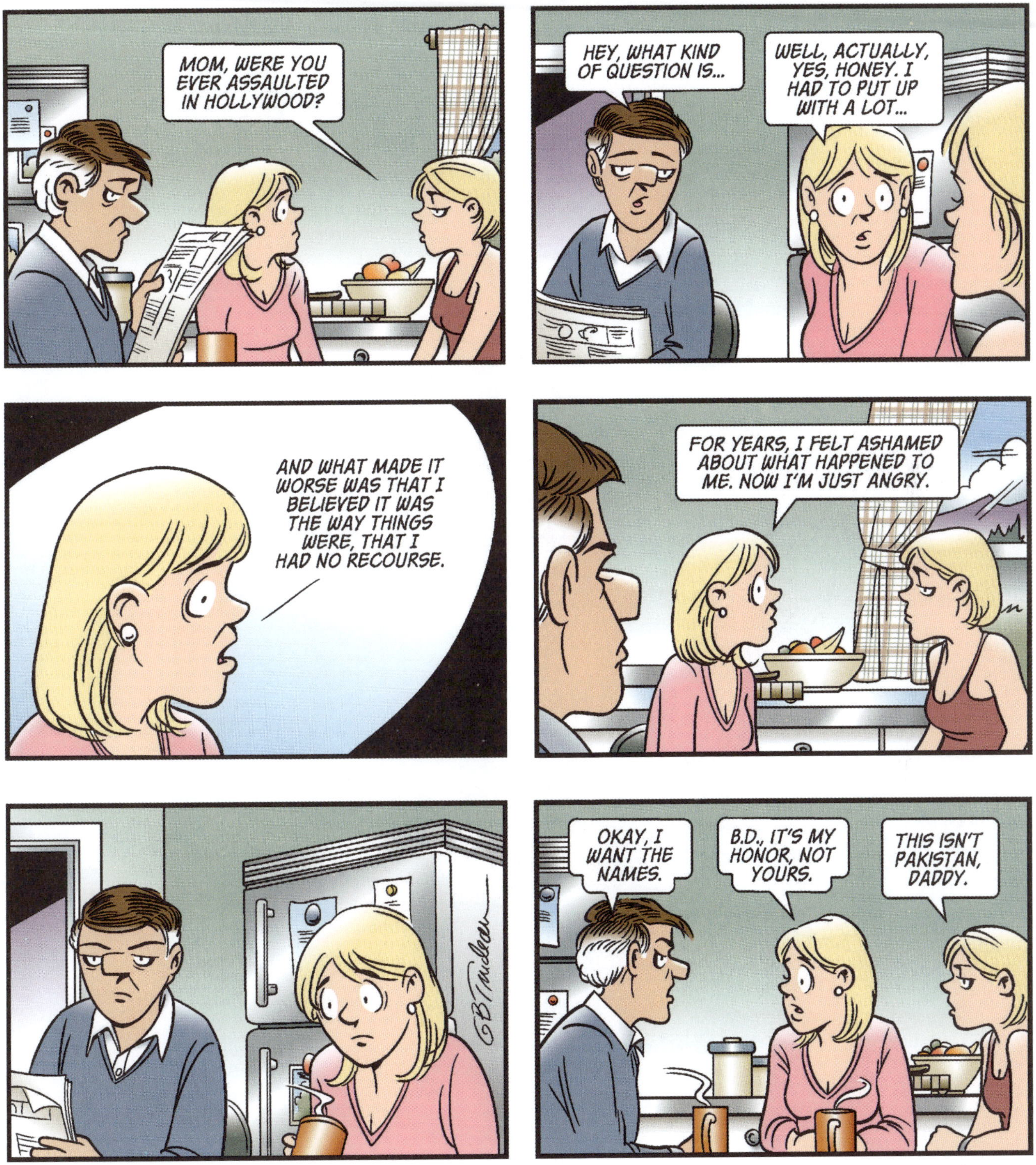
MOM, WERE YOU EVER ASSAULTED IN HOLLYWOOD?
HEY, WHAT KIND OF QUESTION IS...
WELL, ACTUALLY, YES, HONEY. I HAD TO PUT UP WITH A LOT...
AND WHAT MADE IT WORSE WAS THAT I BELIEVED IT WAS THE WAY THINGS WERE, THAT I HAD NO RECOURSE.
FOR YEARS, I FELT ASHAMED ABOUT WHAT HAPPENED TO ME. NOW I'M JUST ANGRY.
GBTrudeau
OKAY, I WANT THE NAMES.
B.D., IT'S MY HONOR, NOT YOURS.
THIS ISN'T PAKISTAN, DADDY.

November 27, 2016

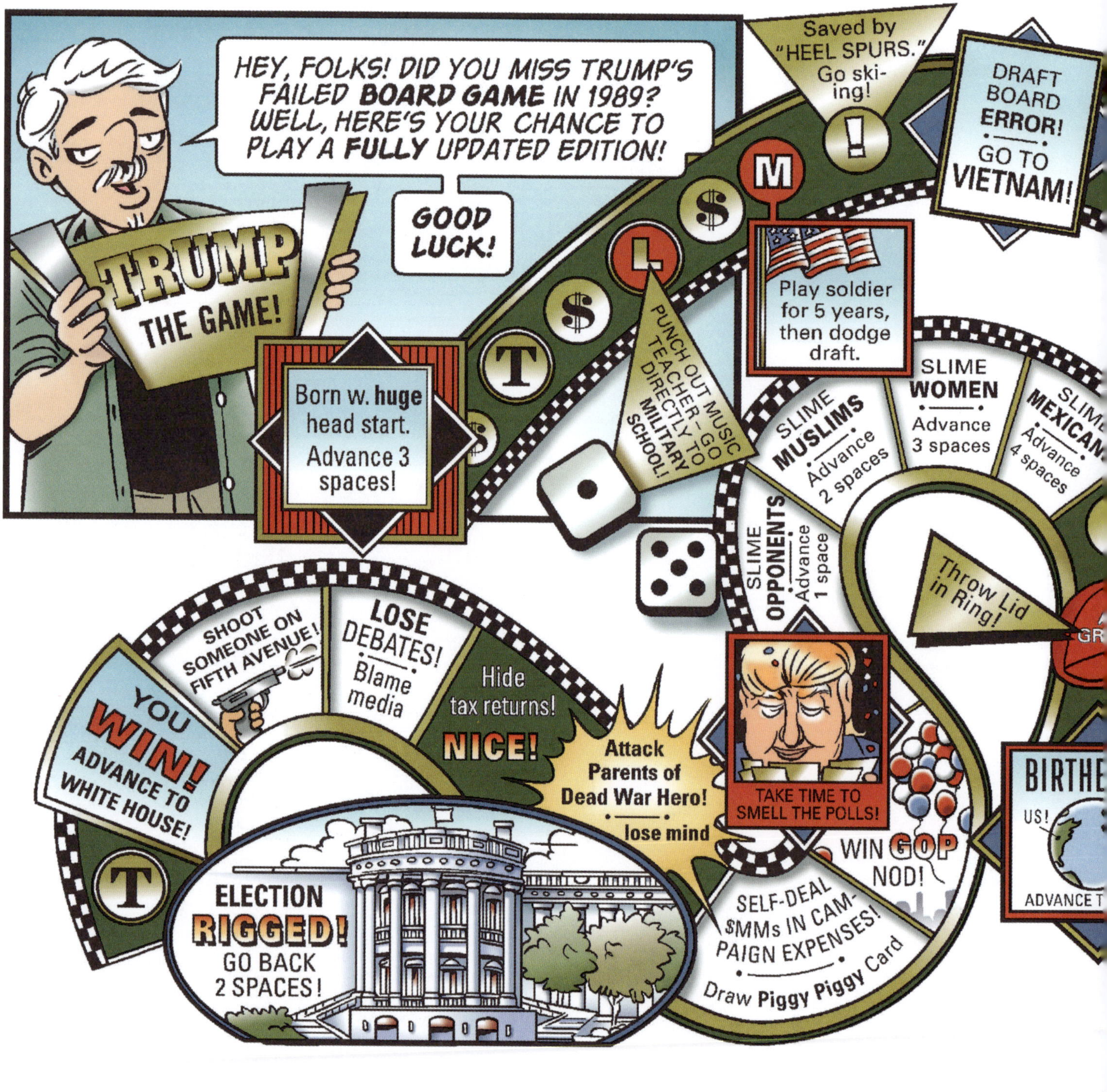
HEY, FOLKS! DID YOU MISS TRUMP'S FAILED BOARD GAME IN 1989? WELL, HERE'S YOUR CHANCE TO PLAY A FULLY UPDATED EDITION!
GOOD LUCK!
TRUMP THE GAME!
Born w. huge head start. Advance 3 spaces!
PUNCH OUT MUSIC TEACHER – GO DIRECTLY TO MILITARY SCHOOL!
Play soldier for 5 years, then dodge draft.
Saved by "HEEL SPURS." Go ski-ing!
DRAFT BOARD ERROR! GO TO VIETNAM!
SLIME MUSLIMS Advance 2 spaces
SLIME WOMEN Advance 3 spaces
SLIME MEXICANS Advance 4 spaces
SLIME OPPONENTS Advance 1 space
Throw Lid in Ring!
TAKE TIME TO SMELL THE POLLS!
BIRTHE
US!
ADVANCE T
WIN GOP NOD!
SELF-DEAL $MMs IN CAMPAIGN EXPENSES! Draw Piggy Piggy Card
Attack Parents of Dead War Hero! lose mind
Hide tax returns! NICE!
LOSE DEBATES! Blame media
SHOOT SOMEONE ON FIFTH AVENUE!
YOU WIN! ADVANCE TO WHITE HOUSE!
ELECTION RIGGED! GO BACK 2 SPACES!

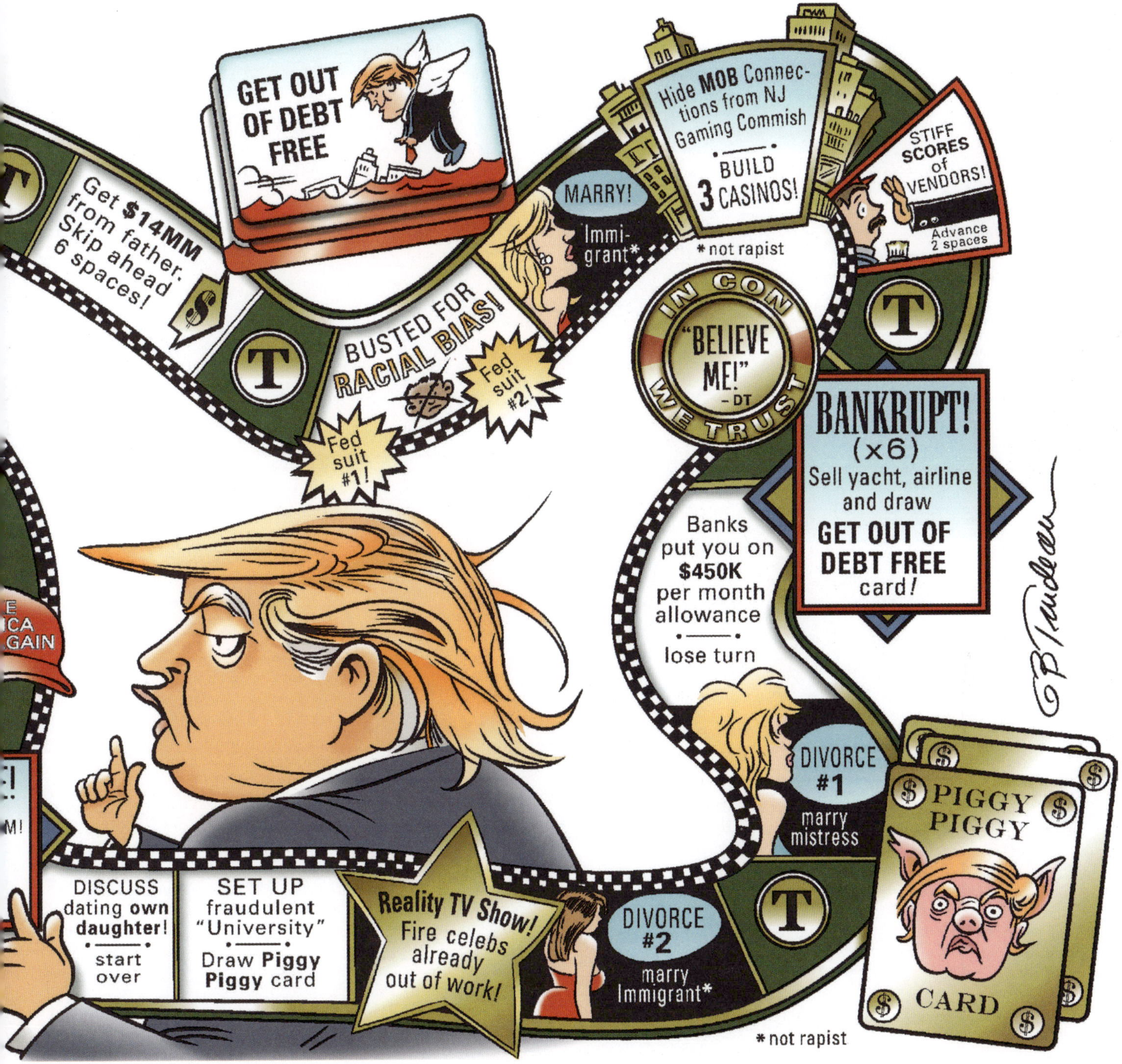
GET OUT OF DEBT FREE
Get $14MM from father. Skip ahead 6 spaces!
BUSTED FOR RACIAL BIAS!
Fed suit #1!
Fed suit #2!
MARRY!
Immi-grant*
Hide MOB Connec-tions from NJ Gaming Commish
BUILD 3 CASINOS!
* not rapist
STIFF SCORES of VENDORS!
Advance 2 spaces
IN CON WE TRUST
"BELIEVE ME!" - DT
BANKRUPT! (x6)
Sell yacht, airline and draw GET OUT OF DEBT FREE card!
Banks put you on $450K per month allowance
lose turn
DIVORCE #1
marry mistress
PIGGY PIGGY CARD
DIVORCE #2
marry Immigrant*
* not rapist
Reality TV Show! Fire celebs already out of work!
SET UP fraudulent "University"
Draw Piggy Piggy card
DISCUSS dating own daughter!
start over
GBTrudeau

November 6, 2016

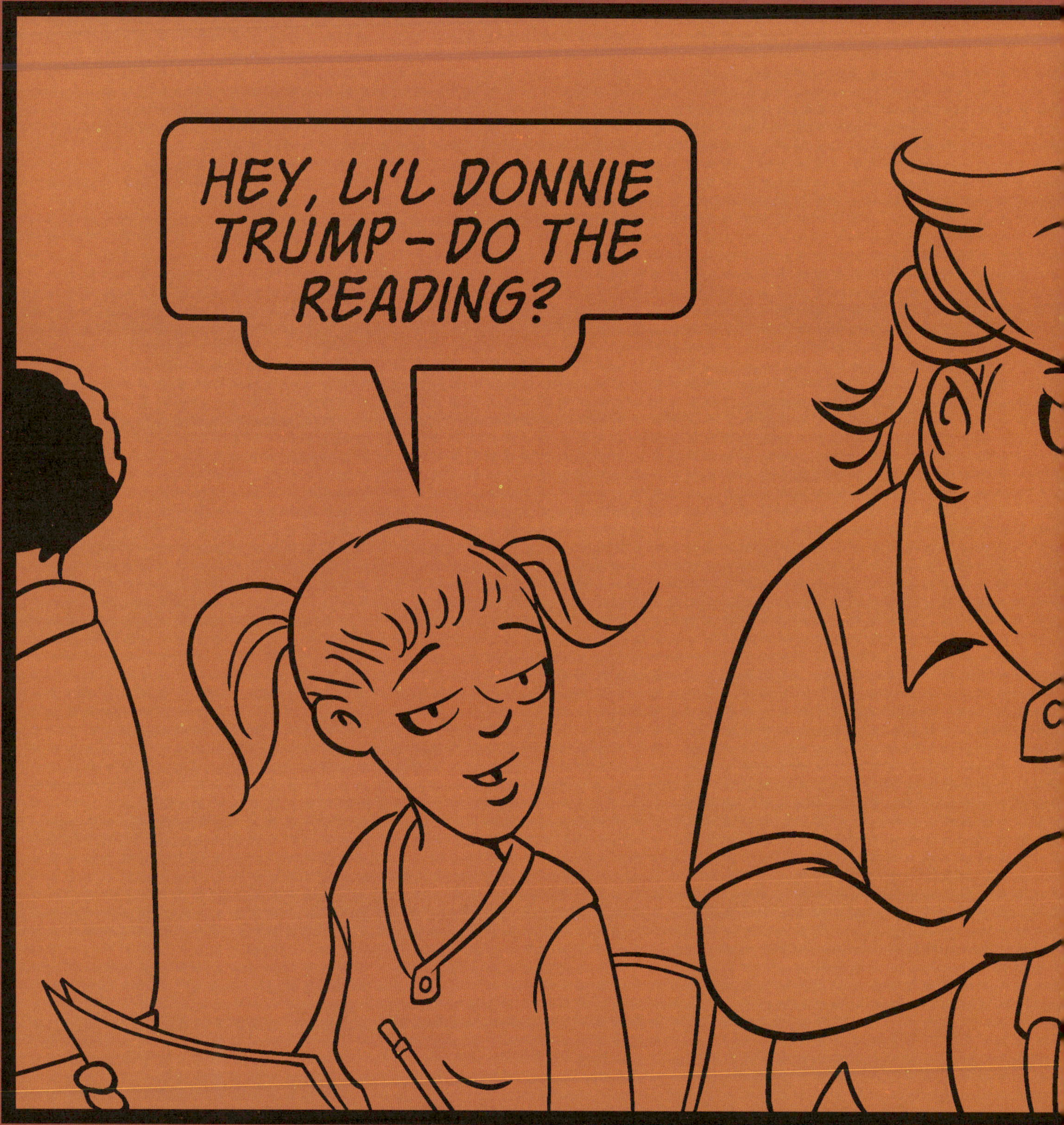
HEY, LI'L DONNIE TRUMP – DO THE READING?

PART 2
American Carnage

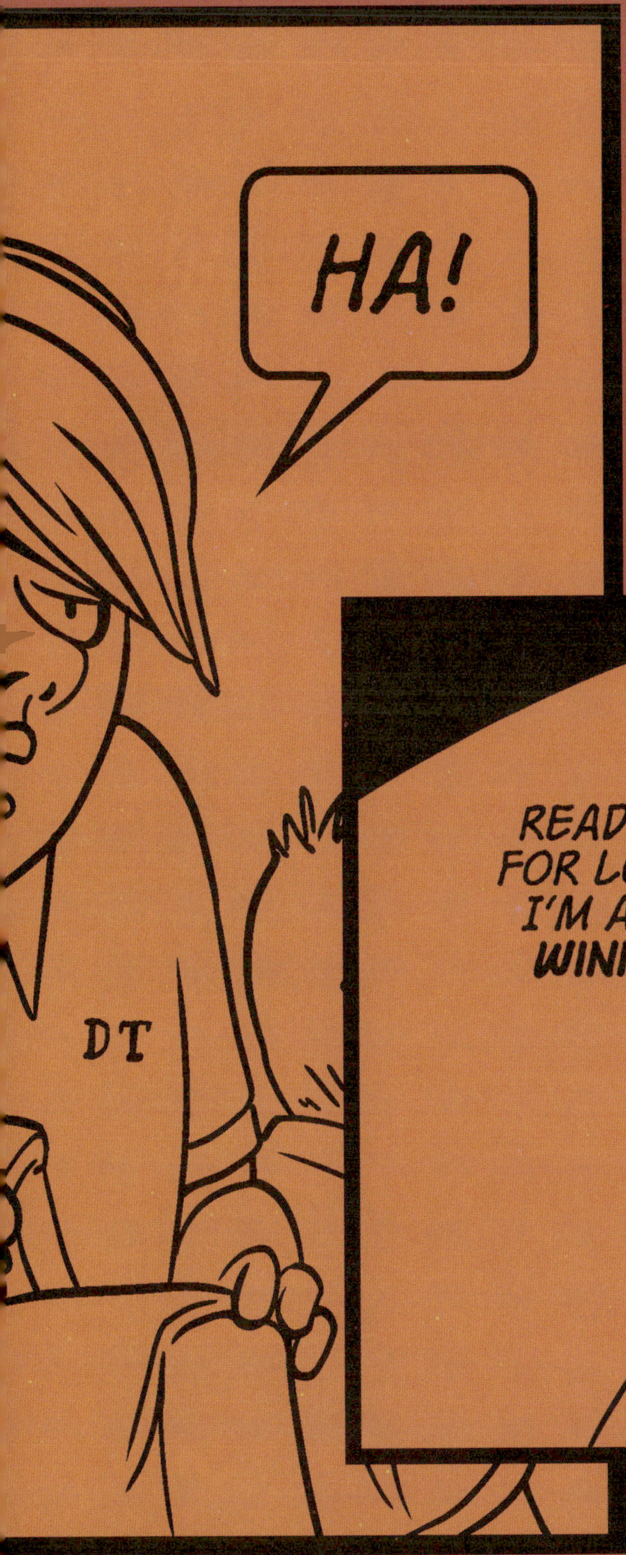

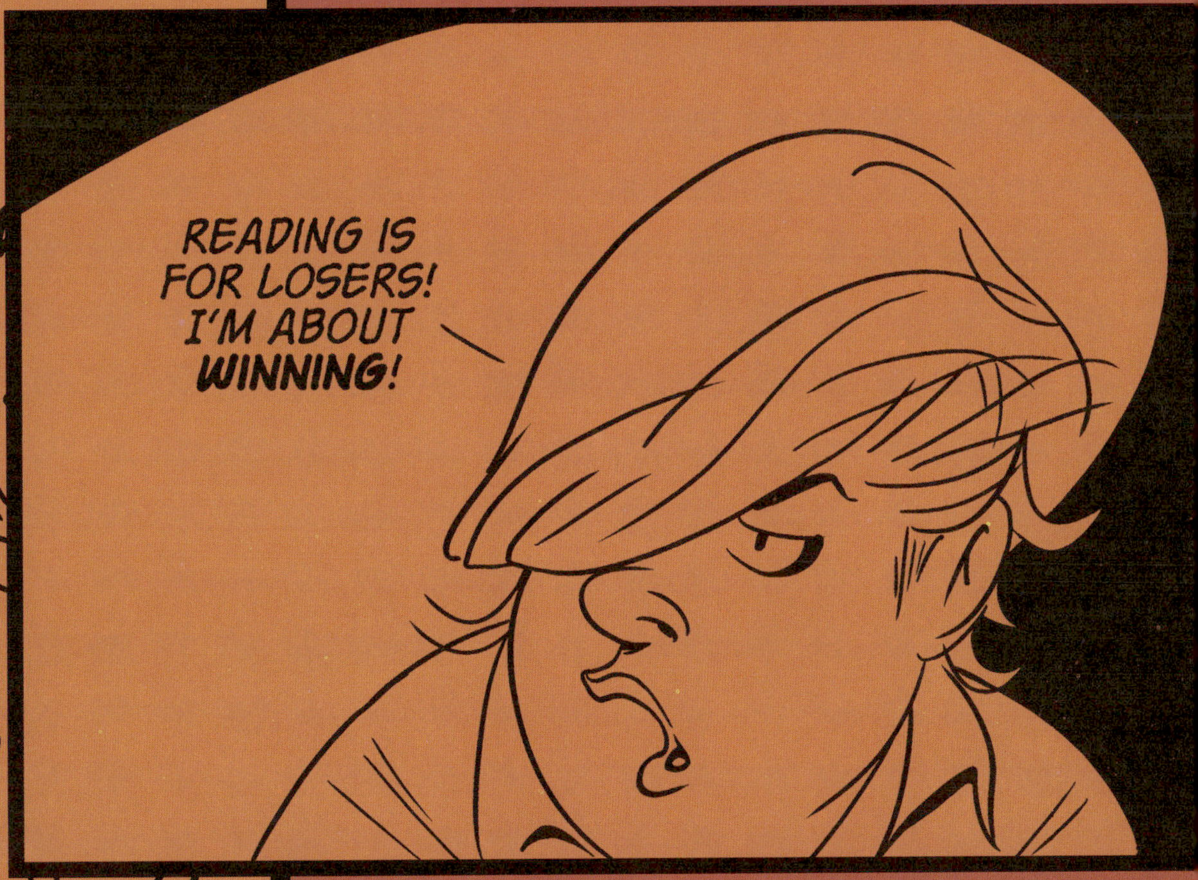

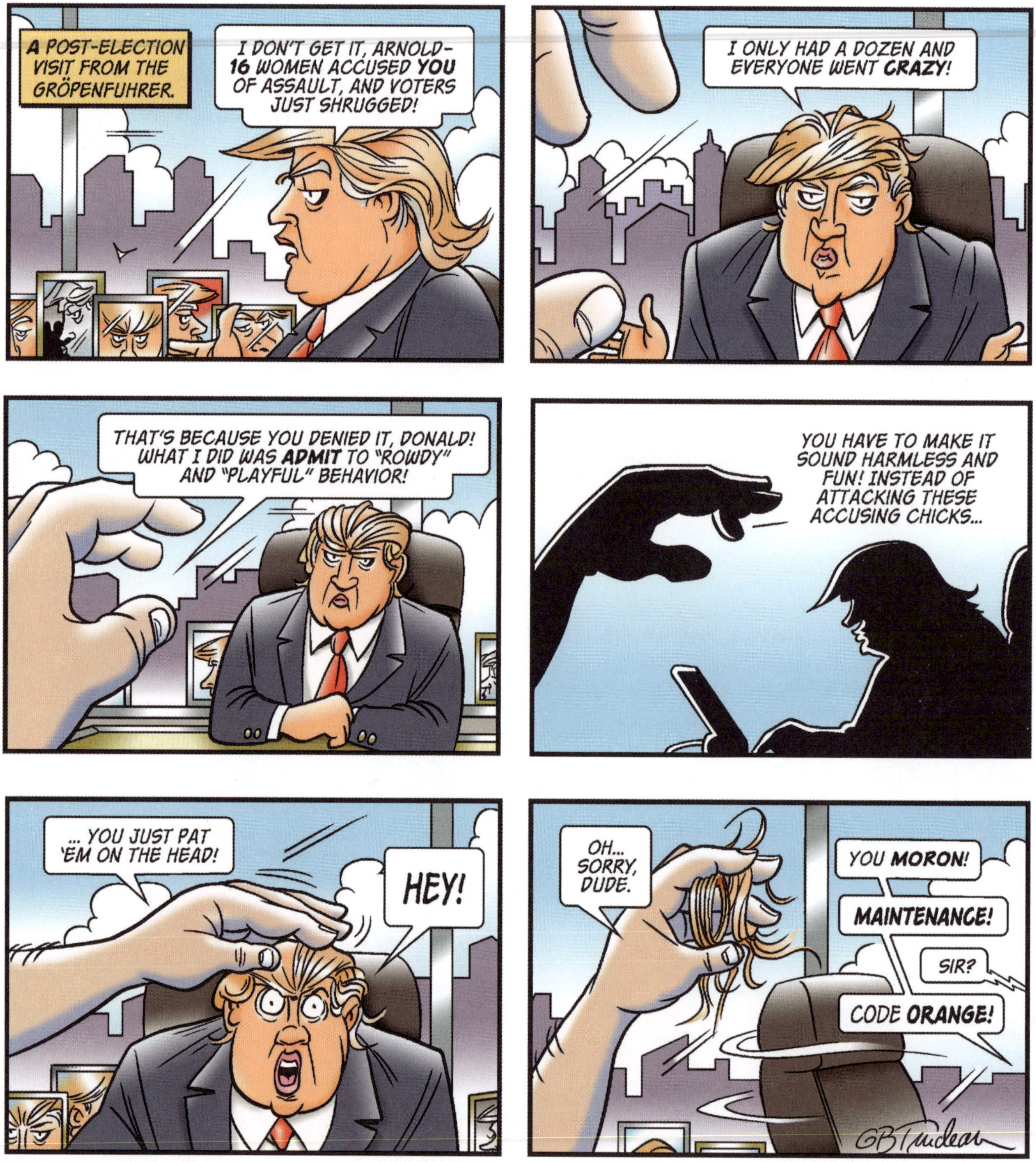
A POST-ELECTION VISIT FROM THE GRÖPENFUHRER.
I DON'T GET IT, ARNOLD– 16 WOMEN ACCUSED YOU OF ASSAULT, AND VOTERS JUST SHRUGGED!
I ONLY HAD A DOZEN AND EVERYONE WENT CRAZY!
THAT'S BECAUSE YOU DENIED IT, DONALD! WHAT I DID WAS ADMIT TO "ROWDY" AND "PLAYFUL" BEHAVIOR!
YOU HAVE TO MAKE IT SOUND HARMLESS AND FUN! INSTEAD OF ATTACKING THESE ACCUSING CHICKS...
... YOU JUST PAT 'EM ON THE HEAD!
HEY!
OH... SORRY, DUDE.
YOU MORON!
MAINTENANCE!
SIR?
CODE ORANGE!
GBTrudeau

November 20, 2016

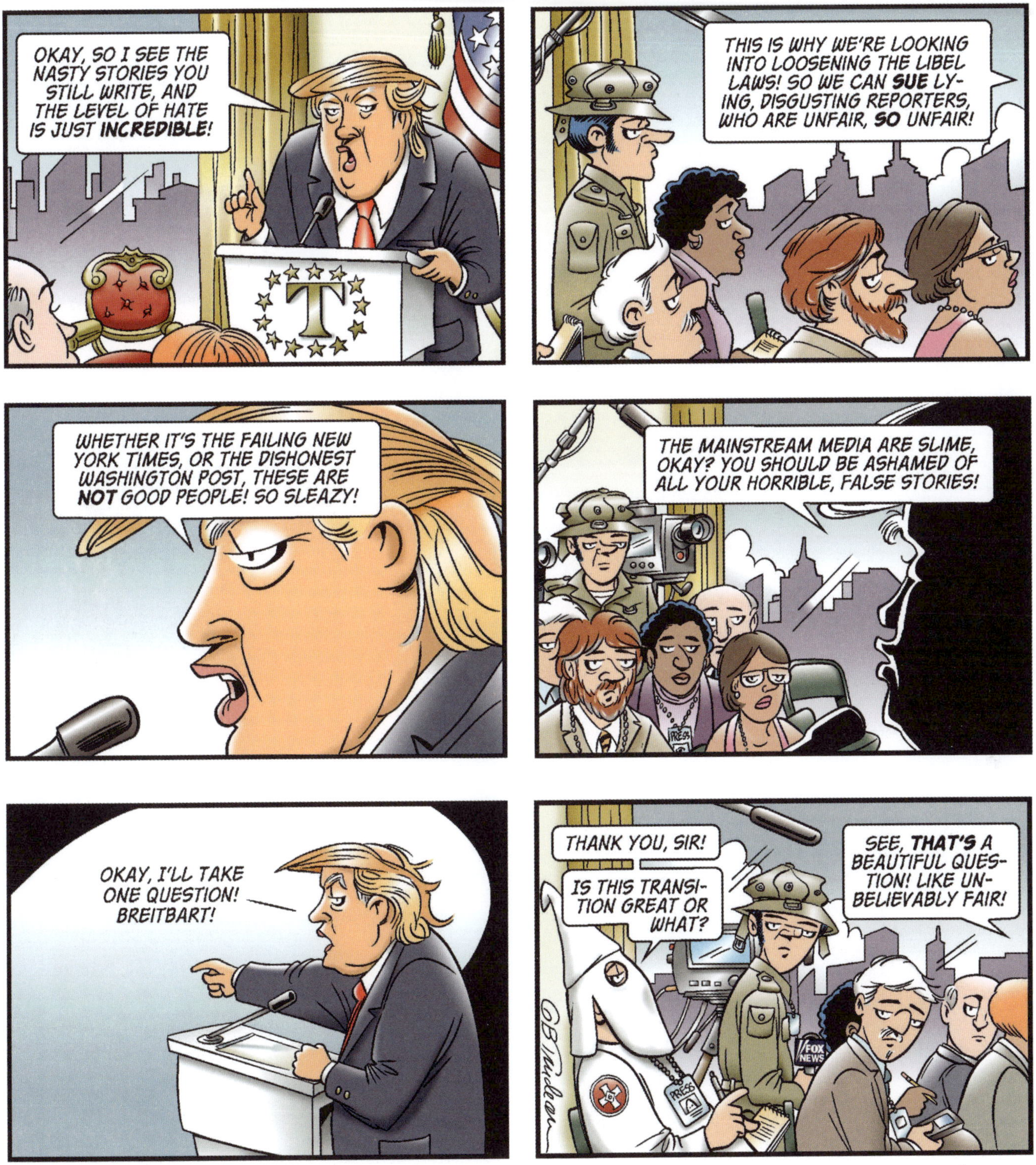
OKAY, SO I SEE THE NASTY STORIES YOU STILL WRITE, AND THE LEVEL OF HATE IS JUST INCREDIBLE!
THIS IS WHY WE'RE LOOKING INTO LOOSENING THE LIBEL LAWS! SO WE CAN SUE LYING, DISGUSTING REPORTERS, WHO ARE UNFAIR, SO UNFAIR!
WHETHER IT'S THE FAILING NEW YORK TIMES, OR THE DISHONEST WASHINGTON POST, THESE ARE NOT GOOD PEOPLE! SO SLEAZY!
THE MAINSTREAM MEDIA ARE SLIME, OKAY? YOU SHOULD BE ASHAMED OF ALL YOUR HORRIBLE, FALSE STORIES!
OKAY, I'LL TAKE ONE QUESTION! BREITBART!
THANK YOU, SIR!
IS THIS TRANSITION GREAT OR WHAT?
SEE, THAT'S A BEAUTIFUL QUESTION! LIKE UNBELIEVABLY FAIR!
PRESS
FOX NEWS
GB Trudeau

December 18, 2016

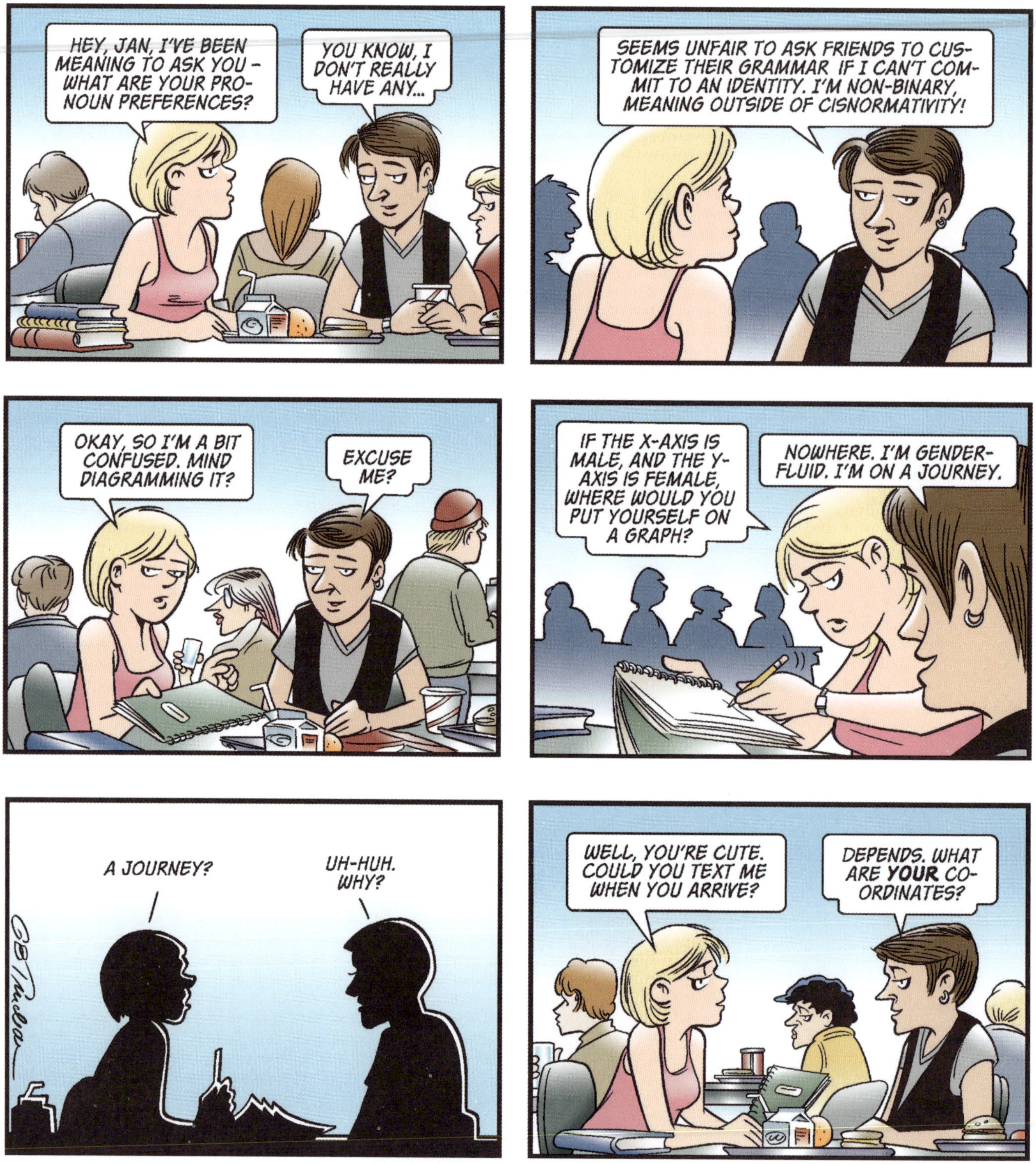
HEY, JAN, I'VE BEEN MEANING TO ASK YOU - WHAT ARE YOUR PRONOUN PREFERENCES?
YOU KNOW, I DON'T REALLY HAVE ANY...
SEEMS UNFAIR TO ASK FRIENDS TO CUSTOMIZE THEIR GRAMMAR IF I CAN'T COMMIT TO AN IDENTITY. I'M NON-BINARY, MEANING OUTSIDE OF CISNORMATIVITY!
OKAY, SO I'M A BIT CONFUSED. MIND DIAGRAMMING IT?
EXCUSE ME?
IF THE X-AXIS IS MALE, AND THE Y-AXIS IS FEMALE, WHERE WOULD YOU PUT YOURSELF ON A GRAPH?
NOWHERE. I'M GENDER-FLUID. I'M ON A JOURNEY.
A JOURNEY?
UH-HUH. WHY?
WELL, YOU'RE CUTE. COULD YOU TEXT ME WHEN YOU ARRIVE?
DEPENDS. WHAT ARE **YOUR** CO-ORDINATES?

December 11, 2016

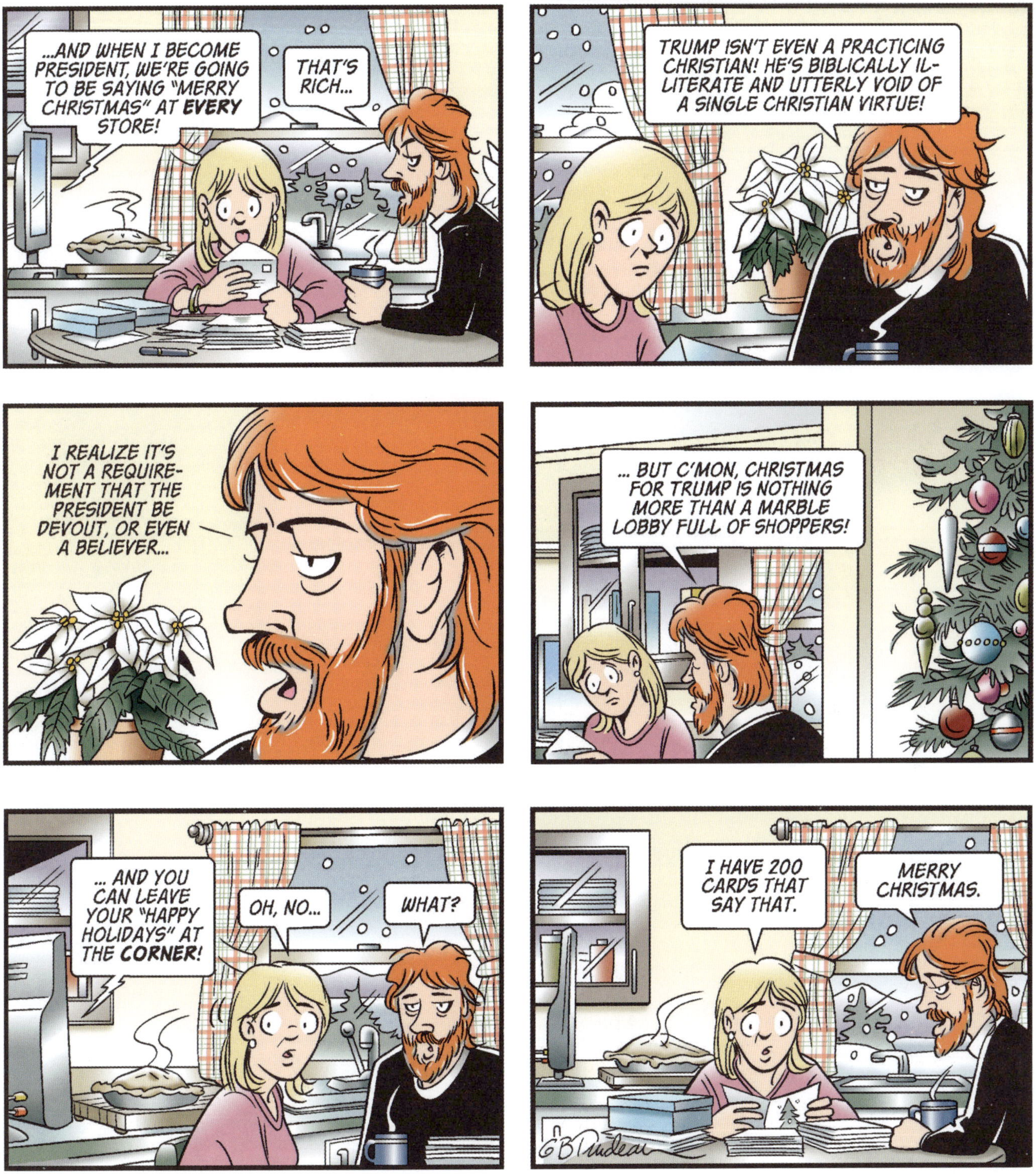
...AND WHEN I BECOME PRESIDENT, WE'RE GOING TO BE SAYING "MERRY CHRISTMAS" AT EVERY STORE!
THAT'S RICH...
TRUMP ISN'T EVEN A PRACTICING CHRISTIAN! HE'S BIBLICALLY ILLITERATE AND UTTERLY VOID OF A SINGLE CHRISTIAN VIRTUE!
I REALIZE IT'S NOT A REQUIREMENT THAT THE PRESIDENT BE DEVOUT, OR EVEN A BELIEVER...
... BUT C'MON, CHRISTMAS FOR TRUMP IS NOTHING MORE THAN A MARBLE LOBBY FULL OF SHOPPERS!
... AND YOU CAN LEAVE YOUR "HAPPY HOLIDAYS" AT THE CORNER!
OH, NO...
WHAT?
I HAVE 200 CARDS THAT SAY THAT.
MERRY CHRISTMAS.
GB Trudeau

December 25, 2016

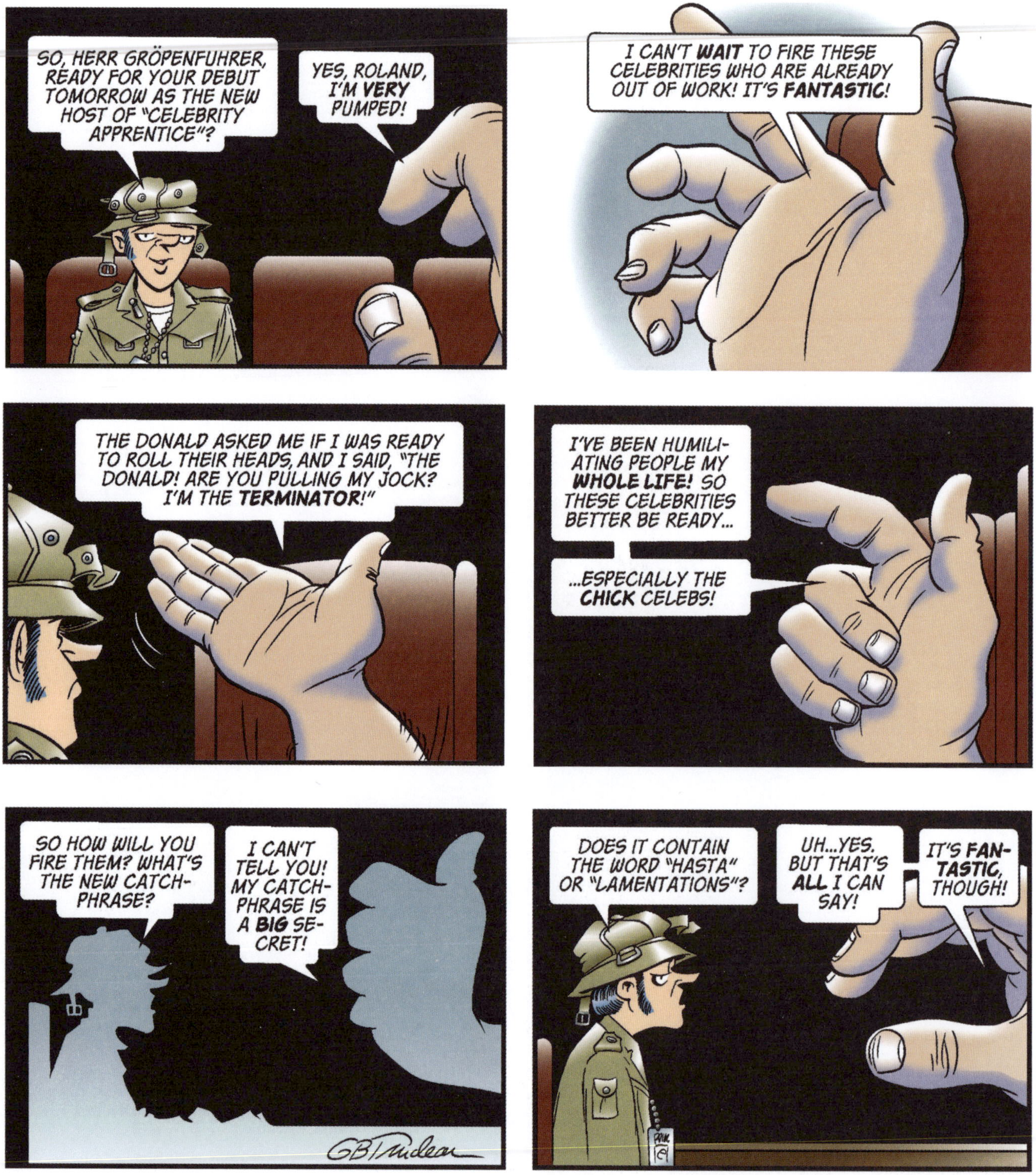
SO, HERR GRÖPENFUHRER, READY FOR YOUR DEBUT TOMORROW AS THE NEW HOST OF "CELEBRITY APPRENTICE"?
YES, ROLAND, I'M VERY PUMPED!
I CAN'T WAIT TO FIRE THESE CELEBRITIES WHO ARE ALREADY OUT OF WORK! IT'S FANTASTIC!
THE DONALD ASKED ME IF I WAS READY TO ROLL THEIR HEADS, AND I SAID, "THE DONALD! ARE YOU PULLING MY JOCK? I'M THE TERMINATOR!"
I'VE BEEN HUMILIATING PEOPLE MY WHOLE LIFE! SO THESE CELEBRITIES BETTER BE READY...
...ESPECIALLY THE CHICK CELEBS!
SO HOW WILL YOU FIRE THEM? WHAT'S THE NEW CATCH-PHRASE?
I CAN'T TELL YOU! MY CATCH-PHRASE IS A BIG SE-CRET!
GBTrudeau
DOES IT CONTAIN THE WORD "HASTA" OR "LAMENTATIONS"?
UH...YES. BUT THAT'S ALL I CAN SAY!
IT'S FAN-TASTIC, THOUGH!

January 1, 2017

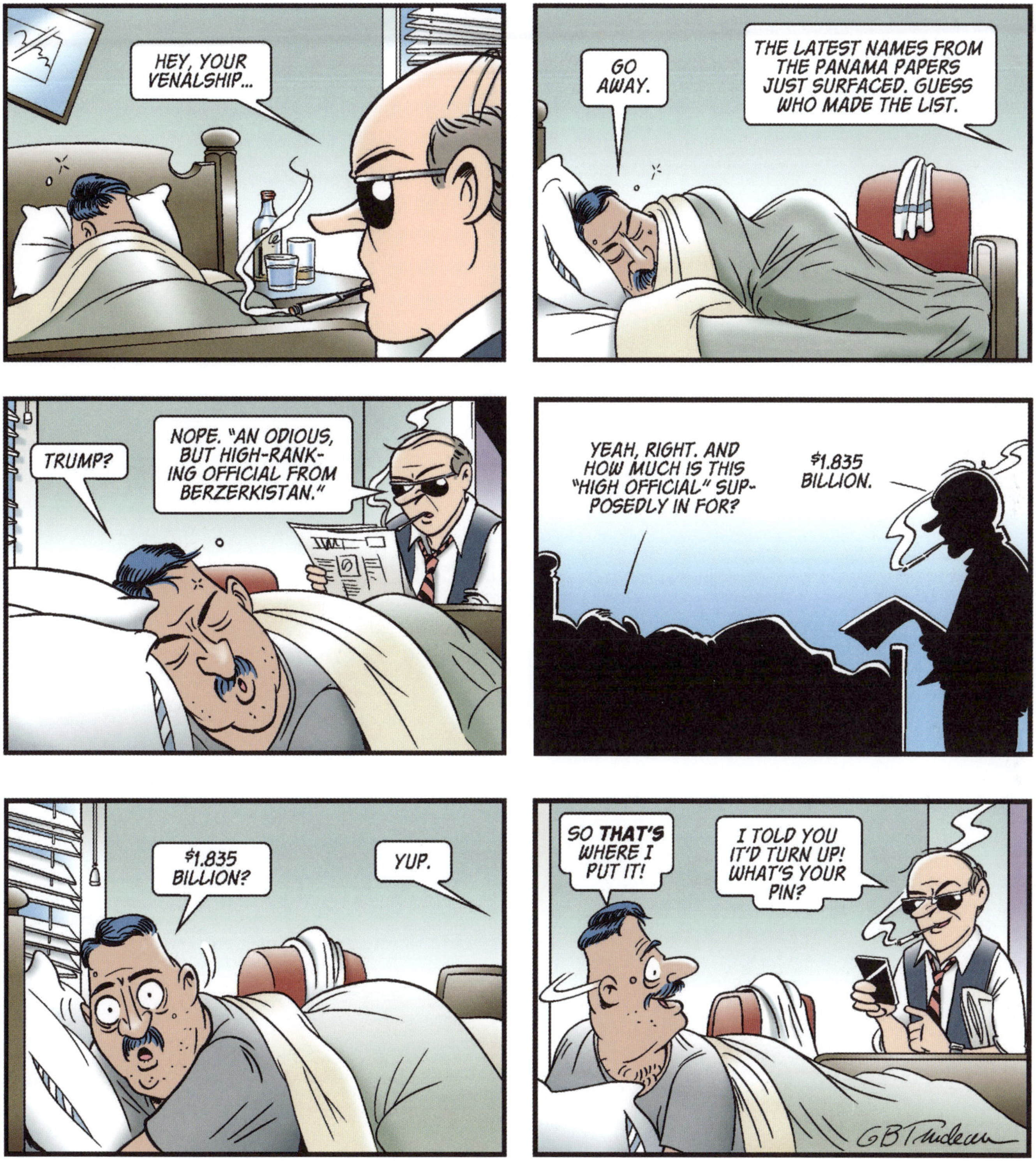
HEY, YOUR VENALSHIP...
GO AWAY.
THE LATEST NAMES FROM THE PANAMA PAPERS JUST SURFACED. GUESS WHO MADE THE LIST.
TRUMP?
NOPE. "AN ODIOUS, BUT HIGH-RANKING OFFICIAL FROM BERZERKISTAN."
YEAH, RIGHT. AND HOW MUCH IS THIS "HIGH OFFICIAL" SUPPOSEDLY IN FOR?
$1.835 BILLION.
$1.835 BILLION?
YUP.
SO **THAT'S** WHERE I PUT IT!
I TOLD YOU IT'D TURN UP! WHAT'S YOUR PIN?
GBTrudeau

May 22, 2016

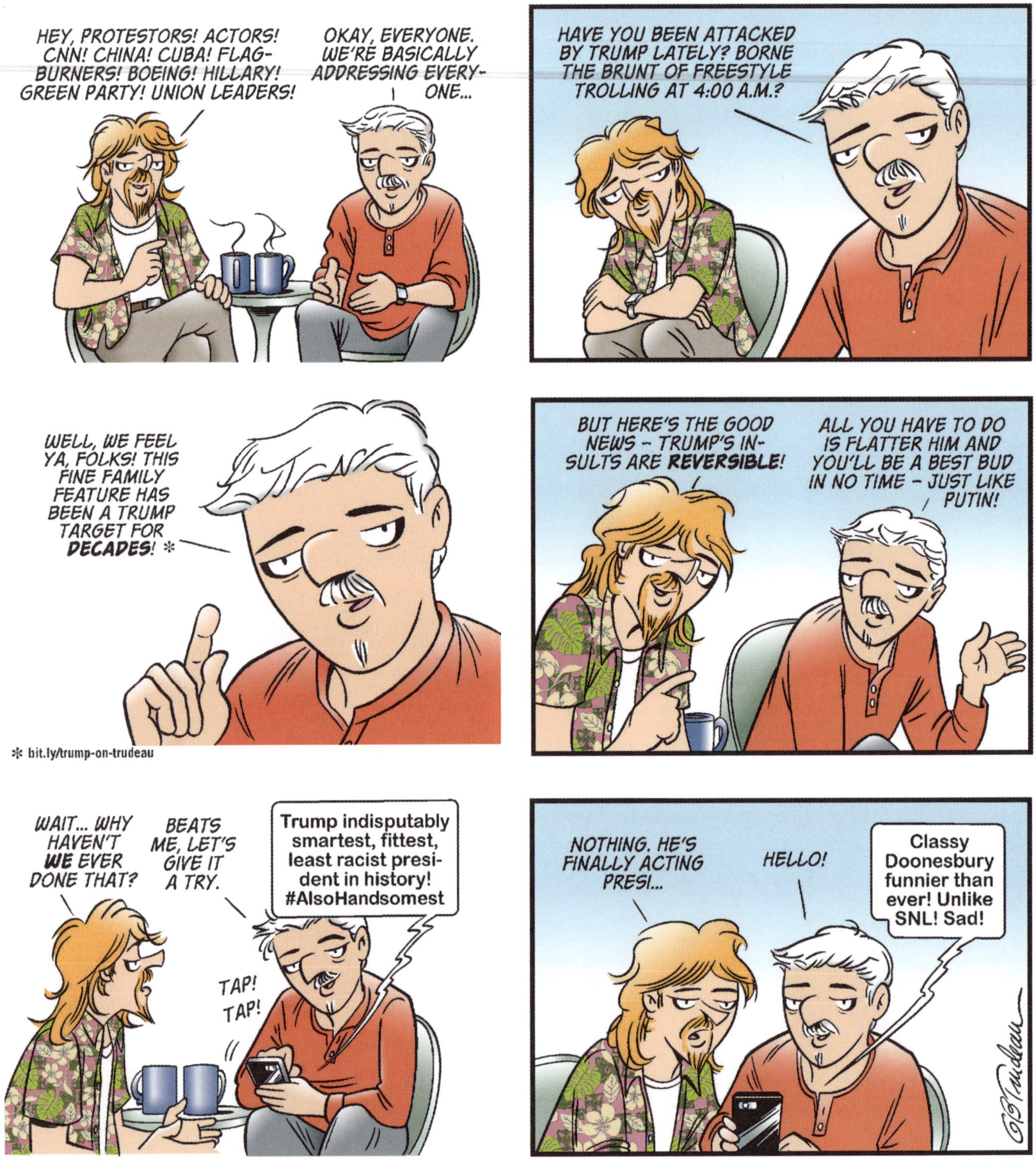
HEY, PROTESTORS! ACTORS! CNN! CHINA! CUBA! FLAG-BURNERS! BOEING! HILLARY! GREEN PARTY! UNION LEADERS!
OKAY, EVERYONE. WE'RE BASICALLY ADDRESSING EVERY-ONE...
HAVE YOU BEEN ATTACKED BY TRUMP LATELY? BORNE THE BRUNT OF FREESTYLE TROLLING AT 4:00 A.M.?
WELL, WE FEEL YA, FOLKS! THIS FINE FAMILY FEATURE HAS BEEN A TRUMP TARGET FOR **DECADES**! *
BUT HERE'S THE GOOD NEWS – TRUMP'S IN-SULTS ARE **REVERSIBLE**!
ALL YOU HAVE TO DO IS FLATTER HIM AND YOU'LL BE A BEST BUD IN NO TIME – JUST LIKE PUTIN!
WAIT... WHY HAVEN'T **WE** EVER DONE THAT?
BEATS ME, LET'S GIVE IT A TRY.
Trump indisputably smartest, fittest, least racist president in history! #AlsoHandsomest
TAP! TAP!
NOTHING. HE'S FINALLY ACTING PRESI...
HELLO!
Classy Doonesbury funnier than ever! Unlike SNL! Sad!
GBTrudeau

* bit.ly/trump-on-trudeau

January 8, 2017

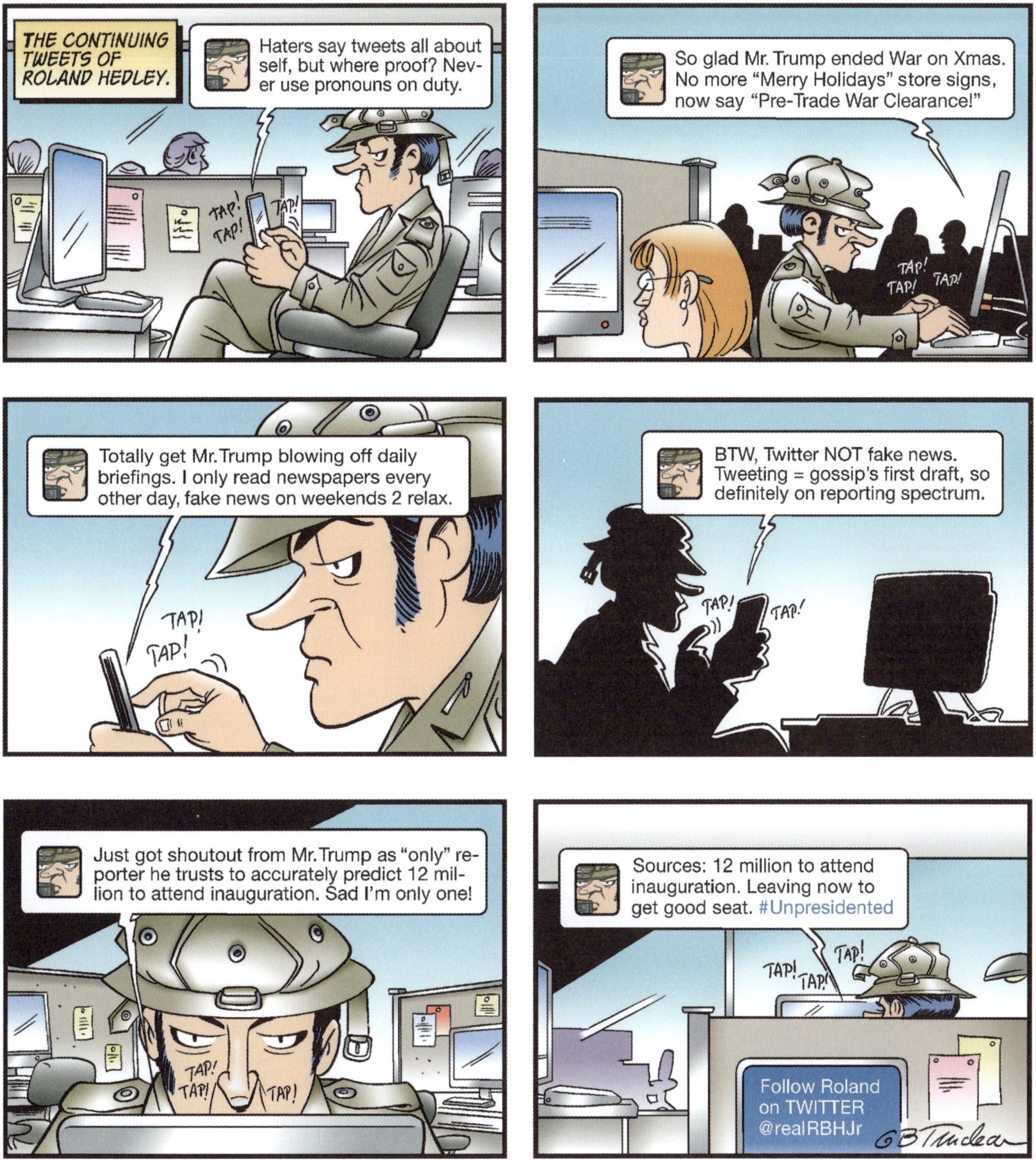
THE CONTINUING TWEETS OF ROLAND HEDLEY.
Haters say tweets all about self, but where proof? Never use pronouns on duty.
TAP! TAP! TAP!
So glad Mr. Trump ended War on Xmas. No more "Merry Holidays" store signs, now say "Pre-Trade War Clearance!"
TAP! TAP! TAP!
Totally get Mr. Trump blowing off daily briefings. I only read newspapers every other day, fake news on weekends 2 relax.
TAP! TAP!
BTW, Twitter NOT fake news. Tweeting = gossip's first draft, so definitely on reporting spectrum.
TAP! TAP!
Just got shoutout from Mr. Trump as "only" reporter he trusts to accurately predict 12 million to attend inauguration. Sad I'm only one!
TAP! TAP! TAP!
Sources: 12 million to attend inauguration. Leaving now to get good seat. #Unpresidented
TAP! TAP! TAP!
Follow Roland on TWITTER @realRBHJr
G B Trudeau

January 15, 2017

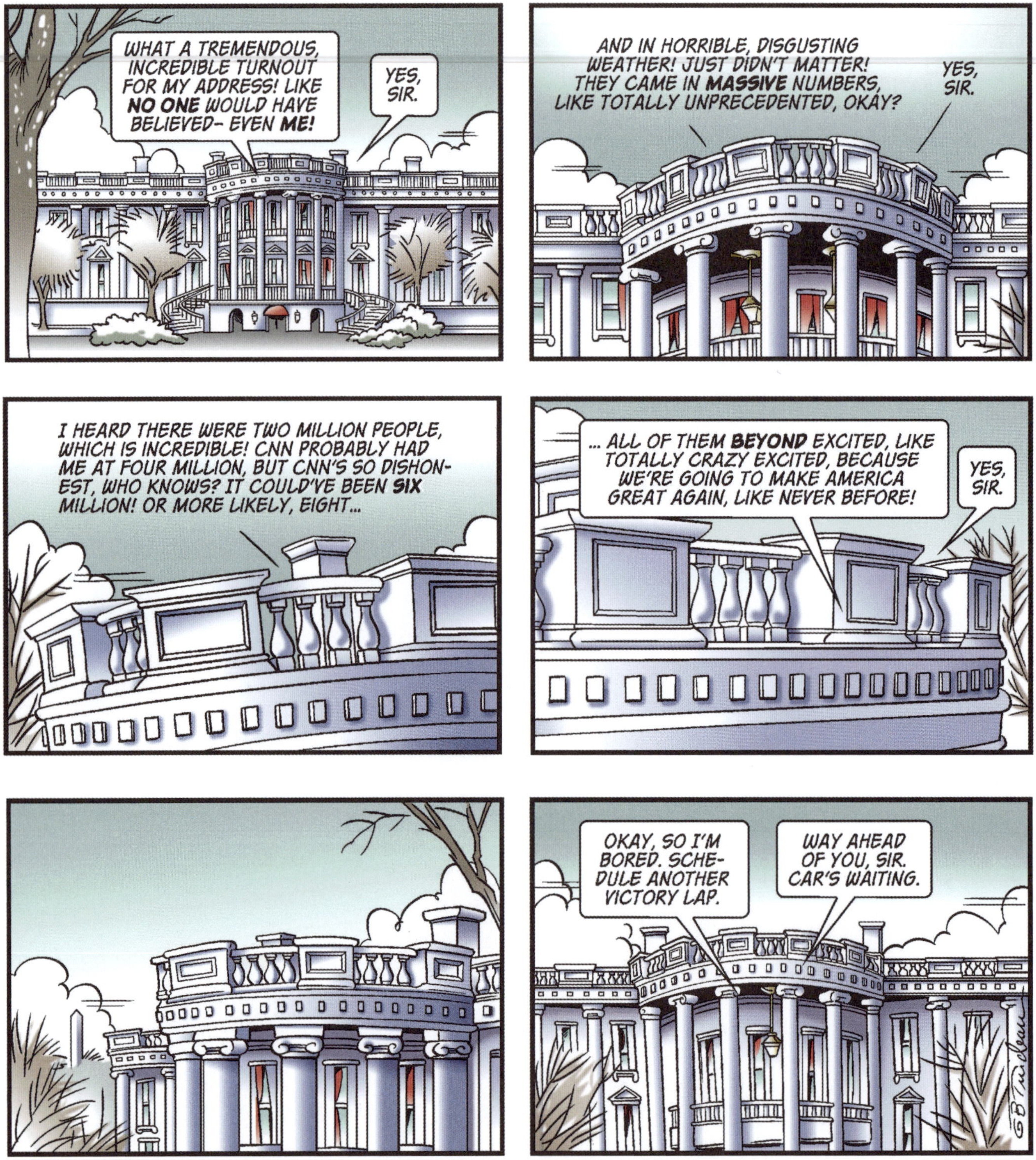
WHAT A TREMENDOUS, INCREDIBLE TURNOUT FOR MY ADDRESS! LIKE **NO ONE** WOULD HAVE BELIEVED– EVEN **ME!**
YES, SIR.
AND IN HORRIBLE, DISGUSTING WEATHER! JUST DIDN'T MATTER! THEY CAME IN **MASSIVE** NUMBERS, LIKE TOTALLY UNPRECEDENTED, OKAY?
YES, SIR.
I HEARD THERE WERE TWO MILLION PEOPLE, WHICH IS INCREDIBLE! CNN PROBABLY HAD ME AT FOUR MILLION, BUT CNN'S SO DISHON-EST, WHO KNOWS? IT COULD'VE BEEN **SIX** MILLION! OR MORE LIKELY, EIGHT...
... ALL OF THEM **BEYOND** EXCITED, LIKE TOTALLY CRAZY EXCITED, BECAUSE WE'RE GOING TO MAKE AMERICA GREAT AGAIN, LIKE NEVER BEFORE!
YES, SIR.
OKAY, SO I'M BORED. SCHE-DULE ANOTHER VICTORY LAP.
WAY AHEAD OF YOU, SIR. CAR'S WAITING.
GBTrudeau

January 22, 2017

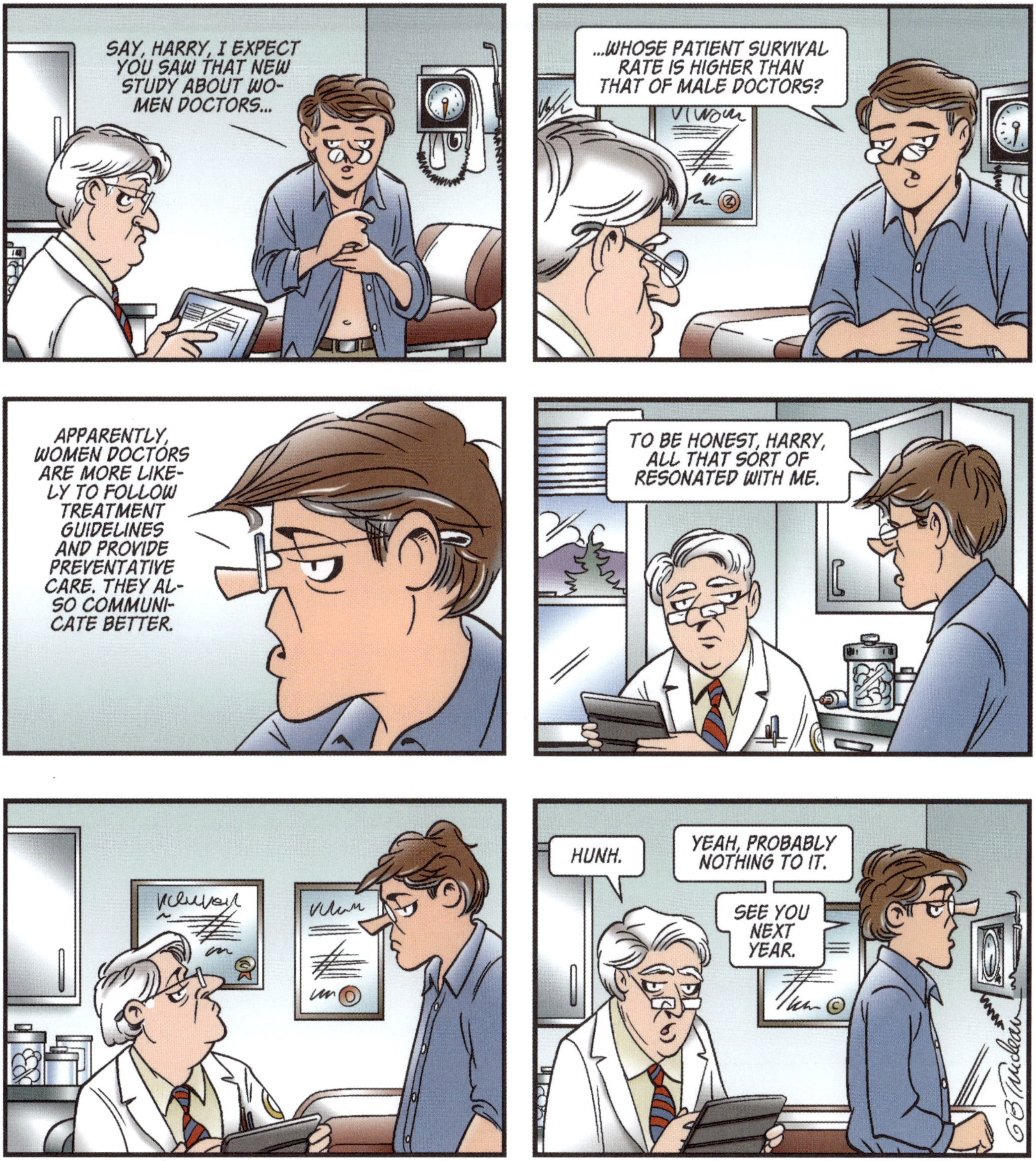
SAY, HARRY, I EXPECT YOU SAW THAT NEW STUDY ABOUT WOMEN DOCTORS...
...WHOSE PATIENT SURVIVAL RATE IS HIGHER THAN THAT OF MALE DOCTORS?
APPARENTLY, WOMEN DOCTORS ARE MORE LIKELY TO FOLLOW TREATMENT GUIDELINES AND PROVIDE PREVENTATIVE CARE. THEY ALSO COMMUNICATE BETTER.
TO BE HONEST, HARRY, ALL THAT SORT OF RESONATED WITH ME.
HUNH.
YEAH, PROBABLY NOTHING TO IT.
SEE YOU NEXT YEAR.
GBTrudeau

January 29, 2017

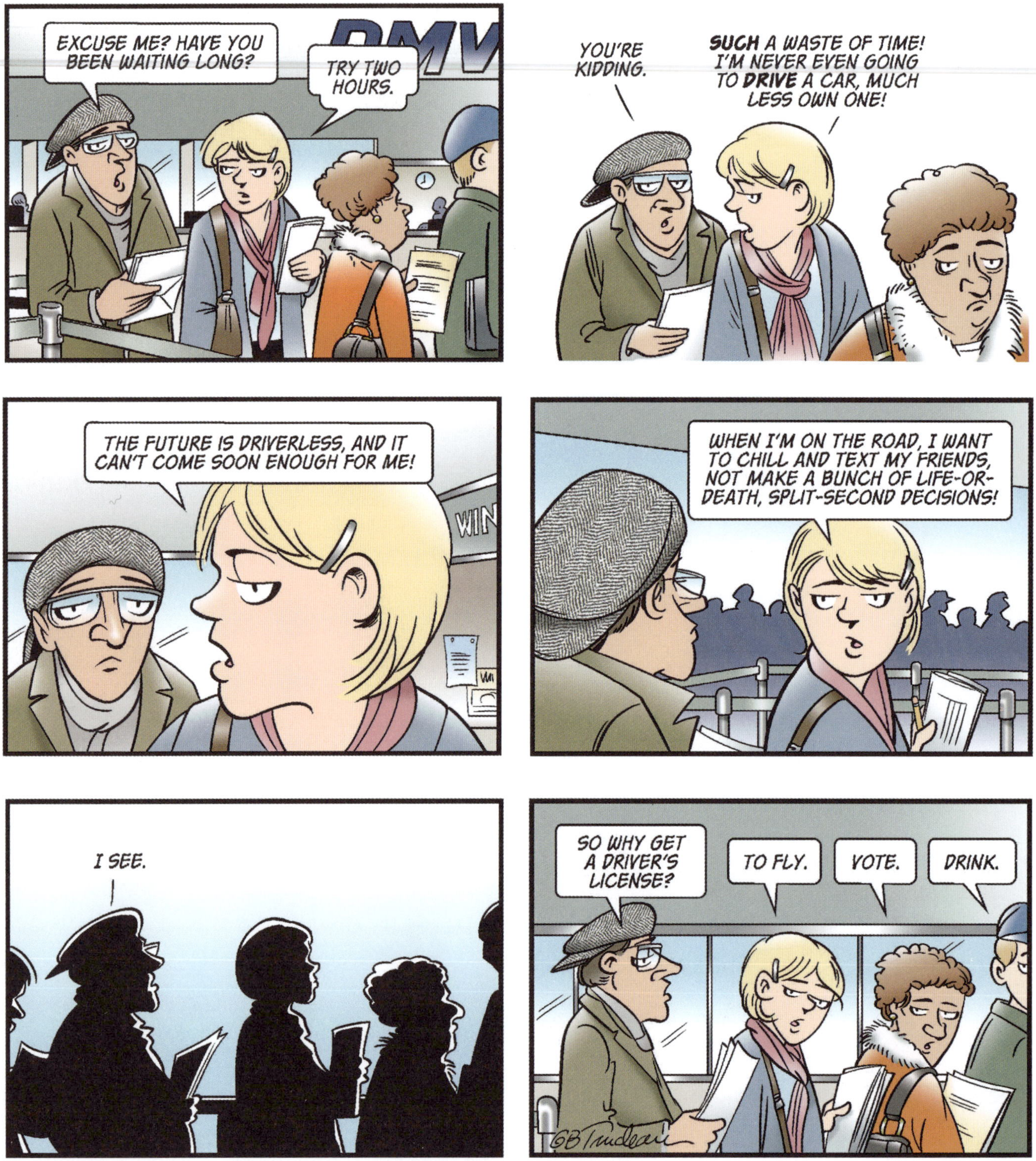
EXCUSE ME? HAVE YOU BEEN WAITING LONG?
TRY TWO HOURS.
DMV
YOU'RE KIDDING.
SUCH A WASTE OF TIME! I'M NEVER EVEN GOING TO **DRIVE** A CAR, MUCH LESS OWN ONE!
THE FUTURE IS DRIVERLESS, AND IT CAN'T COME SOON ENOUGH FOR ME!
WHEN I'M ON THE ROAD, I WANT TO CHILL AND TEXT MY FRIENDS, NOT MAKE A BUNCH OF LIFE-OR-DEATH, SPLIT-SECOND DECISIONS!
I SEE.
SO WHY GET A DRIVER'S LICENSE?
TO FLY.
VOTE.
DRINK.
GBTrudeau

February 5, 2017

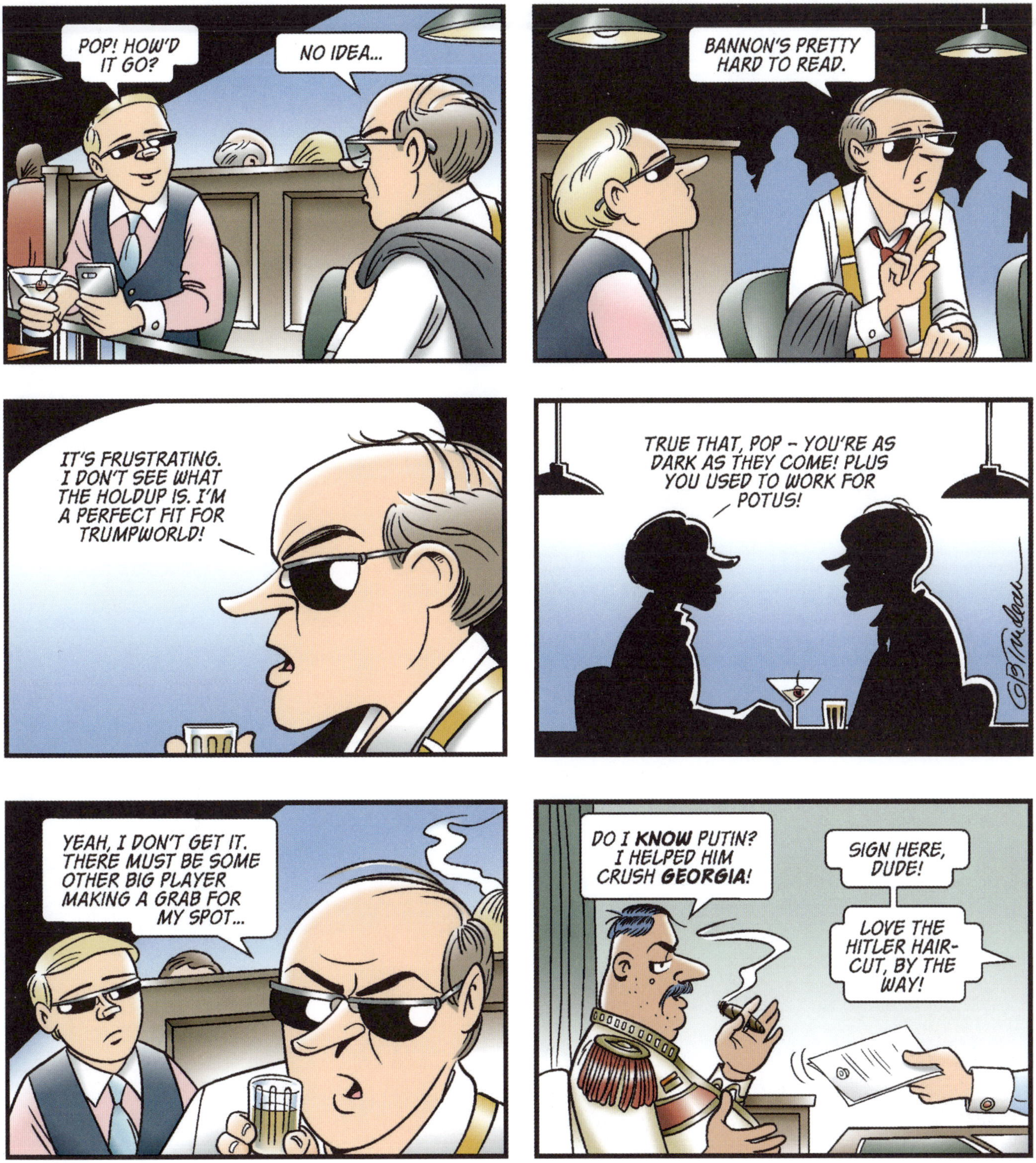
POP! HOW'D IT GO?
NO IDEA...
BANNON'S PRETTY HARD TO READ.
IT'S FRUSTRATING. I DON'T SEE WHAT THE HOLDUP IS. I'M A PERFECT FIT FOR TRUMPWORLD!
TRUE THAT, POP – YOU'RE AS DARK AS THEY COME! PLUS YOU USED TO WORK FOR POTUS!
YEAH, I DON'T GET IT. THERE MUST BE SOME OTHER BIG PLAYER MAKING A GRAB FOR MY SPOT...
DO I **KNOW** PUTIN? I HELPED HIM CRUSH **GEORGIA**!
SIGN HERE, DUDE!
LOVE THE HITLER HAIR-CUT, BY THE WAY!

February 26, 2017

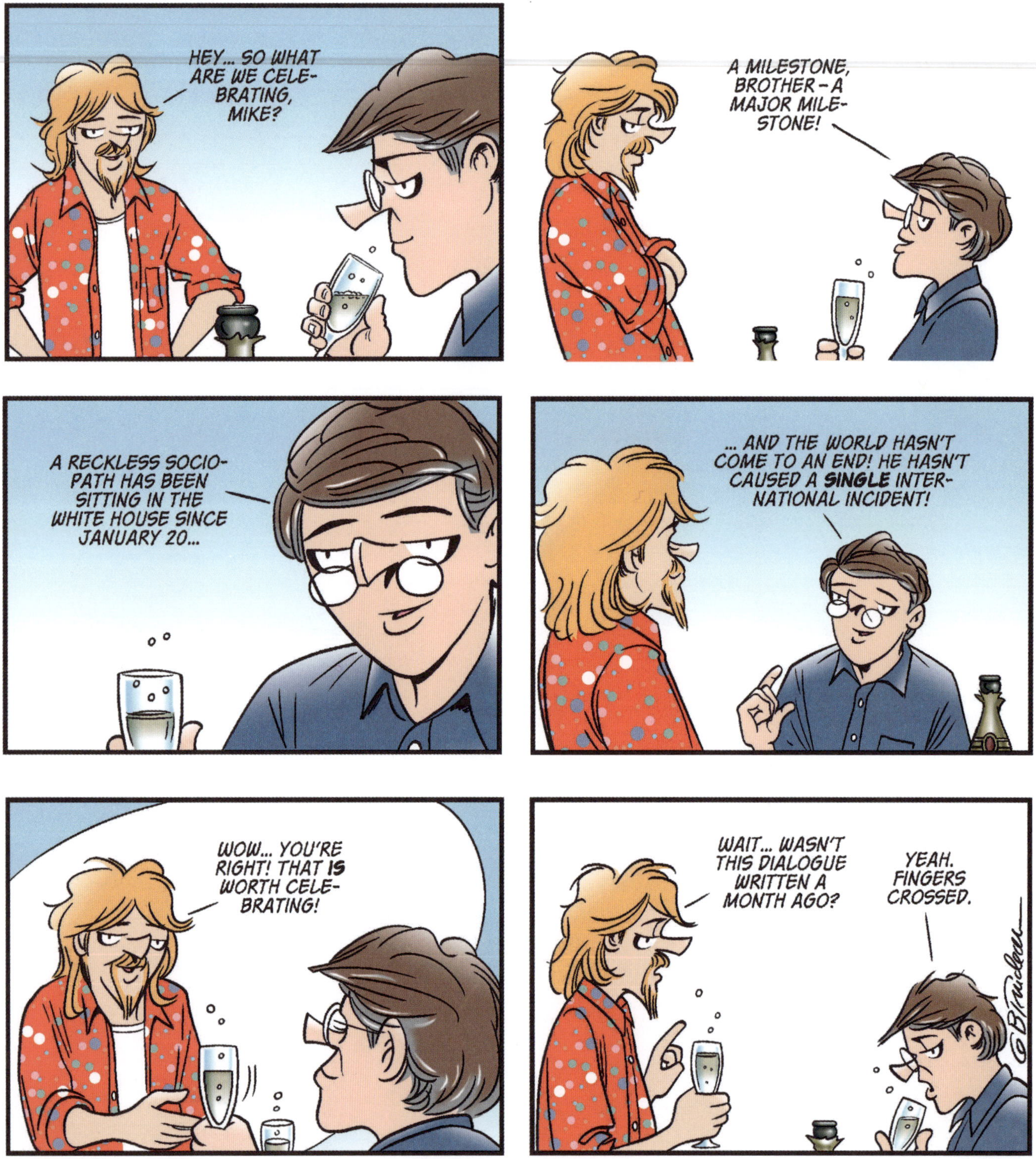
HEY... SO WHAT ARE WE CELE-BRATING, MIKE?
A MILESTONE, BROTHER – A MAJOR MILE-STONE!
A RECKLESS SOCIO-PATH HAS BEEN SITTING IN THE WHITE HOUSE SINCE JANUARY 20...
... AND THE WORLD HASN'T COME TO AN END! HE HASN'T CAUSED A **SINGLE** INTER-NATIONAL INCIDENT!
WOW... YOU'RE RIGHT! THAT **IS** WORTH CELE-BRATING!
WAIT... WASN'T THIS DIALOGUE WRITTEN A MONTH AGO?
YEAH. FINGERS CROSSED.
©GBTrudeau

February 12, 2017

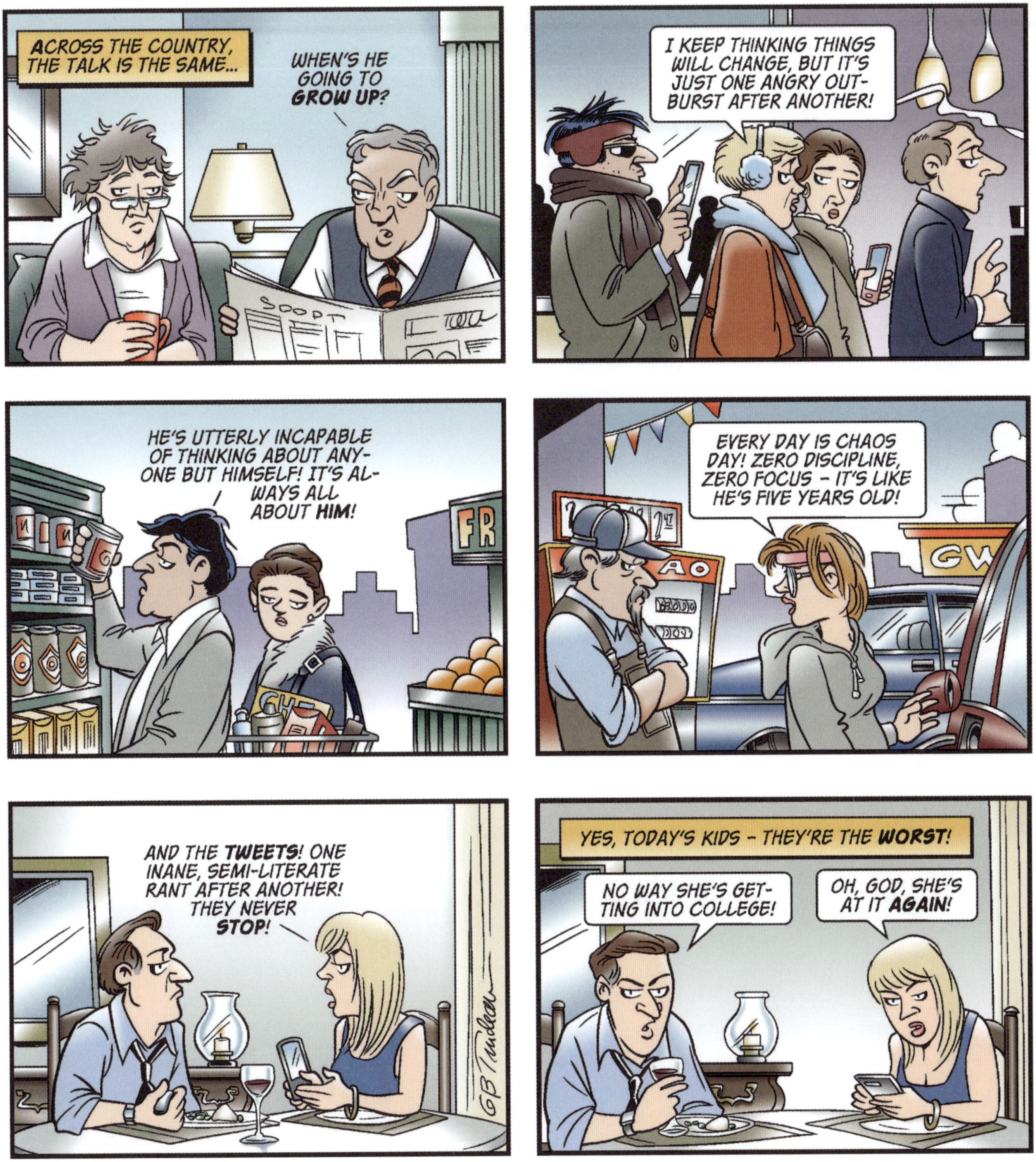
ACROSS THE COUNTRY, THE TALK IS THE SAME...
WHEN'S HE GOING TO GROW UP?
I KEEP THINKING THINGS WILL CHANGE, BUT IT'S JUST ONE ANGRY OUT-BURST AFTER ANOTHER!
HE'S UTTERLY INCAPABLE OF THINKING ABOUT ANY-ONE BUT HIMSELF! IT'S AL-WAYS ALL ABOUT HIM!
EVERY DAY IS CHAOS DAY! ZERO DISCIPLINE, ZERO FOCUS – IT'S LIKE HE'S FIVE YEARS OLD!
AND THE TWEETS! ONE INANE, SEMI-LITERATE RANT AFTER ANOTHER! THEY NEVER STOP!
GB Trudeau
YES, TODAY'S KIDS – THEY'RE THE WORST!
NO WAY SHE'S GET-TING INTO COLLEGE!
OH, GOD, SHE'S AT IT AGAIN!

February 19, 2017

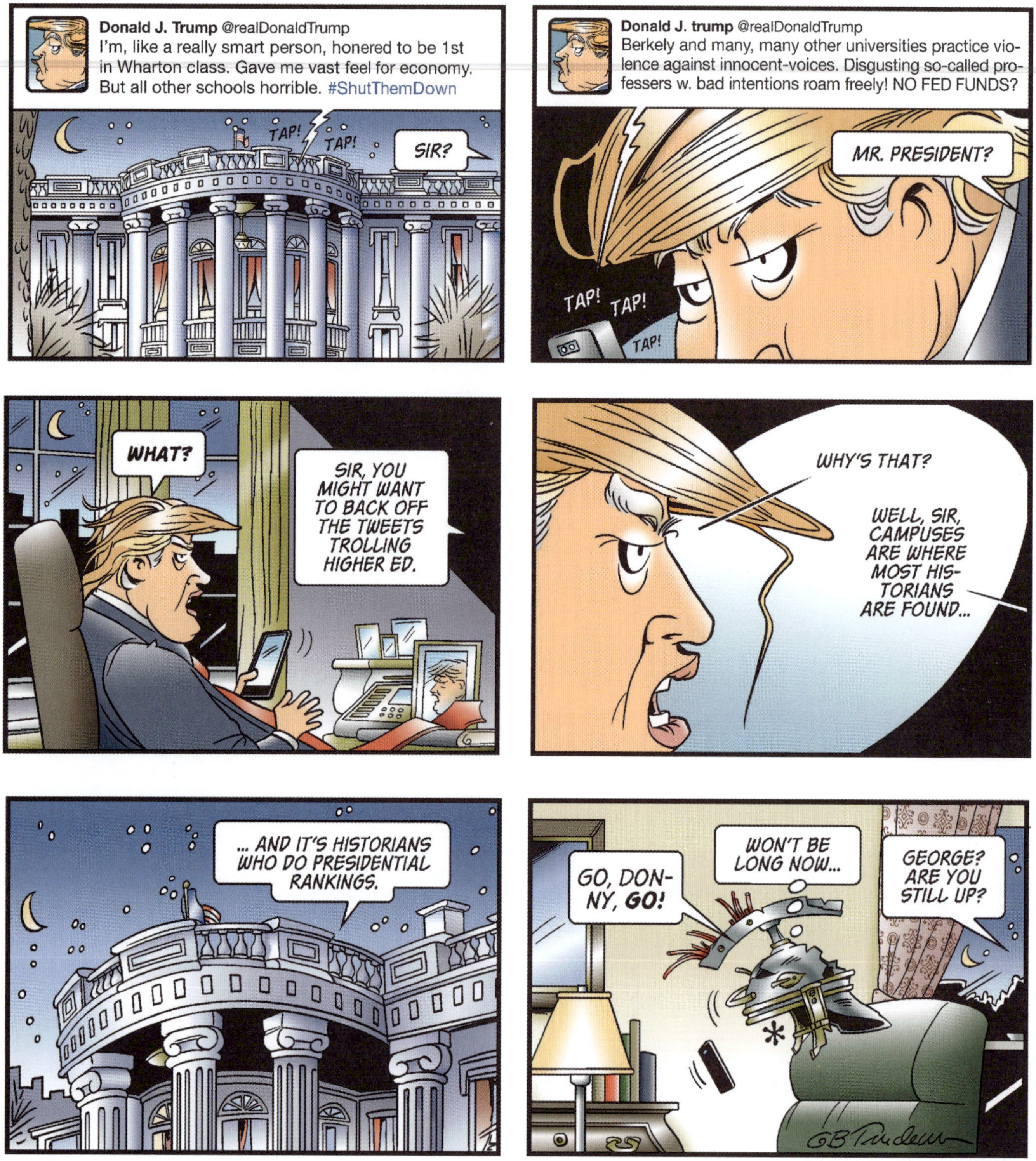
Donald J. Trump @realDonaldTrump
I'm, like a really smart person, honered to be 1st in Wharton class. Gave me vast feel for economy. But all other schools horrible. #ShutThemDown
TAP! TAP!
SIR?
Donald J. trump @realDonaldTrump
Berkely and many, many other universities practice violence against innocent-voices. Disgusting so-called professers w. bad intentions roam freely! NO FED FUNDS?
MR. PRESIDENT?
TAP! TAP! TAP!
WHAT?
SIR, YOU MIGHT WANT TO BACK OFF THE TWEETS TROLLING HIGHER ED.
WHY'S THAT?
WELL, SIR, CAMPUSES ARE WHERE MOST HISTORIANS ARE FOUND...
... AND IT'S HISTORIANS WHO DO PRESIDENTIAL RANKINGS.
GO, DONNY, **GO!**
WON'T BE LONG NOW...
GEORGE? ARE YOU STILL UP?

March 12, 2017

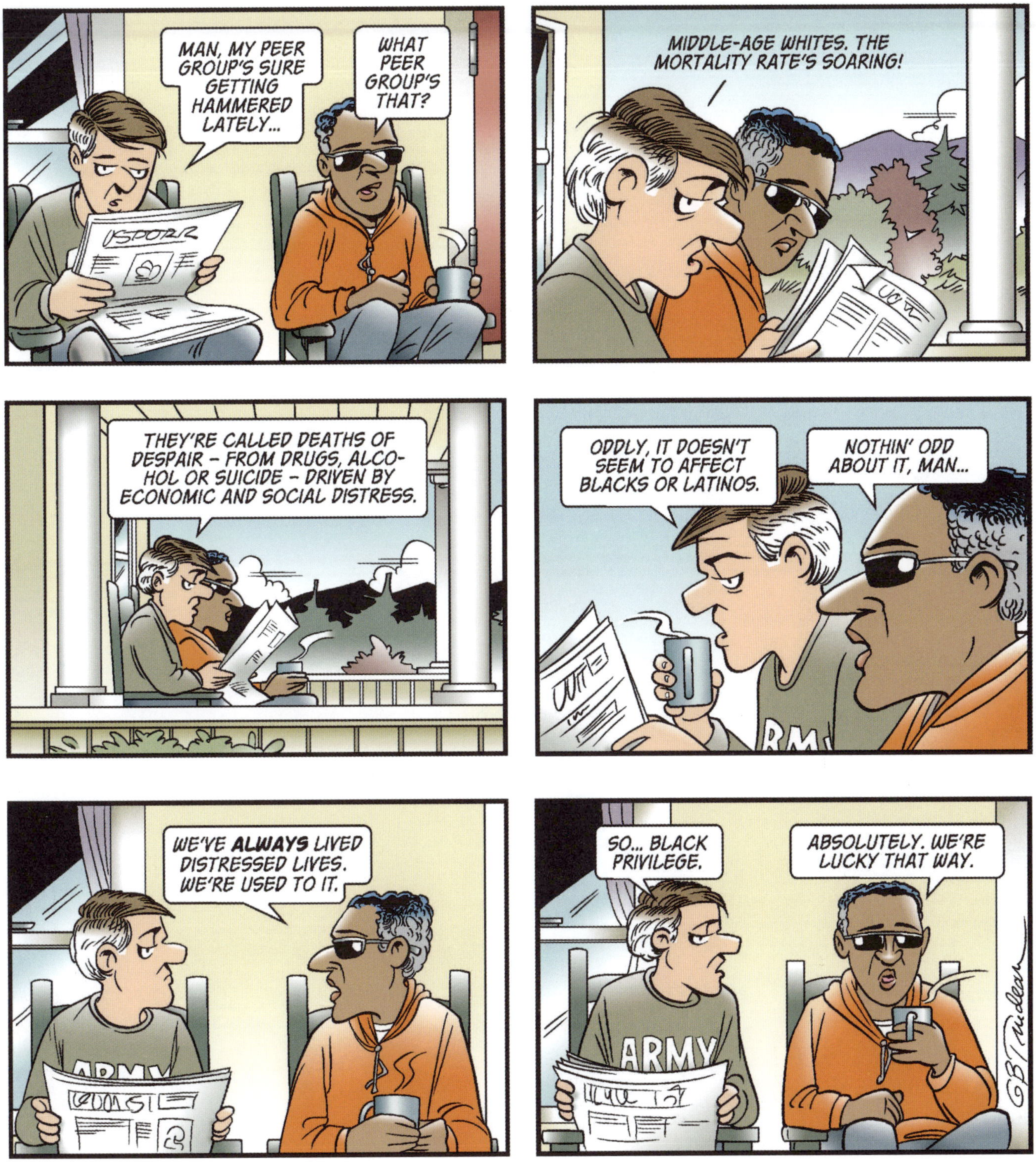
MAN, MY PEER GROUP'S SURE GETTING HAMMERED LATELY...
WHAT PEER GROUP'S THAT?
MIDDLE-AGE WHITES. THE MORTALITY RATE'S SOARING!
THEY'RE CALLED DEATHS OF DESPAIR – FROM DRUGS, ALCOHOL OR SUICIDE – DRIVEN BY ECONOMIC AND SOCIAL DISTRESS.
ODDLY, IT DOESN'T SEEM TO AFFECT BLACKS OR LATINOS.
NOTHIN' ODD ABOUT IT, MAN...
WE'VE **ALWAYS** LIVED DISTRESSED LIVES. WE'RE USED TO IT.
SO... BLACK PRIVILEGE.
ABSOLUTELY. WE'RE LUCKY THAT WAY.
ARMY

March 26, 2017

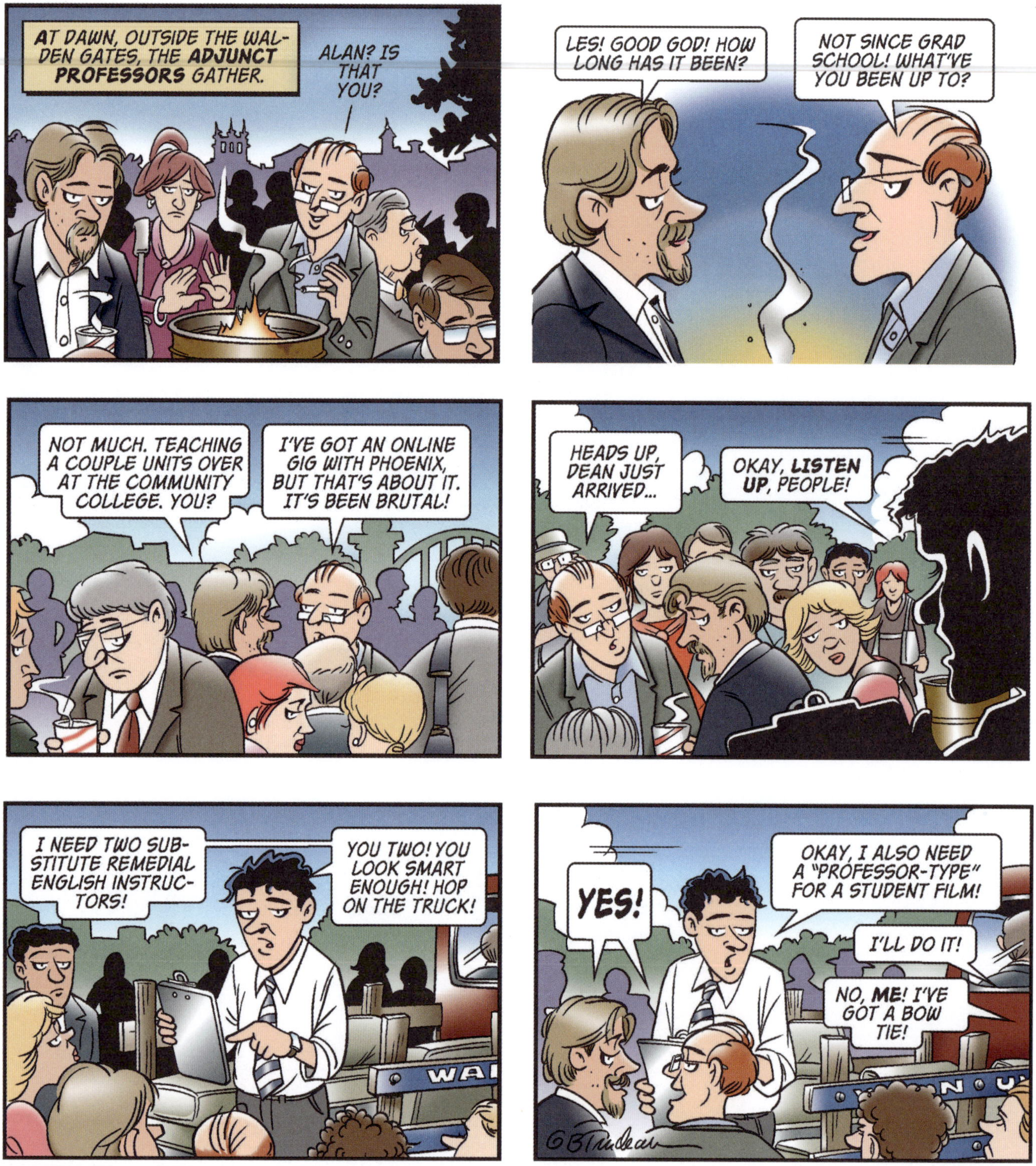
AT DAWN, OUTSIDE THE WALDEN GATES, THE **ADJUNCT PROFESSORS** GATHER.
ALAN? IS THAT YOU?
LES! GOOD GOD! HOW LONG HAS IT BEEN?
NOT SINCE GRAD SCHOOL! WHAT'VE YOU BEEN UP TO?
NOT MUCH. TEACHING A COUPLE UNITS OVER AT THE COMMUNITY COLLEGE. YOU?
I'VE GOT AN ONLINE GIG WITH PHOENIX, BUT THAT'S ABOUT IT. IT'S BEEN BRUTAL!
HEADS UP, DEAN JUST ARRIVED...
OKAY, **LISTEN UP**, PEOPLE!
I NEED TWO SUBSTITUTE REMEDIAL ENGLISH INSTRUCTORS!
YOU TWO! YOU LOOK SMART ENOUGH! HOP ON THE TRUCK!
YES!
OKAY, I ALSO NEED A "PROFESSOR-TYPE" FOR A STUDENT FILM!
I'LL DO IT!
NO, **ME**! I'VE GOT A BOW TIE!
GBTrudeau

September 6, 2015

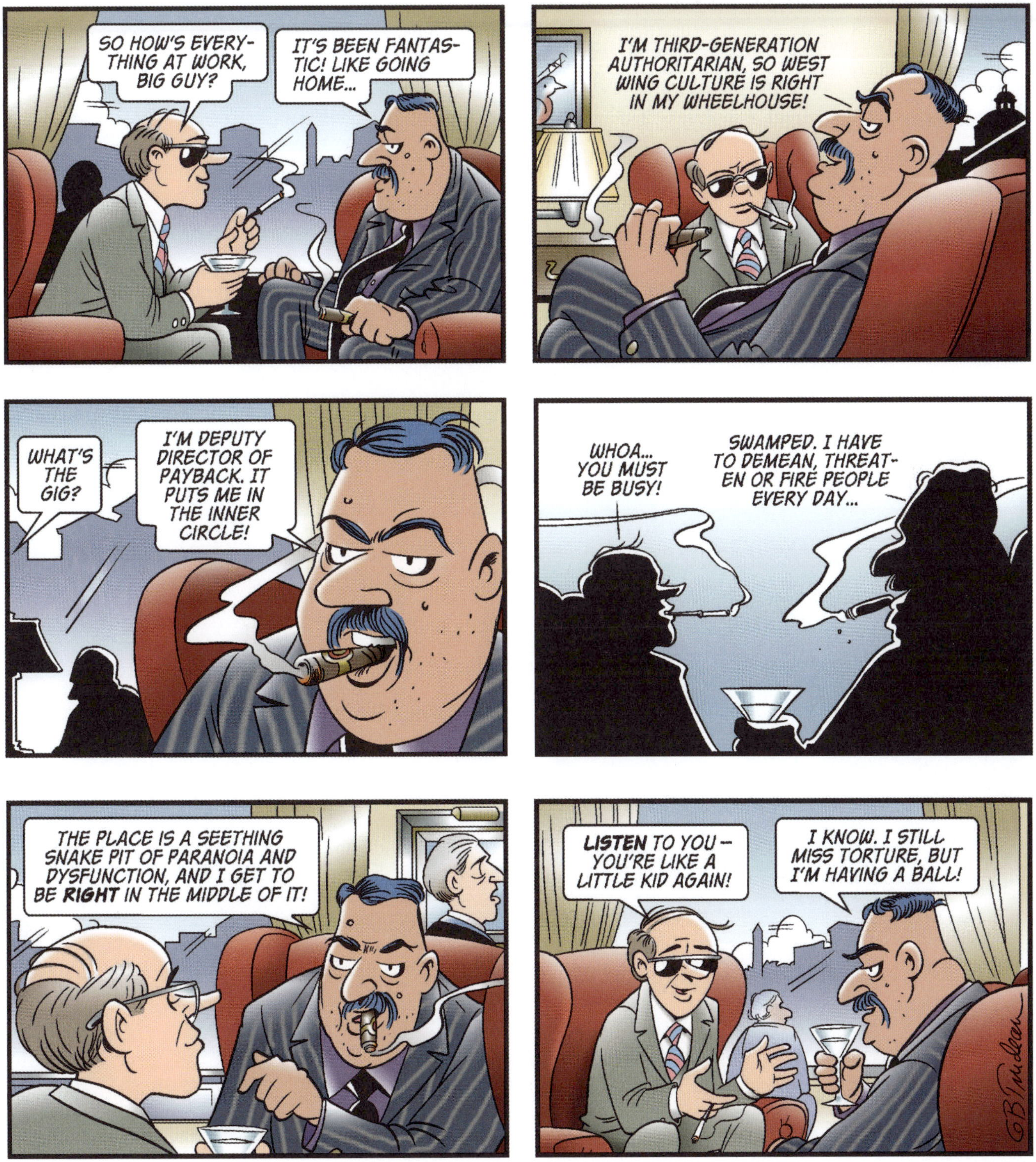
SO HOW'S EVERY-THING AT WORK, BIG GUY?
IT'S BEEN FANTAS-TIC! LIKE GOING HOME...
I'M THIRD-GENERATION AUTHORITARIAN, SO WEST WING CULTURE IS RIGHT IN MY WHEELHOUSE!
WHAT'S THE GIG?
I'M DEPUTY DIRECTOR OF PAYBACK. IT PUTS ME IN THE INNER CIRCLE!
WHOA... YOU MUST BE BUSY!
SWAMPED. I HAVE TO DEMEAN, THREAT-EN OR FIRE PEOPLE EVERY DAY...
THE PLACE IS A SEETHING SNAKE PIT OF PARANOIA AND DYSFUNCTION, AND I GET TO BE **RIGHT** IN THE MIDDLE OF IT!
LISTEN TO YOU – YOU'RE LIKE A LITTLE KID AGAIN!
I KNOW. I STILL MISS TORTURE, BUT I'M HAVING A BALL!
©B Trudeau

March 19, 2017

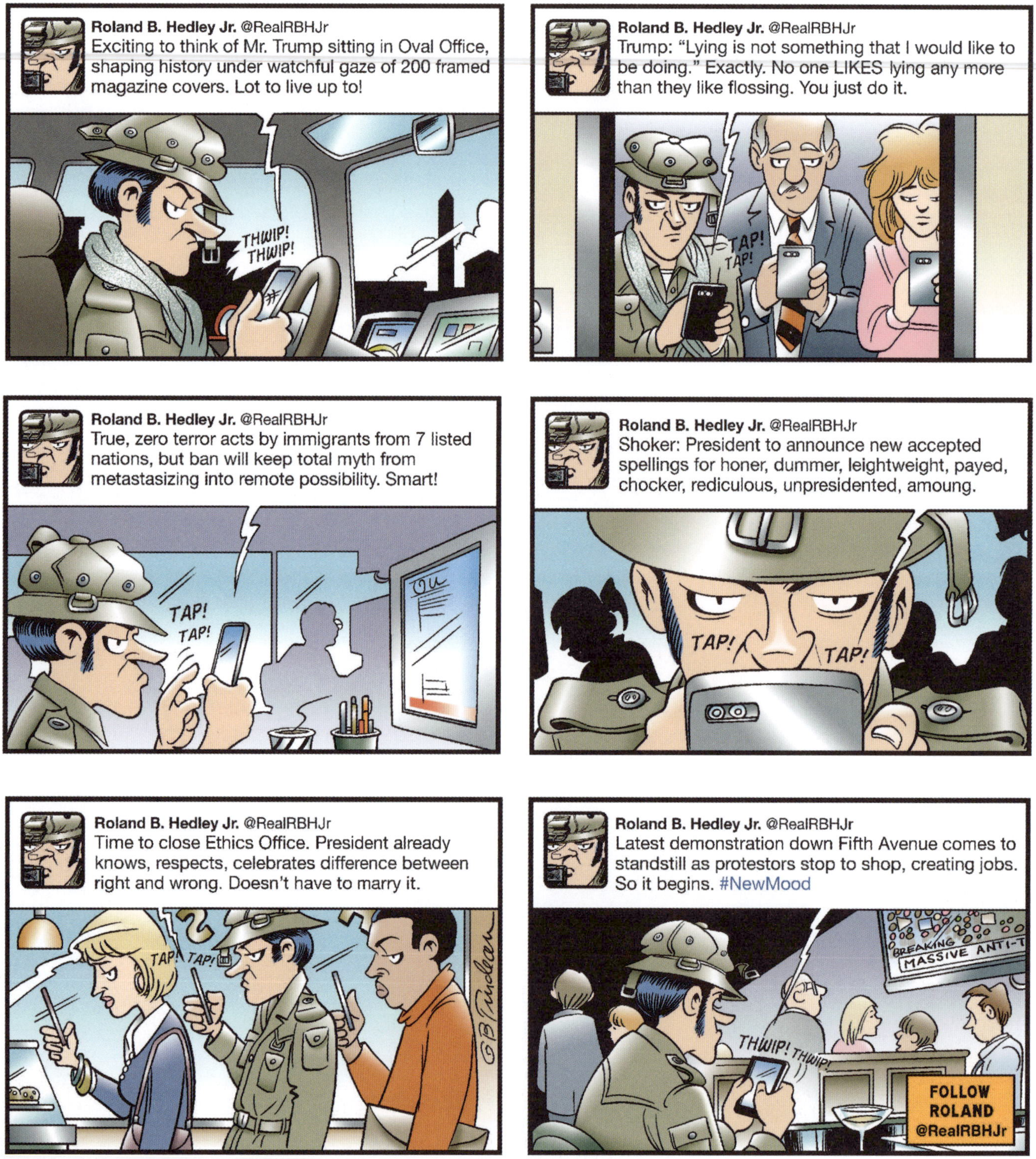
Roland B. Hedley Jr. @RealRBHJr
Exciting to think of Mr. Trump sitting in Oval Office, shaping history under watchful gaze of 200 framed magazine covers. Lot to live up to!
THWIP! THWIP!
Roland B. Hedley Jr. @RealRBHJr
Trump: "Lying is not something that I would like to be doing." Exactly. No one LIKES lying any more than they like flossing. You just do it.
TAP! TAP!
Roland B. Hedley Jr. @RealRBHJr
True, zero terror acts by immigrants from 7 listed nations, but ban will keep total myth from metastasizing into remote possibility. Smart!
TAP! TAP!
Roland B. Hedley Jr. @RealRBHJr
Shoker: President to announce new accepted spellings for honer, dummer, leightweight, payed, chocker, rediculous, unpresidented, amoung.
TAP! TAP!
Roland B. Hedley Jr. @RealRBHJr
Time to close Ethics Office. President already knows, respects, celebrates difference between right and wrong. Doesn't have to marry it.
TAP! TAP!
Roland B. Hedley Jr. @RealRBHJr
Latest demonstration down Fifth Avenue comes to standstill as protestors stop to shop, creating jobs. So it begins. #NewMood
BREAKING
MASSIVE ANTI-T
THWIP! THWIP!
FOLLOW ROLAND @RealRBHJr

March 5, 2017

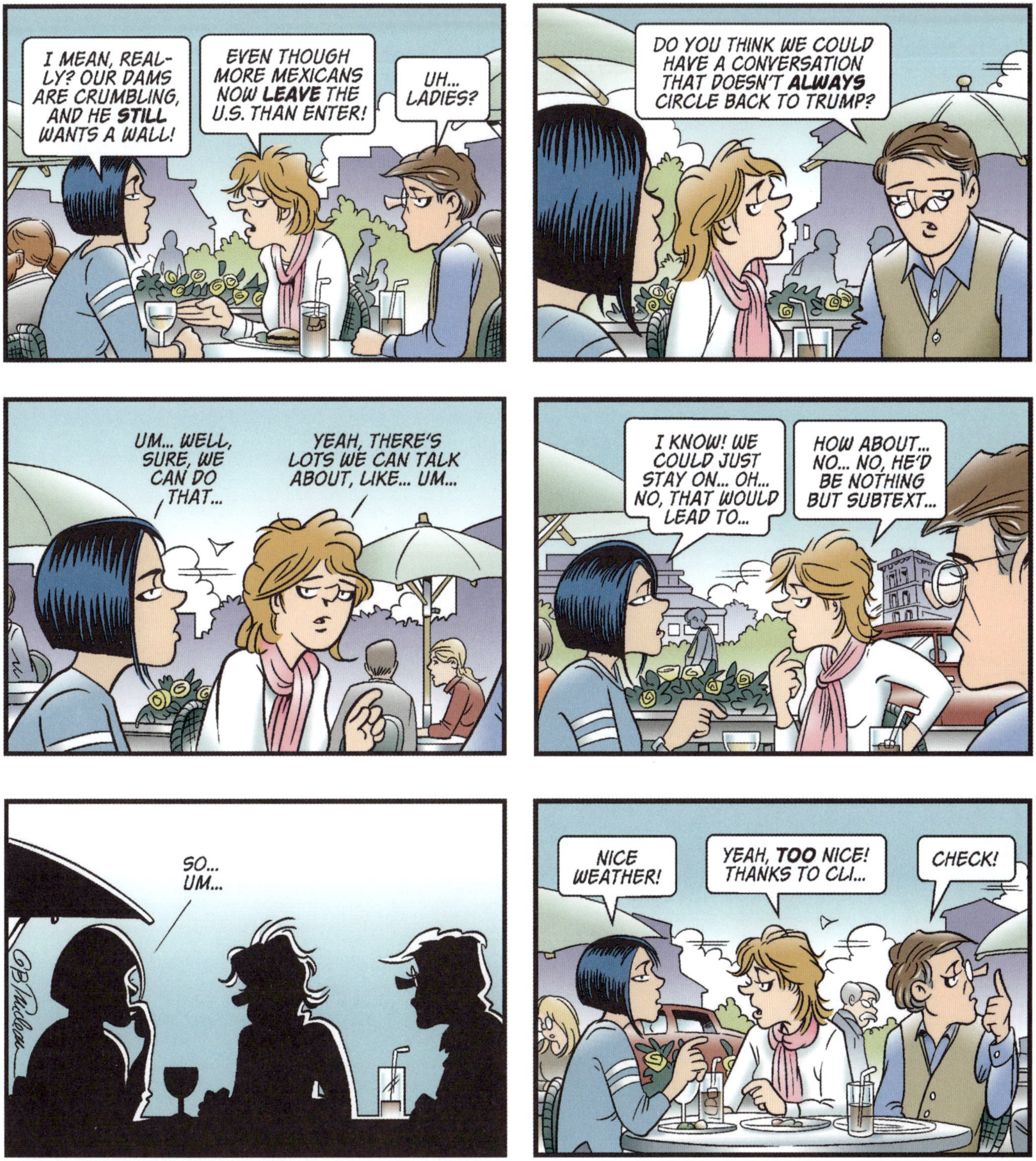
I MEAN, REAL-LY? OUR DAMS ARE CRUMBLING, AND HE **STILL** WANTS A WALL!
EVEN THOUGH MORE MEXICANS NOW **LEAVE** THE U.S. THAN ENTER!
UH... LADIES?
DO YOU THINK WE COULD HAVE A CONVERSATION THAT DOESN'T **ALWAYS** CIRCLE BACK TO TRUMP?
UM... WELL, SURE, WE CAN DO THAT...
YEAH, THERE'S LOTS WE CAN TALK ABOUT, LIKE... UM...
I KNOW! WE COULD JUST STAY ON... OH... NO, THAT WOULD LEAD TO...
HOW ABOUT... NO... NO, HE'D BE NOTHING BUT SUBTEXT...
SO... UM...
NICE WEATHER!
YEAH, **TOO** NICE! THANKS TO CLI...
CHECK!

April 2, 2017

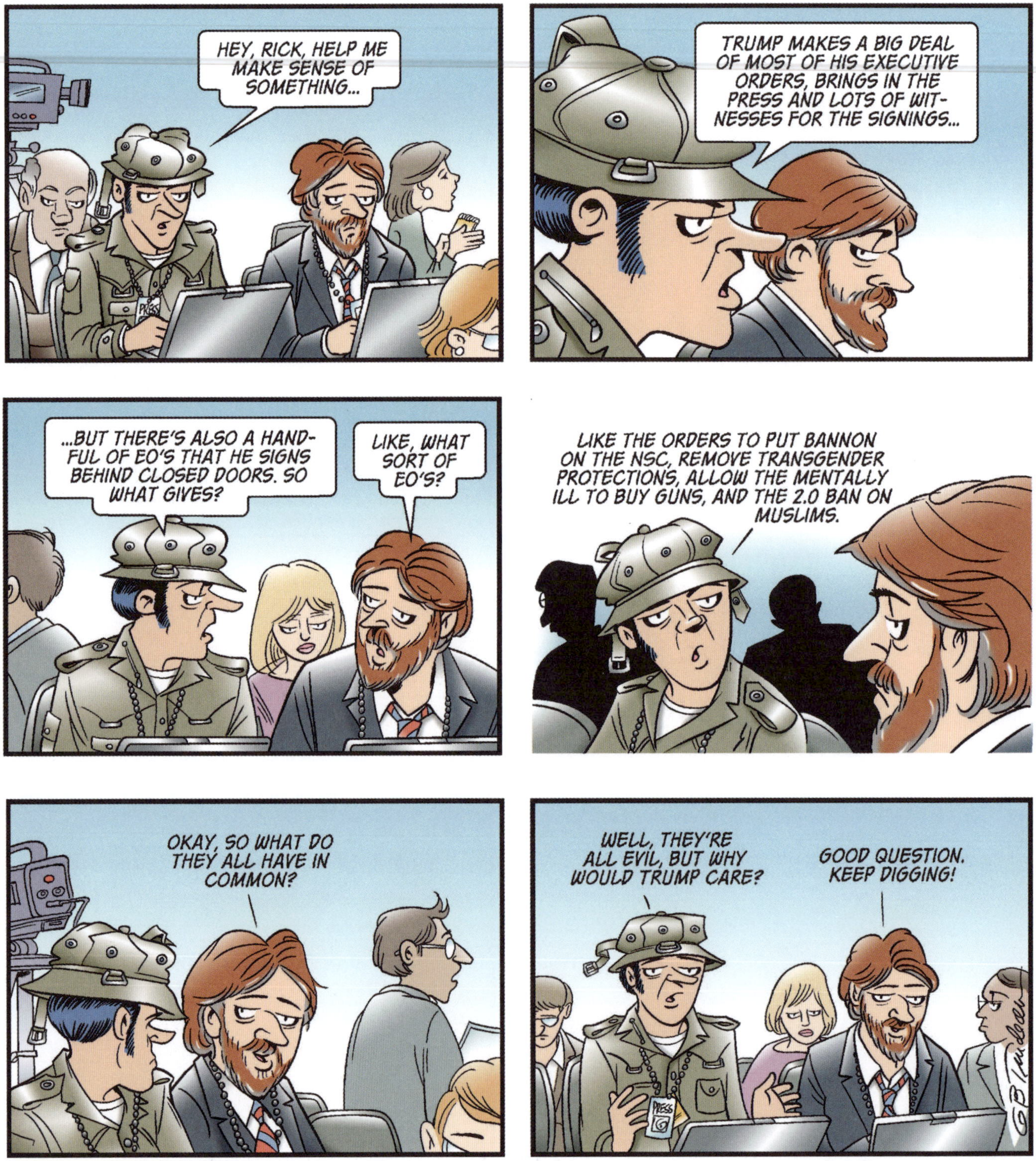
HEY, RICK, HELP ME MAKE SENSE OF SOMETHING...
TRUMP MAKES A BIG DEAL OF MOST OF HIS EXECUTIVE ORDERS, BRINGS IN THE PRESS AND LOTS OF WIT-NESSES FOR THE SIGNINGS...
...BUT THERE'S ALSO A HAND-FUL OF EO'S THAT HE SIGNS BEHIND CLOSED DOORS. SO WHAT GIVES?
LIKE, WHAT SORT OF EO'S?
LIKE THE ORDERS TO PUT BANNON ON THE NSC, REMOVE TRANSGENDER PROTECTIONS, ALLOW THE MENTALLY ILL TO BUY GUNS, AND THE 2.0 BAN ON MUSLIMS.
OKAY, SO WHAT DO THEY ALL HAVE IN COMMON?
WELL, THEY'RE ALL EVIL, BUT WHY WOULD TRUMP CARE?
GOOD QUESTION. KEEP DIGGING!

April 9, 2017

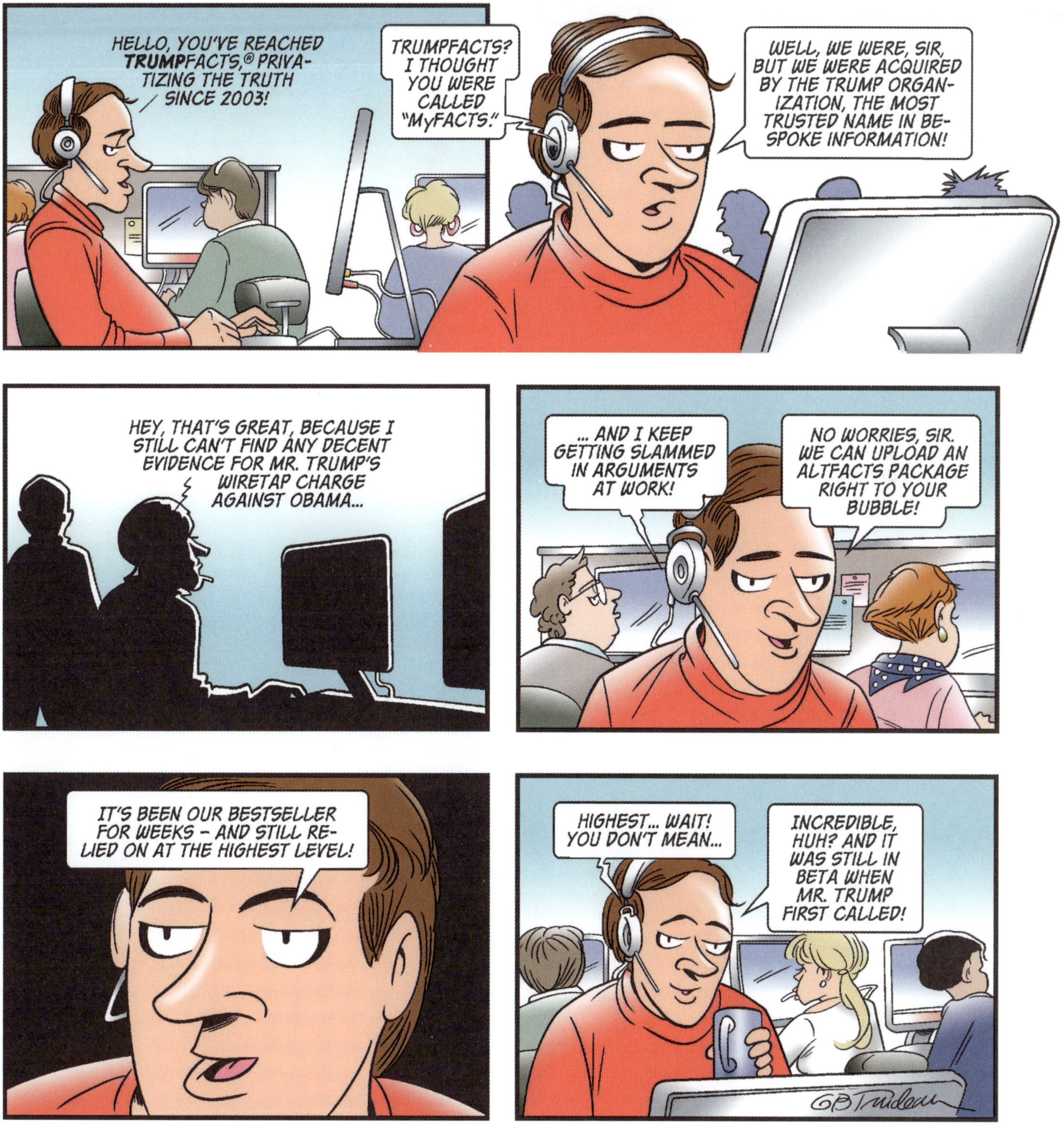
HELLO, YOU'VE REACHED TRUMPFACTS,® PRIVATIZING THE TRUTH SINCE 2003!
TRUMPFACTS? I THOUGHT YOU WERE CALLED "MyFACTS."
WELL, WE WERE, SIR, BUT WE WERE ACQUIRED BY THE TRUMP ORGANIZATION, THE MOST TRUSTED NAME IN BESPOKE INFORMATION!
HEY, THAT'S GREAT, BECAUSE I STILL CAN'T FIND ANY DECENT EVIDENCE FOR MR. TRUMP'S WIRETAP CHARGE AGAINST OBAMA...
... AND I KEEP GETTING SLAMMED IN ARGUMENTS AT WORK!
NO WORRIES, SIR. WE CAN UPLOAD AN ALTFACTS PACKAGE RIGHT TO YOUR BUBBLE!
IT'S BEEN OUR BESTSELLER FOR WEEKS – AND STILL RELIED ON AT THE HIGHEST LEVEL!
HIGHEST... WAIT! YOU DON'T MEAN...
INCREDIBLE, HUH? AND IT WAS STILL IN BETA WHEN MR. TRUMP FIRST CALLED!
GBTrudeau

April 16, 2017

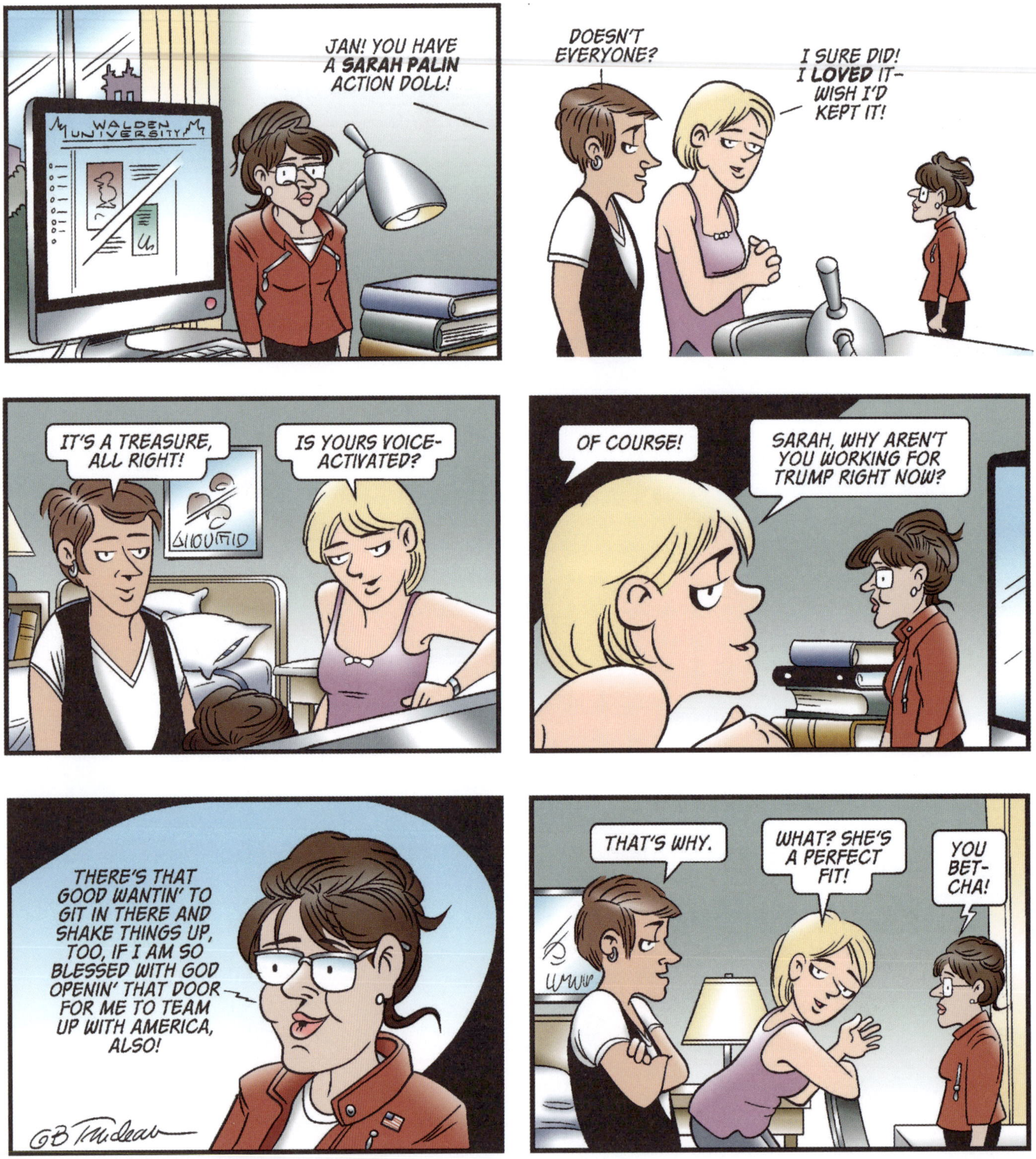
JAN! YOU HAVE A **SARAH PALIN** ACTION DOLL!
WALDEN UNIVERSITY
DOESN'T EVERYONE?
I SURE DID! I **LOVED** IT—WISH I'D KEPT IT!
IT'S A TREASURE, ALL RIGHT!
IS YOURS VOICE-ACTIVATED?
OF COURSE!
SARAH, WHY AREN'T YOU WORKING FOR TRUMP RIGHT NOW?
THERE'S THAT GOOD WANTIN' TO GIT IN THERE AND SHAKE THINGS UP, TOO, IF I AM SO BLESSED WITH GOD OPENIN' THAT DOOR FOR ME TO TEAM UP WITH AMERICA, ALSO!
GB Trudeau
THAT'S WHY.
WHAT? SHE'S A PERFECT FIT!
YOU BET-CHA!

April 23, 2017

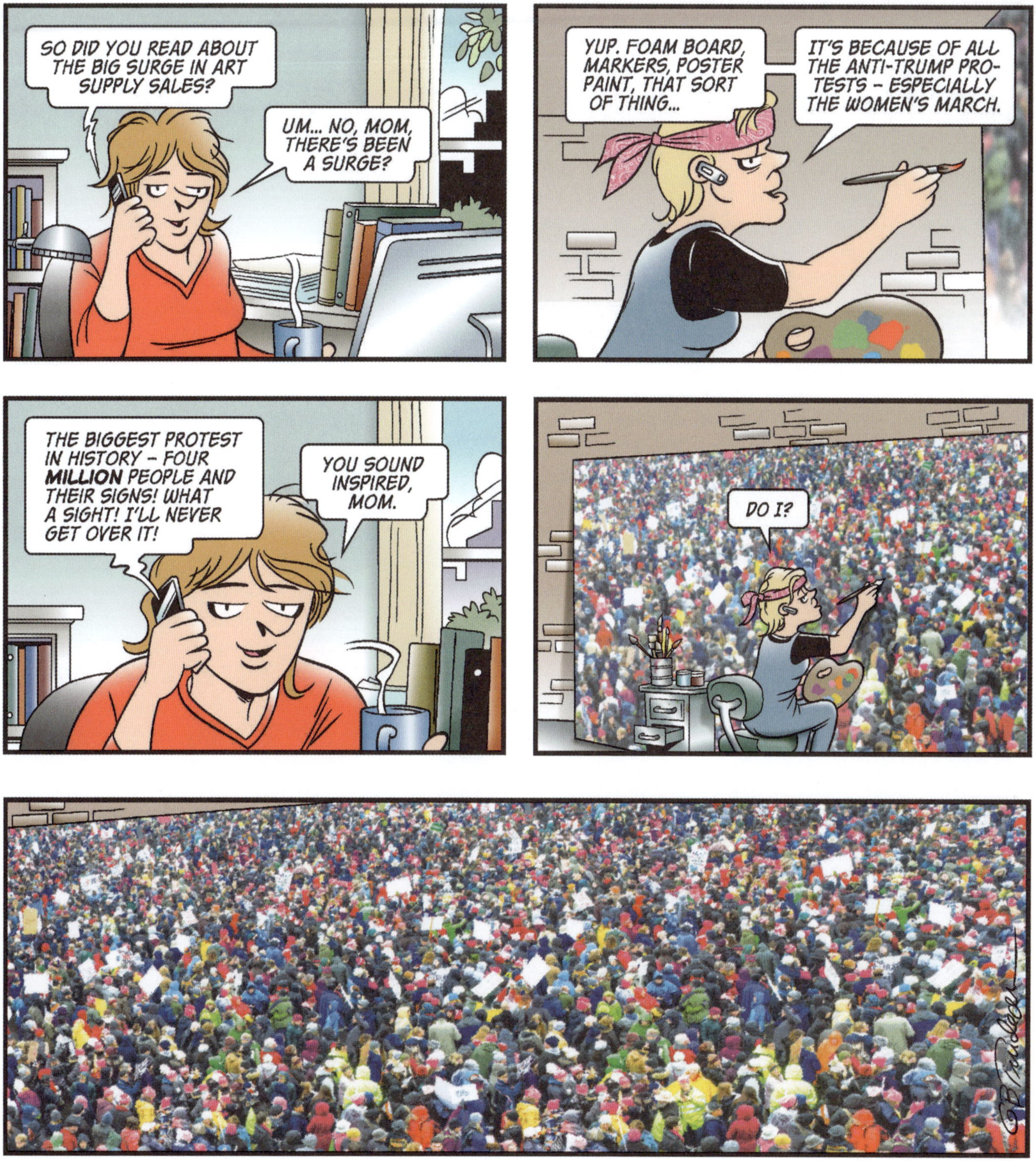

SO DID YOU READ ABOUT THE BIG SURGE IN ART SUPPLY SALES?
UM... NO, MOM, THERE'S BEEN A SURGE?
YUP. FOAM BOARD, MARKERS, POSTER PAINT, THAT SORT OF THING...
IT'S BECAUSE OF ALL THE ANTI-TRUMP PROTESTS – ESPECIALLY THE WOMEN'S MARCH.
THE BIGGEST PROTEST IN HISTORY – FOUR **MILLION** PEOPLE AND THEIR SIGNS! WHAT A SIGHT! I'LL NEVER GET OVER IT!
YOU SOUND INSPIRED, MOM.
DO I?

April 30, 2017

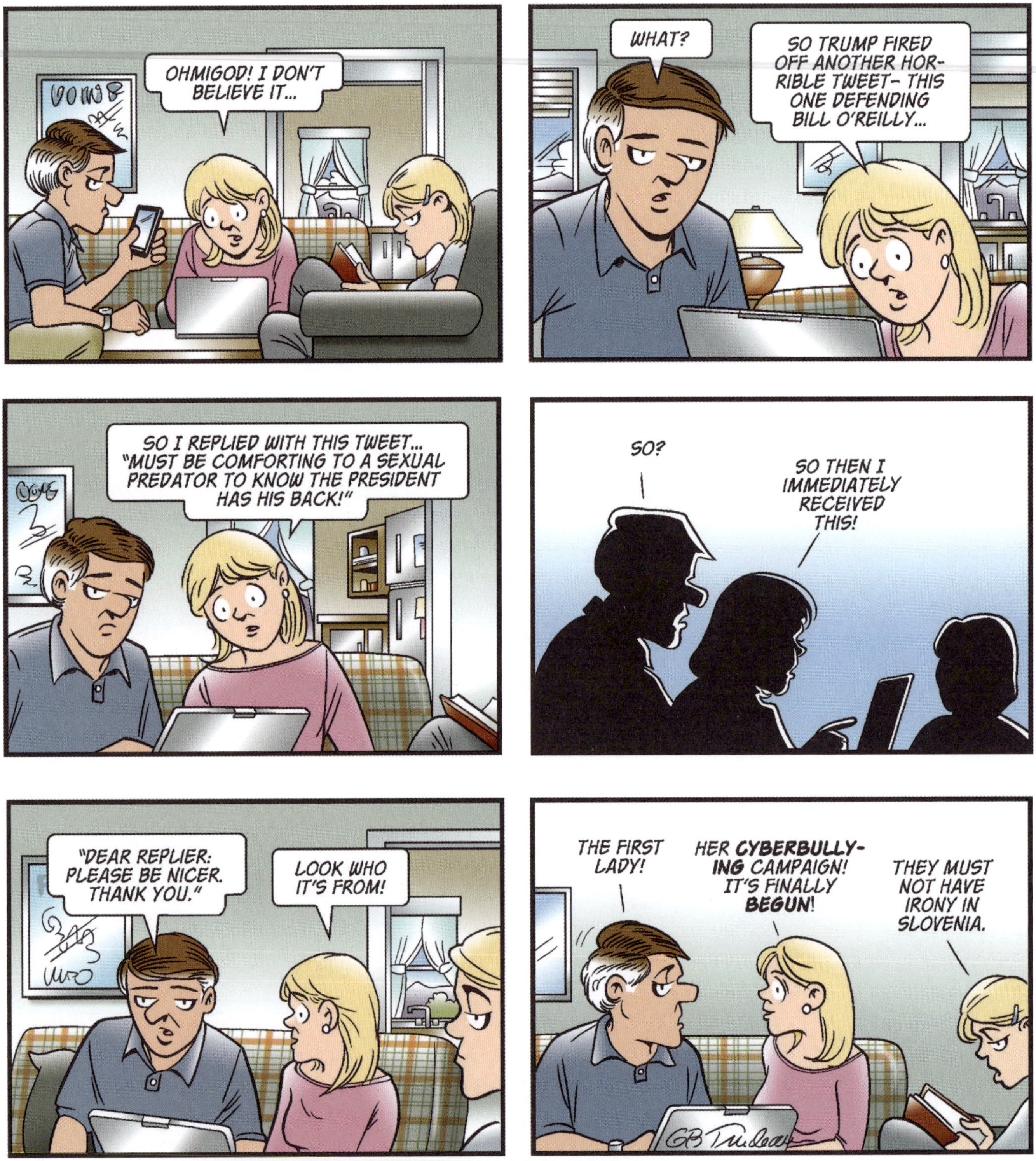
OHMIGOD! I DON'T BELIEVE IT...
WHAT?
SO TRUMP FIRED OFF ANOTHER HOR-RIBLE TWEET- THIS ONE DEFENDING BILL O'REILLY...
SO I REPLIED WITH THIS TWEET... "MUST BE COMFORTING TO A SEXUAL PREDATOR TO KNOW THE PRESIDENT HAS HIS BACK!"
SO?
SO THEN I IMMEDIATELY RECEIVED THIS!
"DEAR REPLIER: PLEASE BE NICER. THANK YOU."
LOOK WHO IT'S FROM!
THE FIRST LADY!
HER **CYBERBULLY-ING** CAMPAIGN! IT'S FINALLY **BEGUN**!
THEY MUST NOT HAVE IRONY IN SLOVENIA.
GB Trudeau

May 7, 2017

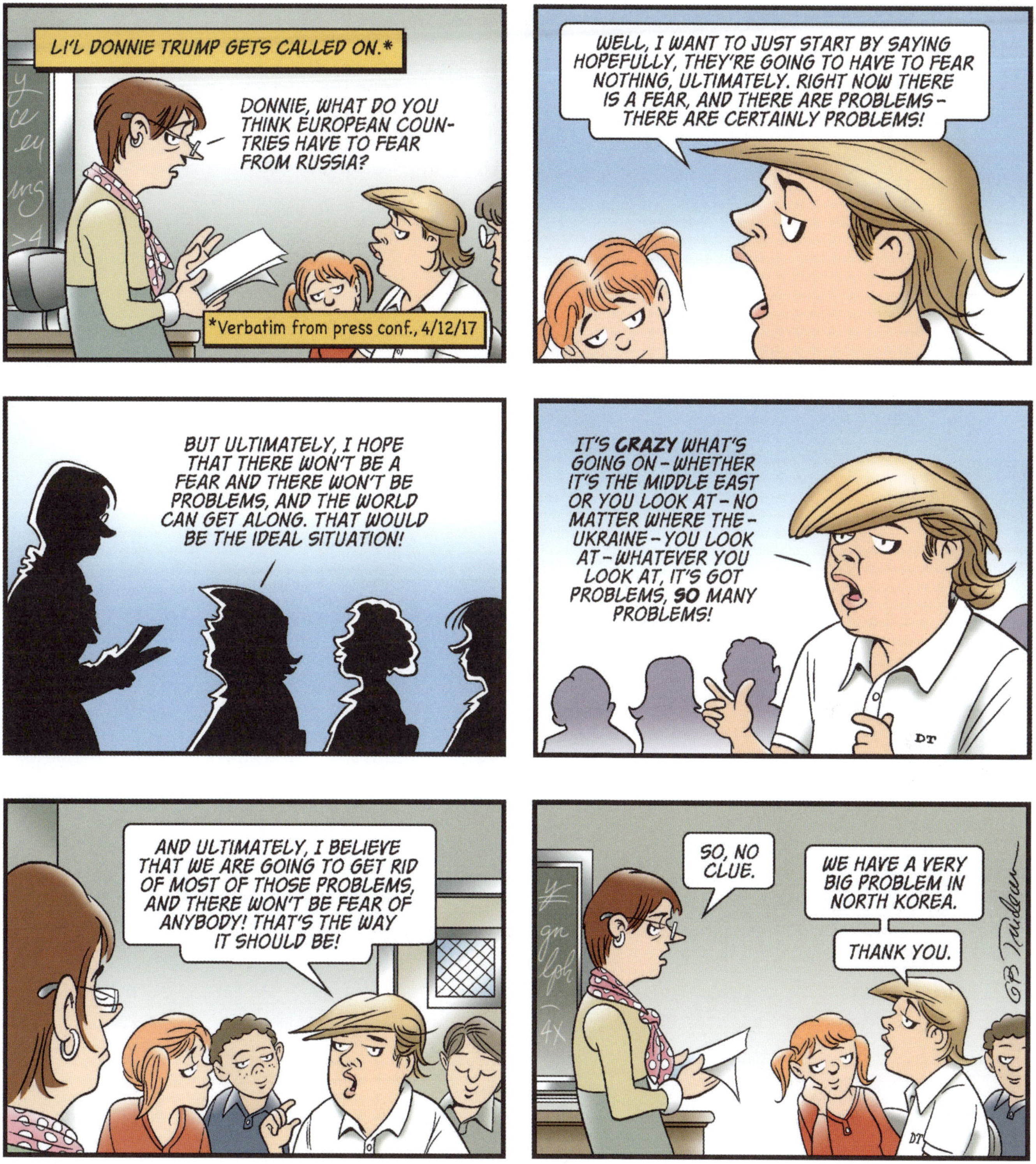
LI'L DONNIE TRUMP GETS CALLED ON.*
DONNIE, WHAT DO YOU THINK EUROPEAN COUNTRIES HAVE TO FEAR FROM RUSSIA?
*Verbatim from press conf., 4/12/17
WELL, I WANT TO JUST START BY SAYING HOPEFULLY, THEY'RE GOING TO HAVE TO FEAR NOTHING, ULTIMATELY. RIGHT NOW THERE IS A FEAR, AND THERE ARE PROBLEMS – THERE ARE CERTAINLY PROBLEMS!
BUT ULTIMATELY, I HOPE THAT THERE WON'T BE A FEAR AND THERE WON'T BE PROBLEMS, AND THE WORLD CAN GET ALONG. THAT WOULD BE THE IDEAL SITUATION!
IT'S CRAZY WHAT'S GOING ON – WHETHER IT'S THE MIDDLE EAST OR YOU LOOK AT – NO MATTER WHERE THE – UKRAINE – YOU LOOK AT – WHATEVER YOU LOOK AT, IT'S GOT PROBLEMS, SO MANY PROBLEMS!
DT
AND ULTIMATELY, I BELIEVE THAT WE ARE GOING TO GET RID OF MOST OF THOSE PROBLEMS, AND THERE WON'T BE FEAR OF ANYBODY! THAT'S THE WAY IT SHOULD BE!
SO, NO CLUE.
WE HAVE A VERY BIG PROBLEM IN NORTH KOREA.
THANK YOU.
GBTrudeau
DT

May 14, 2017

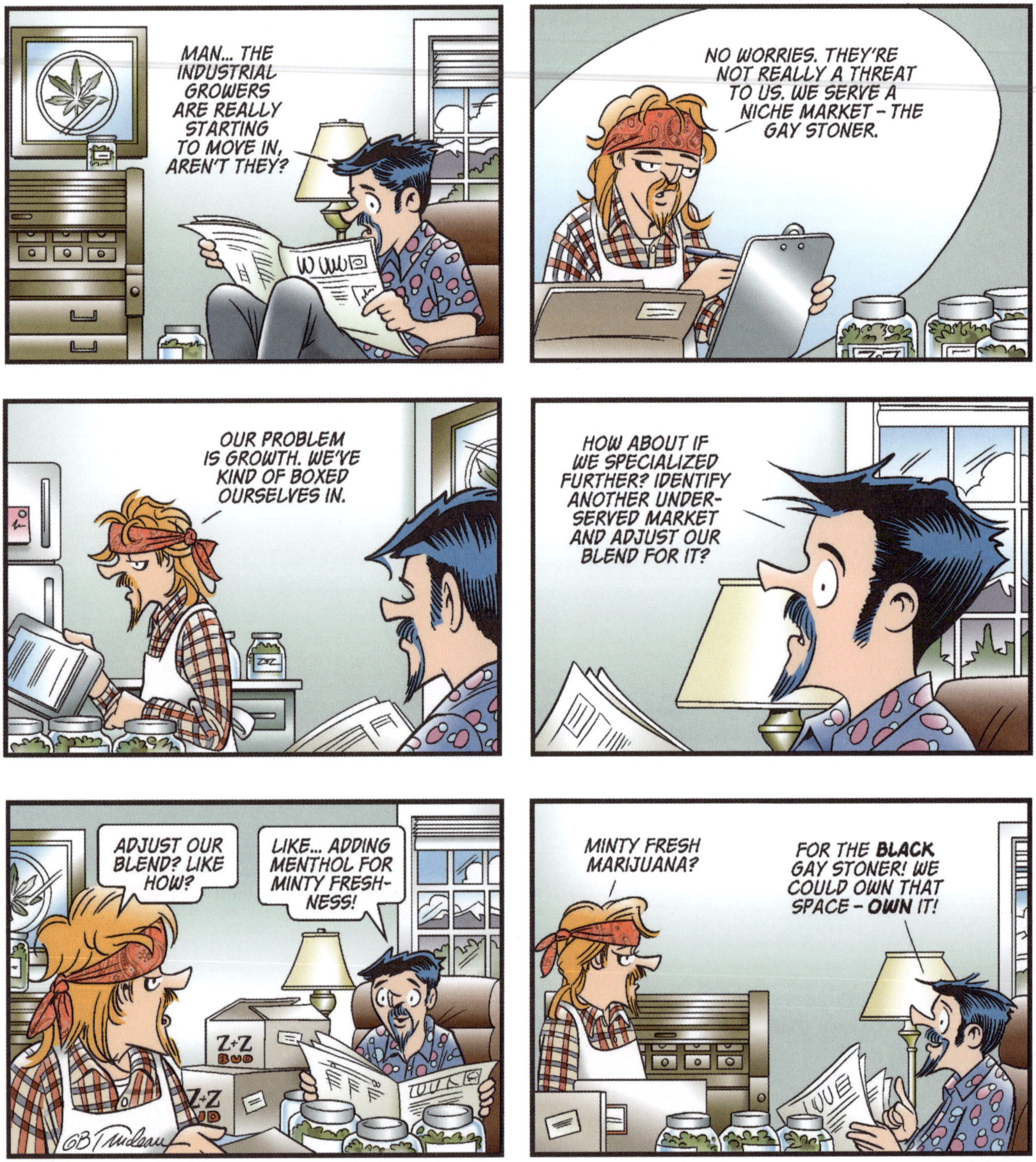
MAN... THE INDUSTRIAL GROWERS ARE REALLY STARTING TO MOVE IN, AREN'T THEY?
NO WORRIES. THEY'RE NOT REALLY A THREAT TO US. WE SERVE A NICHE MARKET – THE GAY STONER.
OUR PROBLEM IS GROWTH. WE'VE KIND OF BOXED OURSELVES IN.
HOW ABOUT IF WE SPECIALIZED FURTHER? IDENTIFY ANOTHER UNDER-SERVED MARKET AND ADJUST OUR BLEND FOR IT?
ADJUST OUR BLEND? LIKE HOW?
LIKE... ADDING MENTHOL FOR MINTY FRESH-NESS!
MINTY FRESH MARIJUANA?
FOR THE **BLACK** GAY STONER! WE COULD OWN THAT SPACE – **OWN** IT!
Z+Z BUD
GB Trudeau
May 21, 2017

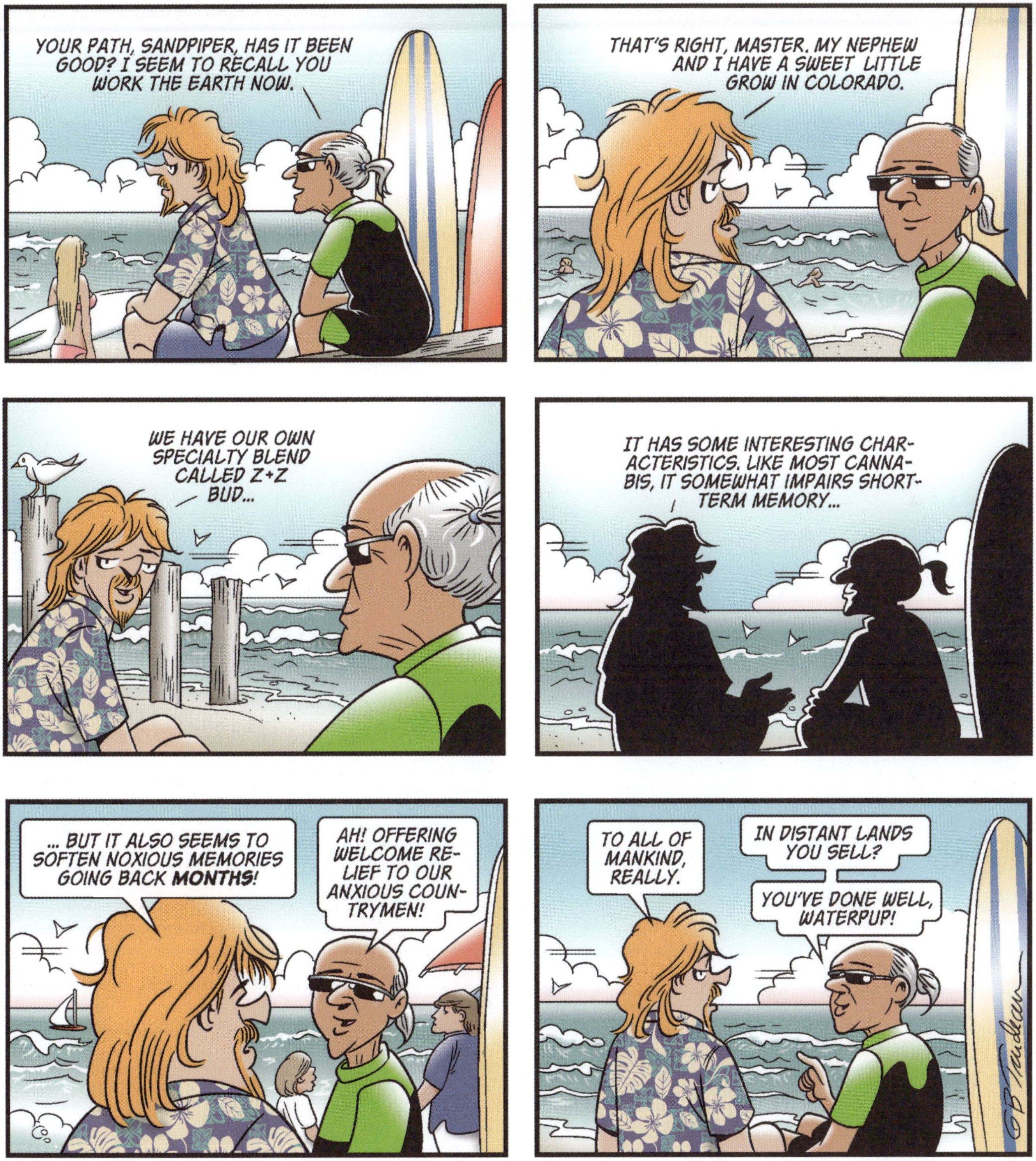
YOUR PATH, SANDPIPER, HAS IT BEEN GOOD? I SEEM TO RECALL YOU WORK THE EARTH NOW.
THAT'S RIGHT, MASTER. MY NEPHEW AND I HAVE A SWEET LITTLE GROW IN COLORADO.
WE HAVE OUR OWN SPECIALTY BLEND CALLED Z+Z BUD...
IT HAS SOME INTERESTING CHAR-ACTERISTICS. LIKE MOST CANNA-BIS, IT SOMEWHAT IMPAIRS SHORT-TERM MEMORY...
... BUT IT ALSO SEEMS TO SOFTEN NOXIOUS MEMORIES GOING BACK **MONTHS**!
AH! OFFERING WELCOME RE-LIEF TO OUR ANXIOUS COUN-TRYMEN!
TO ALL OF MANKIND, REALLY.
IN DISTANT LANDS YOU SELL?
YOU'VE DONE WELL, WATERPUP!
GB Trudeau

June 4, 2017

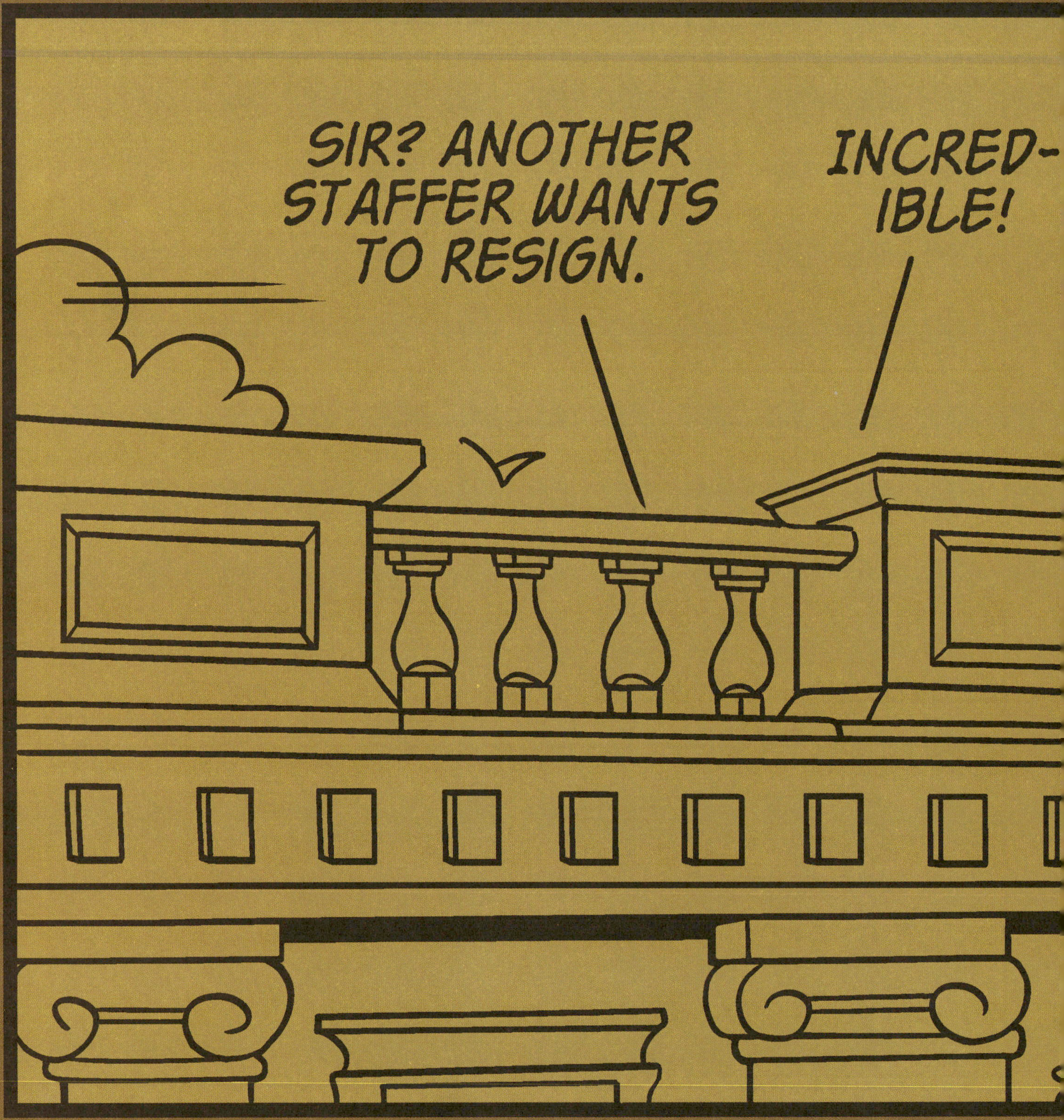
SIR? ANOTHER STAFFER WANTS TO RESIGN.
INCRED-IBLE!

PART 3

Team of Deplorables

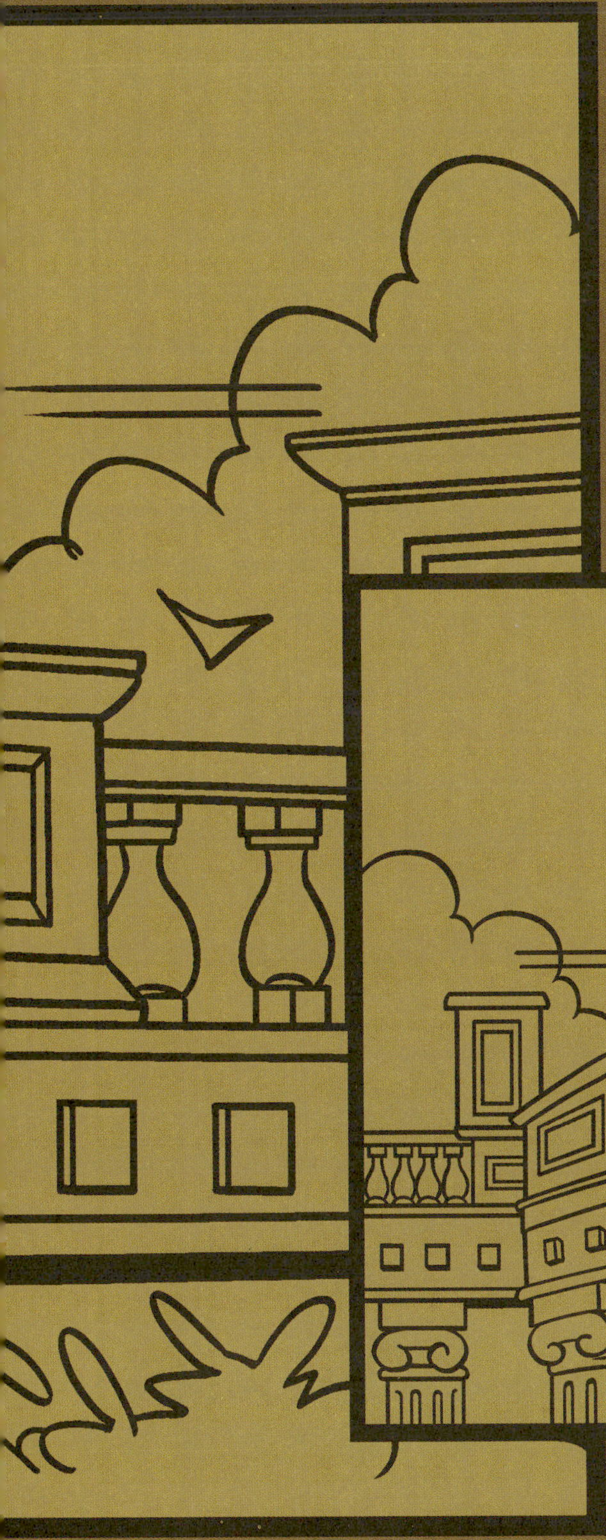

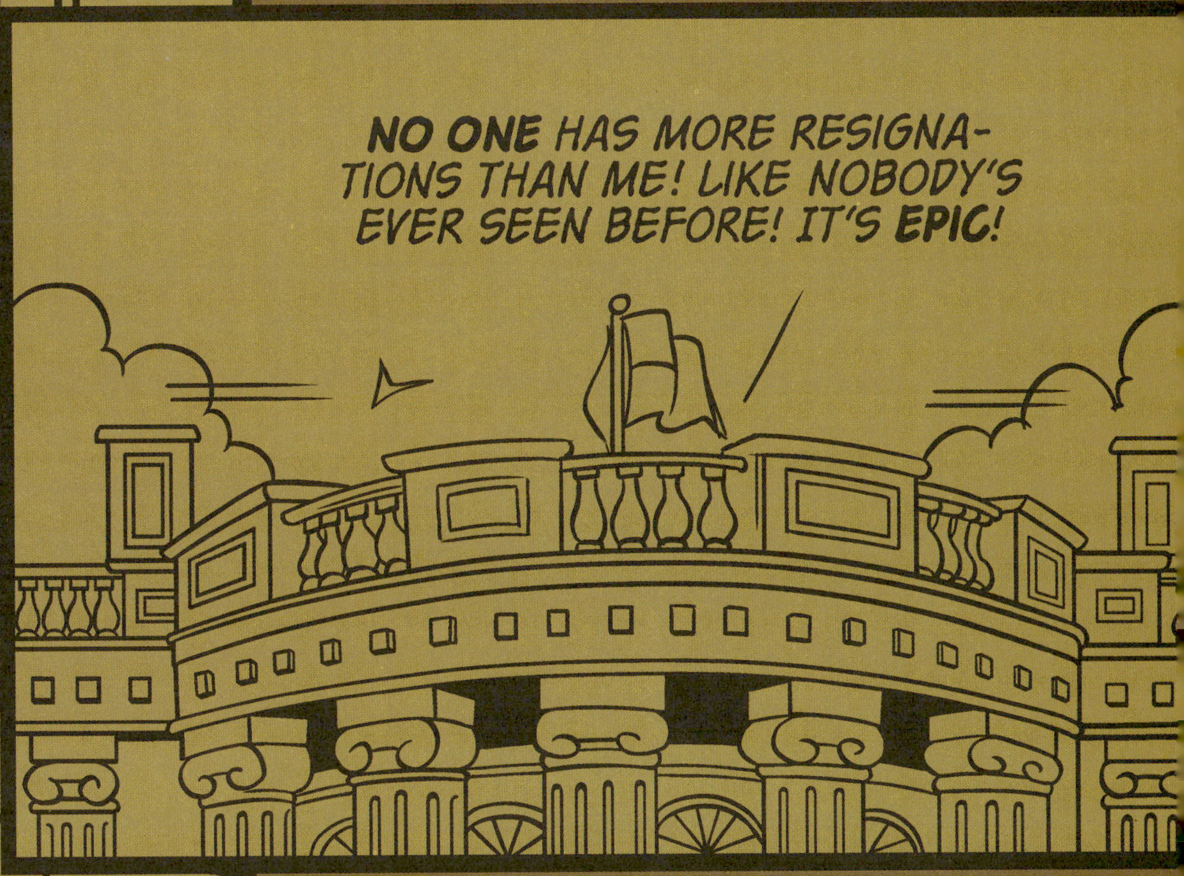
NO ONE HAS MORE RESIGNATIONS THAN ME! LIKE NOBODY'S EVER SEEN BEFORE! IT'S EPIC!

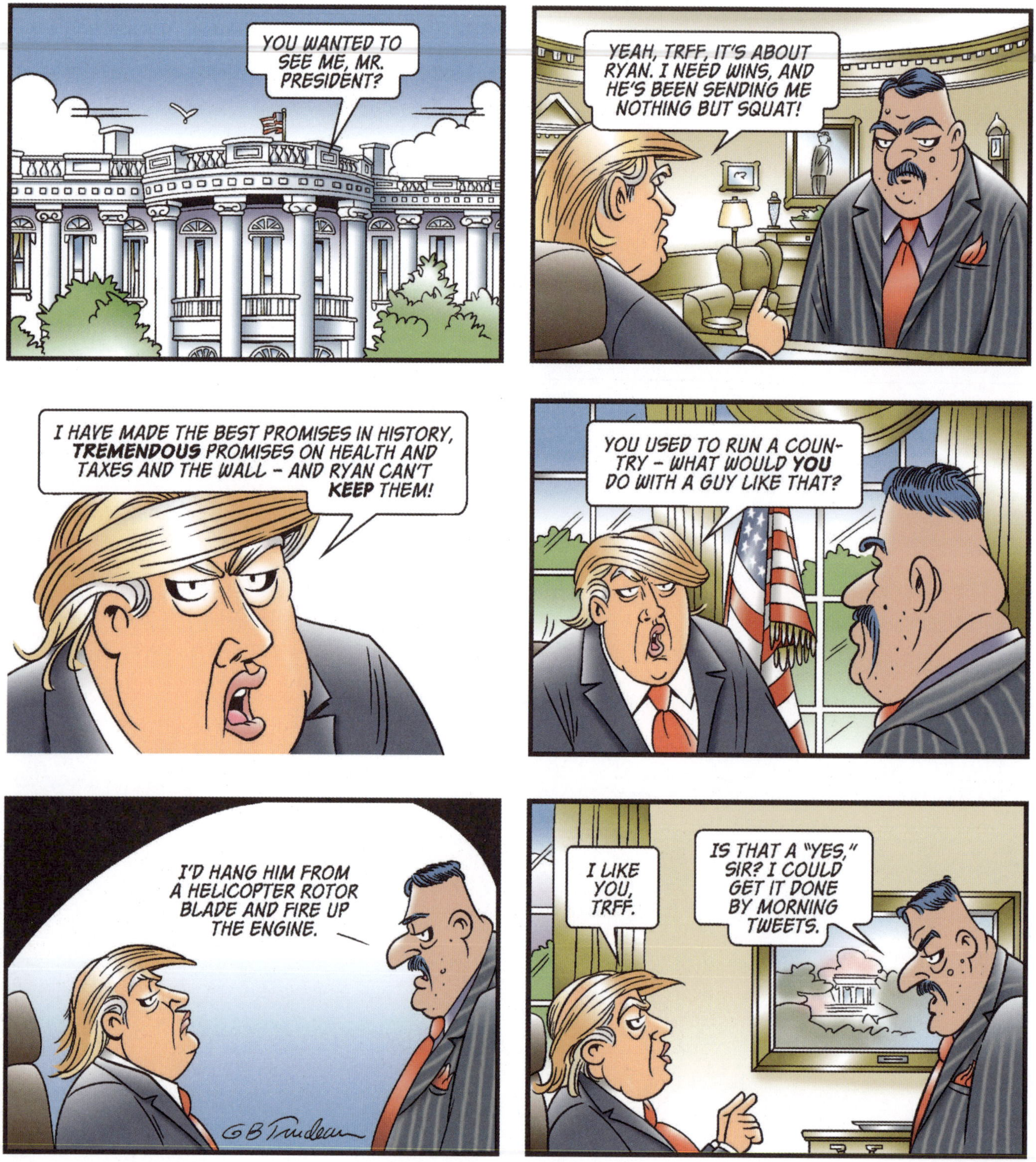
YOU WANTED TO SEE ME, MR. PRESIDENT?
YEAH, TRFF, IT'S ABOUT RYAN. I NEED WINS, AND HE'S BEEN SENDING ME NOTHING BUT SQUAT!
I HAVE MADE THE BEST PROMISES IN HISTORY, **TREMENDOUS** PROMISES ON HEALTH AND TAXES AND THE WALL – AND RYAN CAN'T **KEEP** THEM!
YOU USED TO RUN A COUNTRY – WHAT WOULD **YOU** DO WITH A GUY LIKE THAT?
I'D HANG HIM FROM A HELICOPTER ROTOR BLADE AND FIRE UP THE ENGINE.
GB Trudeau
I LIKE YOU, TRFF.
IS THAT A "YES," SIR? I COULD GET IT DONE BY MORNING TWEETS.

May 28, 2017

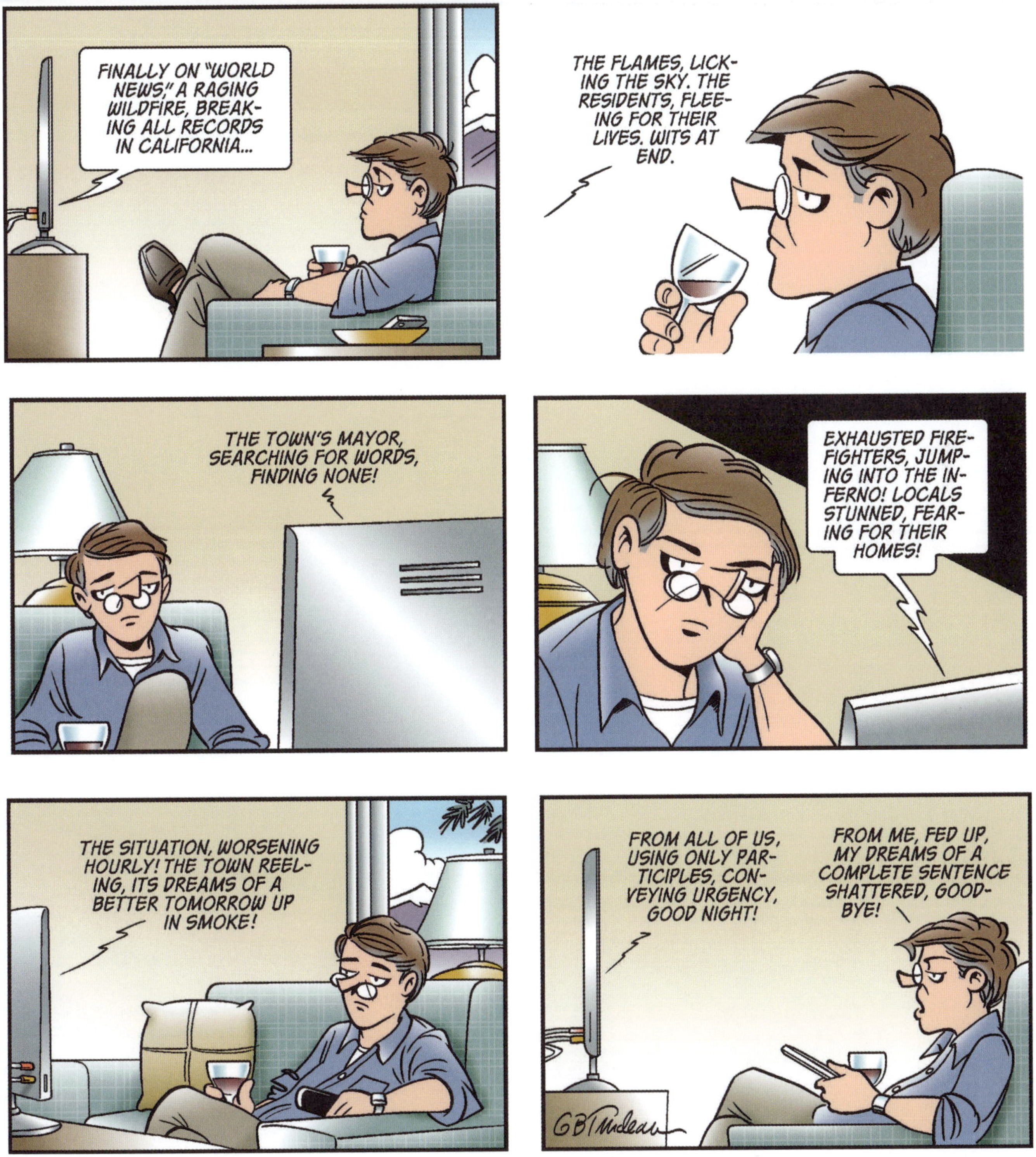
FINALLY ON "WORLD NEWS," A RAGING WILDFIRE, BREAKING ALL RECORDS IN CALIFORNIA...
THE FLAMES, LICKING THE SKY. THE RESIDENTS, FLEEING FOR THEIR LIVES. WITS AT END.
THE TOWN'S MAYOR, SEARCHING FOR WORDS, FINDING NONE!
EXHAUSTED FIREFIGHTERS, JUMPING INTO THE INFERNO! LOCALS STUNNED, FEARING FOR THEIR HOMES!
THE SITUATION, WORSENING HOURLY! THE TOWN REELING, ITS DREAMS OF A BETTER TOMORROW UP IN SMOKE!
FROM ALL OF US, USING ONLY PARTICIPLES, CONVEYING URGENCY, GOOD NIGHT!
FROM ME, FED UP, MY DREAMS OF A COMPLETE SENTENCE SHATTERED, GOODBYE!
GBTrudeau

September 20, 2015

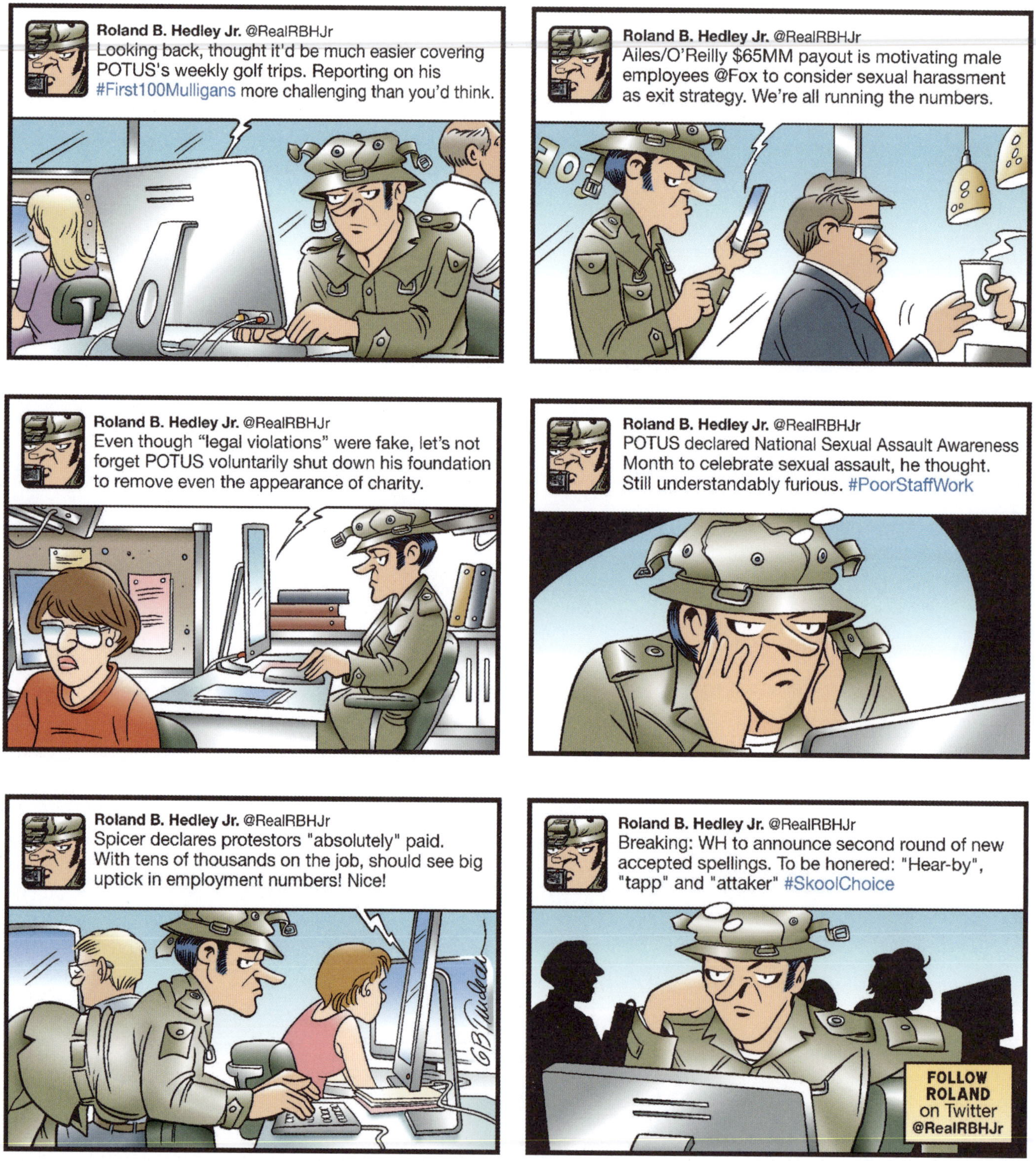

Roland B. Hedley Jr. @RealRBHJr
Looking back, thought it'd be much easier covering POTUS's weekly golf trips. Reporting on his #First100Mulligans more challenging than you'd think.
Roland B. Hedley Jr. @RealRBHJr
Ailes/O'Reilly $65MM payout is motivating male employees @Fox to consider sexual harassment as exit strategy. We're all running the numbers.
Roland B. Hedley Jr. @RealRBHJr
Even though "legal violations" were fake, let's not forget POTUS voluntarily shut down his foundation to remove even the appearance of charity.
Roland B. Hedley Jr. @RealRBHJr
POTUS declared National Sexual Assault Awareness Month to celebrate sexual assault, he thought. Still understandably furious. #PoorStaffWork
Roland B. Hedley Jr. @RealRBHJr
Spicer declares protestors "absolutely" paid. With tens of thousands on the job, should see big uptick in employment numbers! Nice!
Roland B. Hedley Jr. @RealRBHJr
Breaking: WH to announce second round of new accepted spellings. To be honered: "Hear-by", "tapp" and "attaker" #SkoolChoice
FOLLOW ROLAND on Twitter @RealRBHJr

June 11, 2017

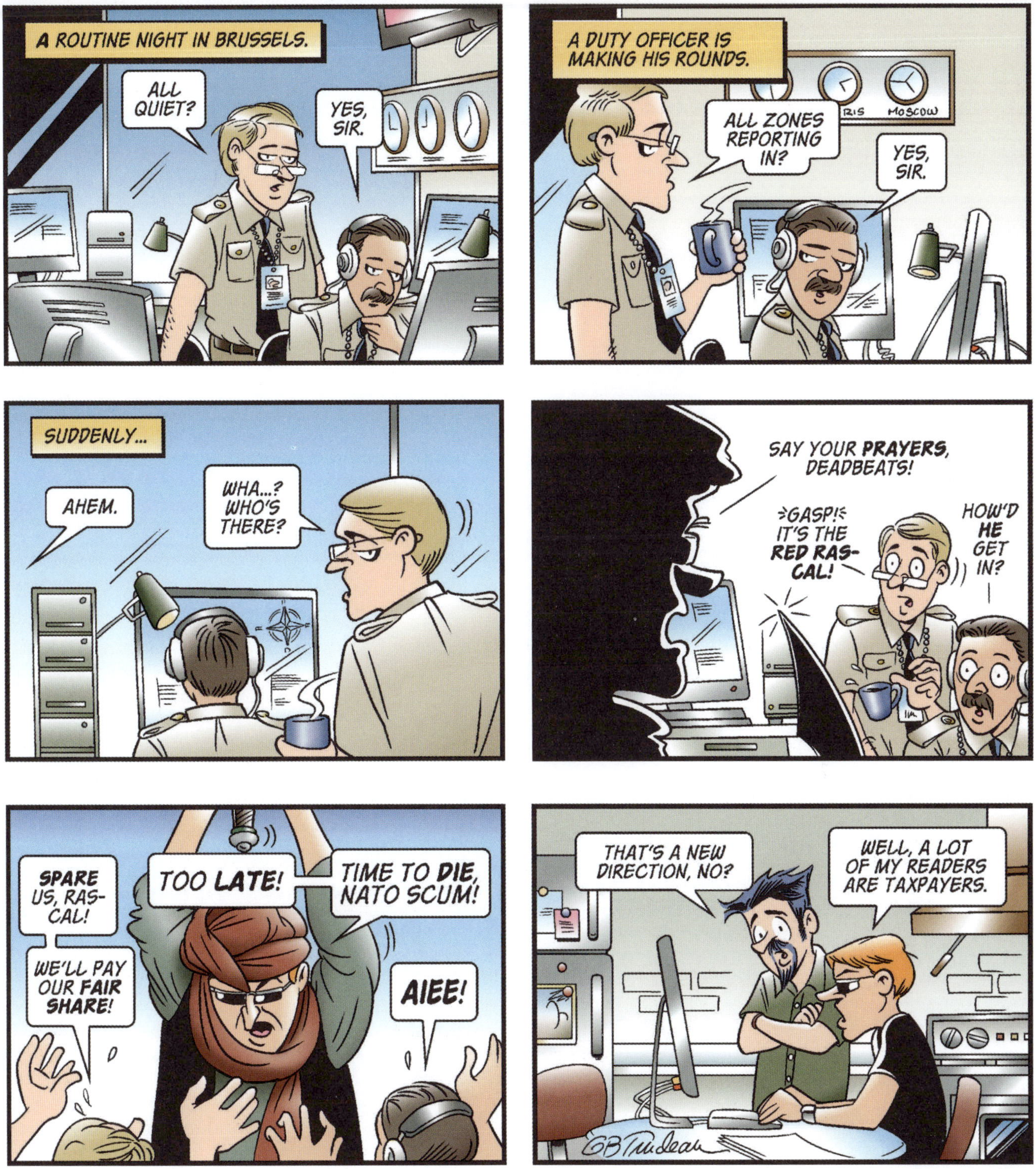
A ROUTINE NIGHT IN BRUSSELS.
ALL QUIET?
YES, SIR.
A DUTY OFFICER IS MAKING HIS ROUNDS.
MOSCOW
ALL ZONES REPORTING IN?
YES, SIR.
SUDDENLY...
AHEM.
WHA...? WHO'S THERE?
SAY YOUR PRAYERS, DEADBEATS!
GASP! IT'S THE RED RASCAL!
HOW'D HE GET IN?
SPARE US, RASCAL!
WE'LL PAY OUR FAIR SHARE!
TOO LATE!
TIME TO DIE, NATO SCUM!
AIEE!
THAT'S A NEW DIRECTION, NO?
WELL, A LOT OF MY READERS ARE TAXPAYERS.
GB Trudeau

June 25, 2017

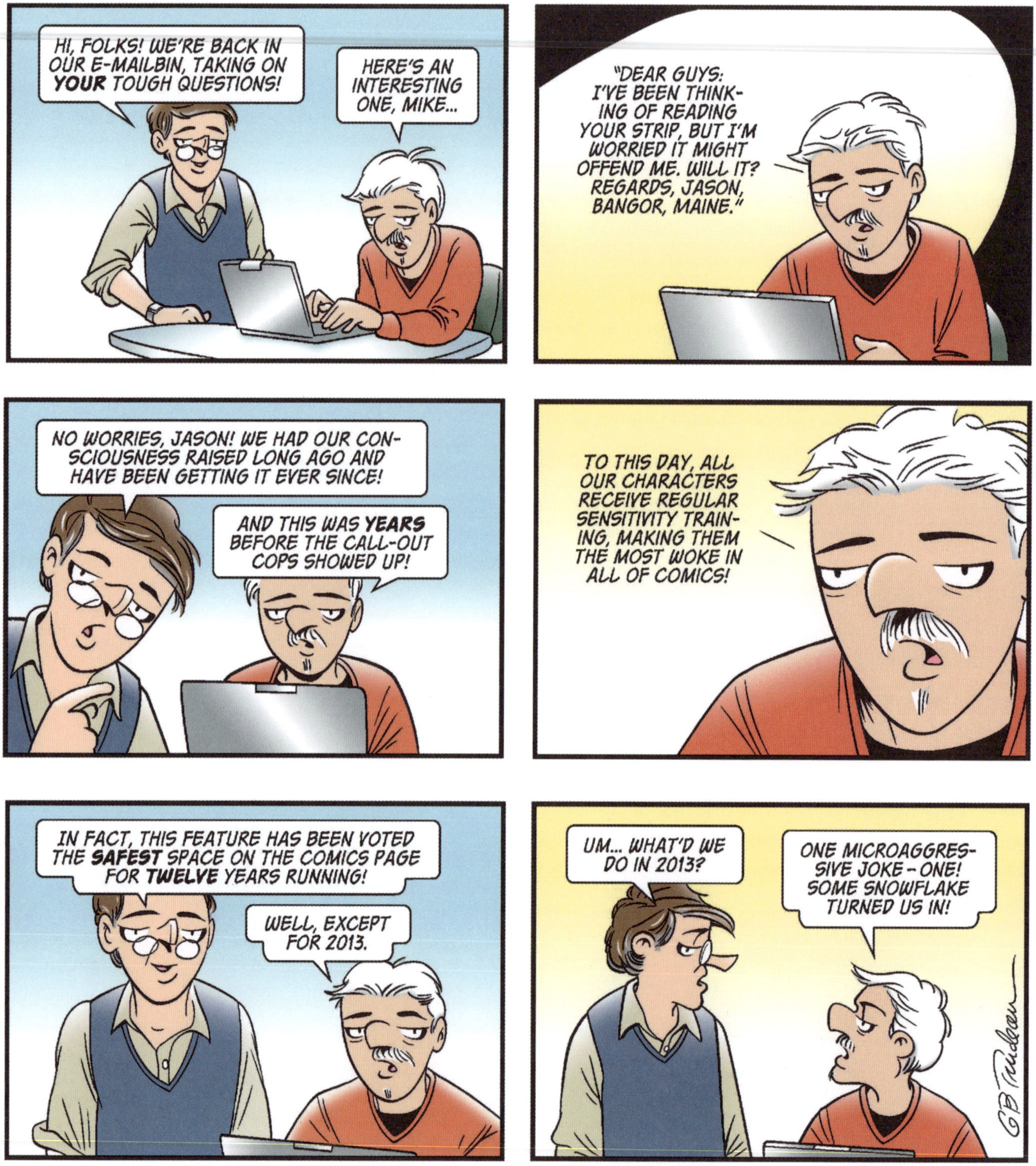
HI, FOLKS! WE'RE BACK IN OUR E-MAILBIN, TAKING ON **YOUR** TOUGH QUESTIONS!
HERE'S AN INTERESTING ONE, MIKE...
"DEAR GUYS: I'VE BEEN THINKING OF READING YOUR STRIP, BUT I'M WORRIED IT MIGHT OFFEND ME. WILL IT? REGARDS, JASON, BANGOR, MAINE."
NO WORRIES, JASON! WE HAD OUR CONSCIOUSNESS RAISED LONG AGO AND HAVE BEEN GETTING IT EVER SINCE!
AND THIS WAS **YEARS** BEFORE THE CALL-OUT COPS SHOWED UP!
TO THIS DAY, ALL OUR CHARACTERS RECEIVE REGULAR SENSITIVITY TRAINING, MAKING THEM THE MOST WOKE IN ALL OF COMICS!
IN FACT, THIS FEATURE HAS BEEN VOTED THE **SAFEST** SPACE ON THE COMICS PAGE FOR **TWELVE** YEARS RUNNING!
WELL, EXCEPT FOR 2013.
UM... WHAT'D WE DO IN 2013?
ONE MICROAGGRESSIVE JOKE – ONE! SOME SNOWFLAKE TURNED US IN!
GB Trudeau

July 2, 2017

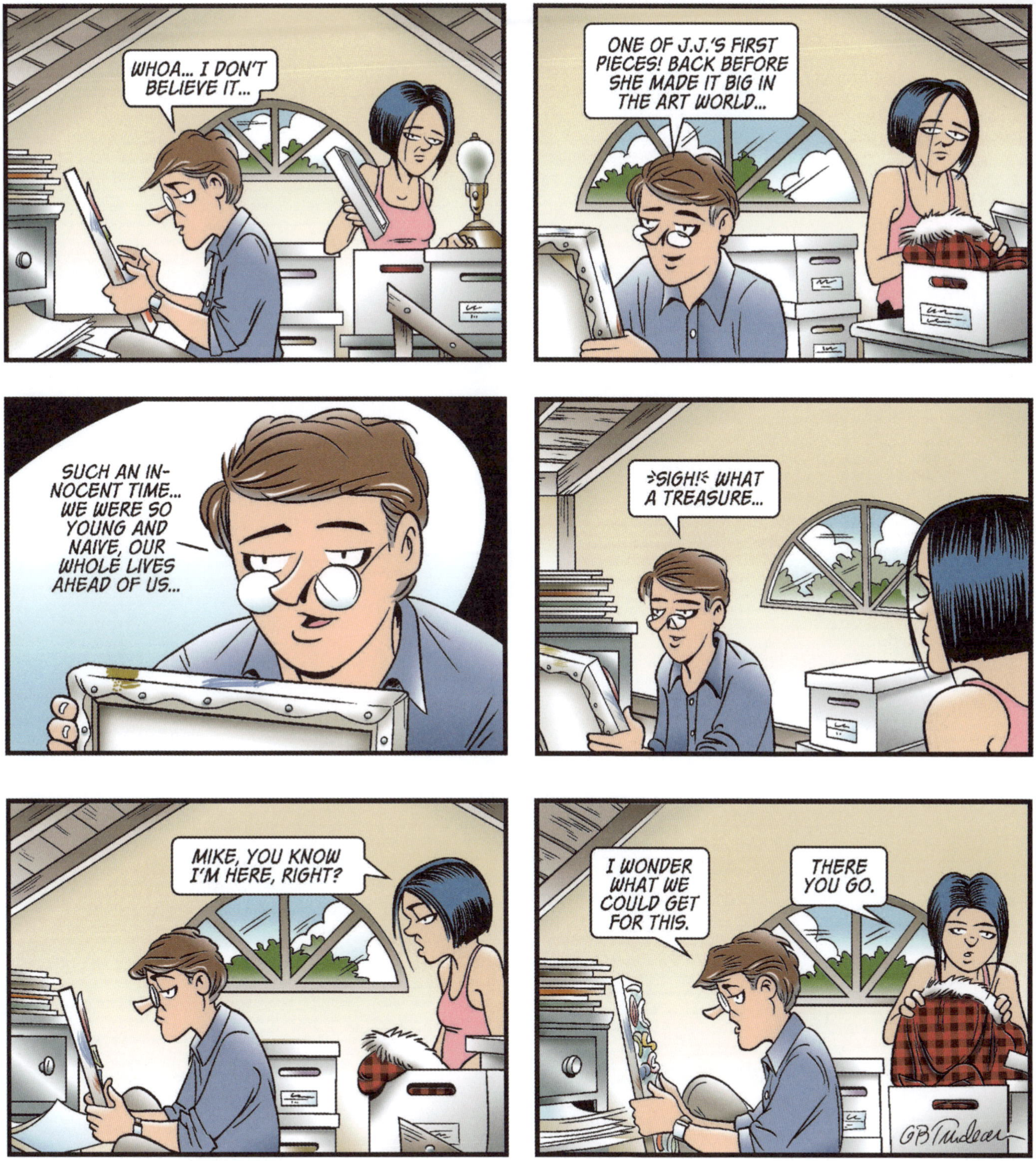
WHOA... I DON'T BELIEVE IT...
ONE OF J.J.'S FIRST PIECES! BACK BEFORE SHE MADE IT BIG IN THE ART WORLD...
SUCH AN IN-NOCENT TIME... WE WERE SO YOUNG AND NAIVE, OUR WHOLE LIVES AHEAD OF US...
SIGH! WHAT A TREASURE...
MIKE, YOU KNOW I'M HERE, RIGHT?
I WONDER WHAT WE COULD GET FOR THIS.
THERE YOU GO.
GB Trudeau

July 9, 2017

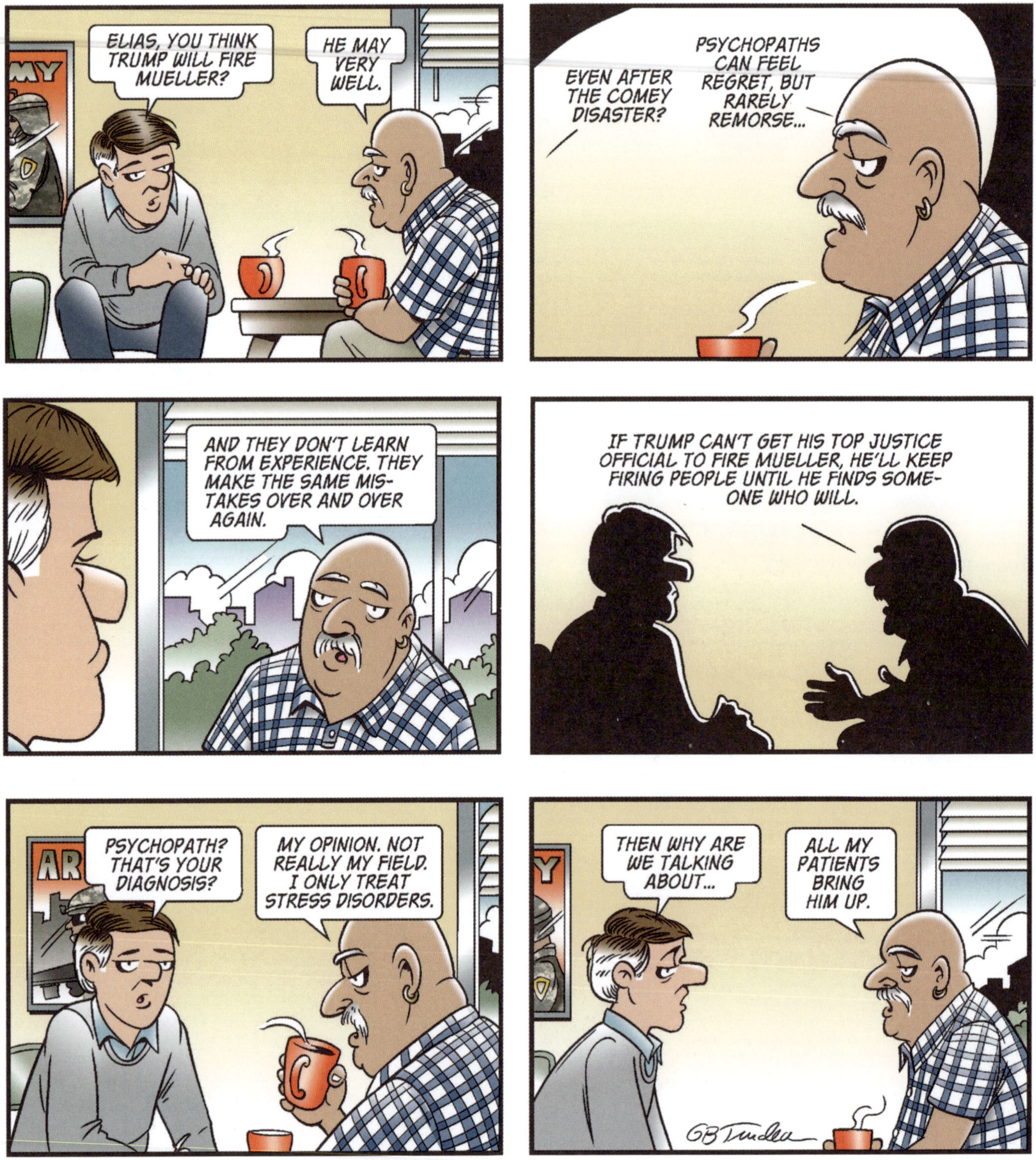
ELIAS, YOU THINK TRUMP WILL FIRE MUELLER?
HE MAY VERY WELL.
EVEN AFTER THE COMEY DISASTER?
PSYCHOPATHS CAN FEEL REGRET, BUT RARELY REMORSE...
AND THEY DON'T LEARN FROM EXPERIENCE. THEY MAKE THE SAME MISTAKES OVER AND OVER AGAIN.
IF TRUMP CAN'T GET HIS TOP JUSTICE OFFICIAL TO FIRE MUELLER, HE'LL KEEP FIRING PEOPLE UNTIL HE FINDS SOMEONE WHO WILL.
PSYCHOPATH? THAT'S YOUR DIAGNOSIS?
MY OPINION. NOT REALLY MY FIELD. I ONLY TREAT STRESS DISORDERS.
THEN WHY ARE WE TALKING ABOUT...
ALL MY PATIENTS BRING HIM UP.
GB Trudeau

July 16, 2017

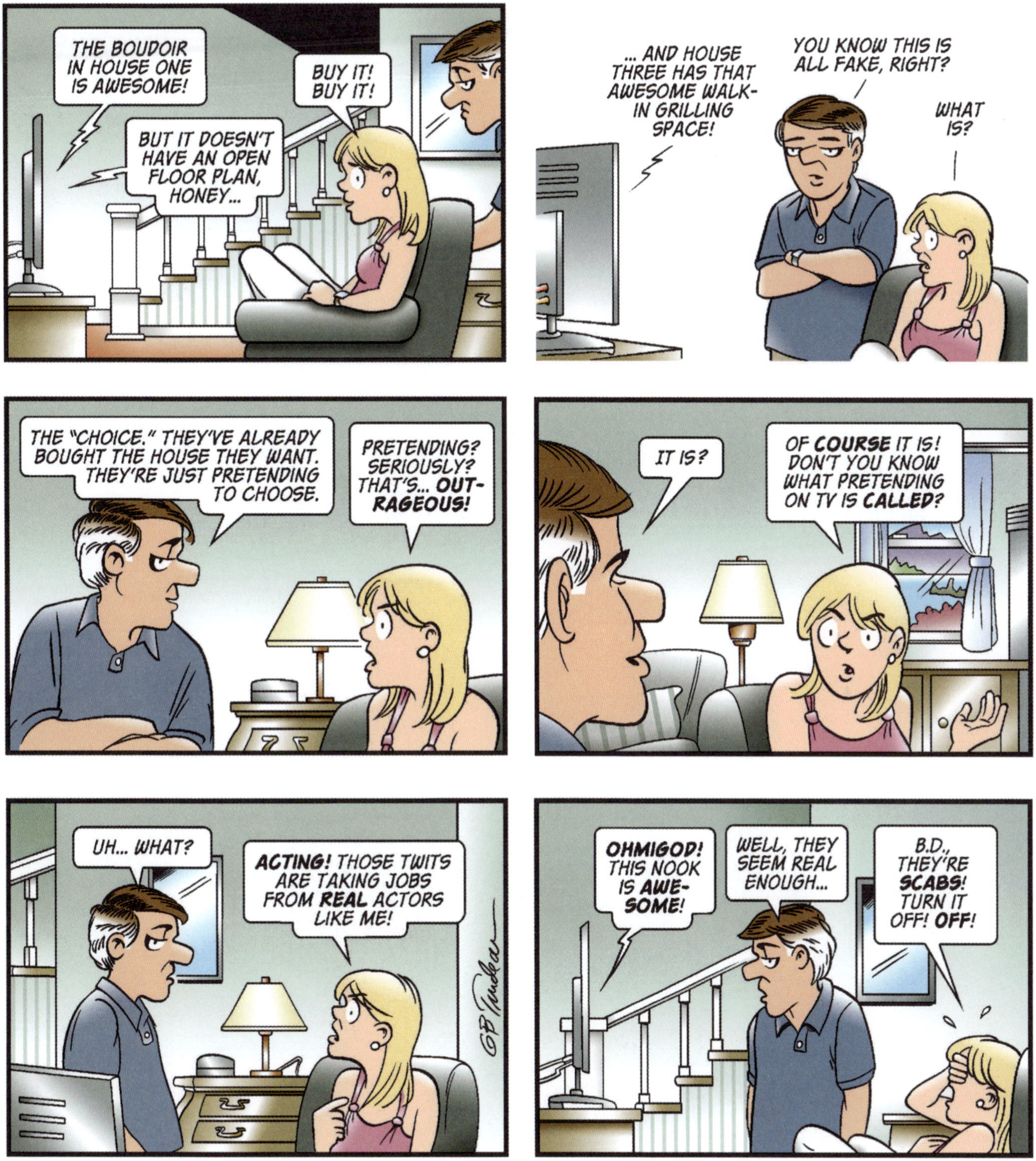
THE BOUDOIR IN HOUSE ONE IS AWESOME!
BUT IT DOESN'T HAVE AN OPEN FLOOR PLAN, HONEY...
BUY IT! BUY IT!
... AND HOUSE THREE HAS THAT AWESOME WALK-IN GRILLING SPACE!
YOU KNOW THIS IS ALL FAKE, RIGHT?
WHAT IS?
THE "CHOICE." THEY'VE ALREADY BOUGHT THE HOUSE THEY WANT. THEY'RE JUST PRETENDING TO CHOOSE.
PRETENDING? SERIOUSLY? THAT'S... OUT-RAGEOUS!
IT IS?
OF COURSE IT IS! DON'T YOU KNOW WHAT PRETENDING ON TV IS CALLED?
UH... WHAT?
ACTING! THOSE TWITS ARE TAKING JOBS FROM REAL ACTORS LIKE ME!
GB Trudeau
OHMIGOD! THIS NOOK IS AWE-SOME!
WELL, THEY SEEM REAL ENOUGH...
B.D., THEY'RE SCABS! TURN IT OFF! OFF!

July 23, 2017

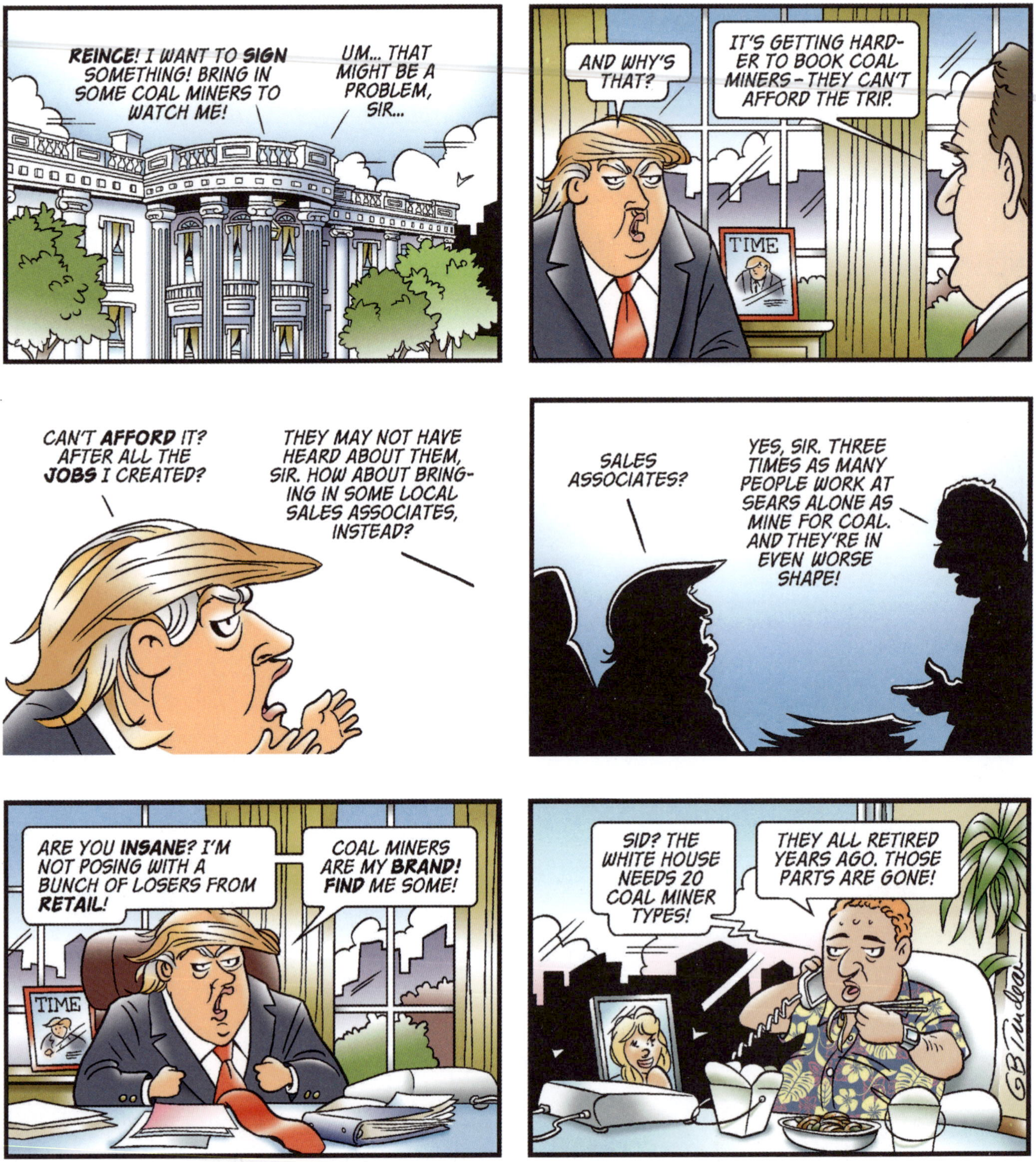
REINCE! I WANT TO SIGN SOMETHING! BRING IN SOME COAL MINERS TO WATCH ME!
UM... THAT MIGHT BE A PROBLEM, SIR...
AND WHY'S THAT?
IT'S GETTING HARDER TO BOOK COAL MINERS - THEY CAN'T AFFORD THE TRIP.
TIME
CAN'T AFFORD IT? AFTER ALL THE JOBS I CREATED?
THEY MAY NOT HAVE HEARD ABOUT THEM, SIR. HOW ABOUT BRINGING IN SOME LOCAL SALES ASSOCIATES, INSTEAD?
SALES ASSOCIATES?
YES, SIR. THREE TIMES AS MANY PEOPLE WORK AT SEARS ALONE AS MINE FOR COAL. AND THEY'RE IN EVEN WORSE SHAPE!
ARE YOU INSANE? I'M NOT POSING WITH A BUNCH OF LOSERS FROM RETAIL!
COAL MINERS ARE MY BRAND! FIND ME SOME!
TIME
SID? THE WHITE HOUSE NEEDS 20 COAL MINER TYPES!
THEY ALL RETIRED YEARS AGO. THOSE PARTS ARE GONE!
GBTrudeau

July 30, 2017

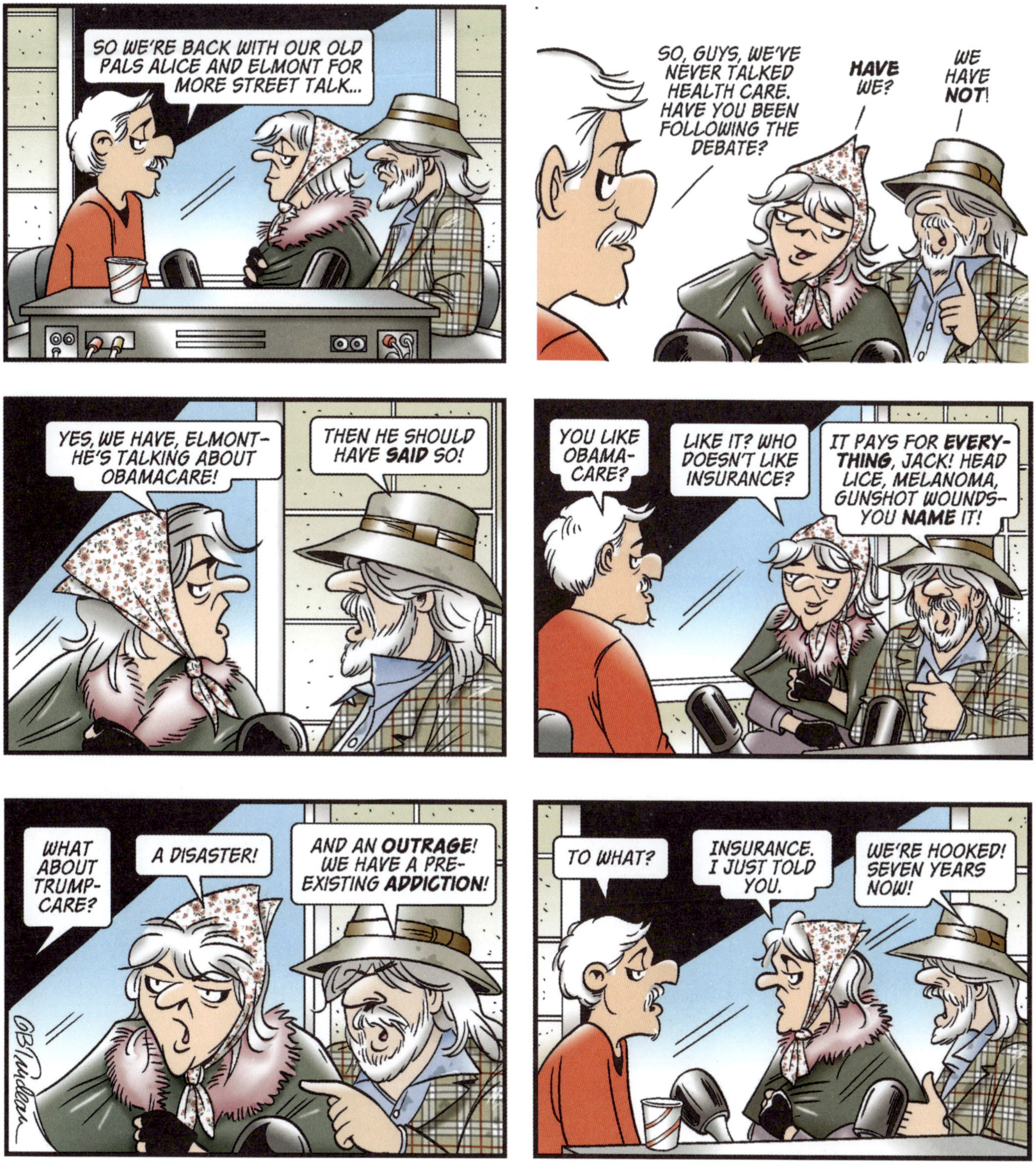
SO WE'RE BACK WITH OUR OLD PALS ALICE AND ELMONT FOR MORE STREET TALK...
SO, GUYS, WE'VE NEVER TALKED HEALTH CARE. HAVE YOU BEEN FOLLOWING THE DEBATE?
HAVE WE?
WE HAVE **NOT**!
YES, WE HAVE, ELMONT- HE'S TALKING ABOUT OBAMACARE!
THEN HE SHOULD HAVE **SAID** SO!
YOU LIKE OBAMA-CARE?
LIKE IT? WHO DOESN'T LIKE INSURANCE?
IT PAYS FOR **EVERY-THING**, JACK! HEAD LICE, MELANOMA, GUNSHOT WOUNDS- YOU **NAME** IT!
WHAT ABOUT TRUMP-CARE?
A DISASTER!
AND AN **OUTRAGE**! WE HAVE A PRE-EXISTING **ADDICTION**!
TO WHAT?
INSURANCE. I JUST TOLD YOU.
WE'RE HOOKED! SEVEN YEARS NOW!

August 6, 2017

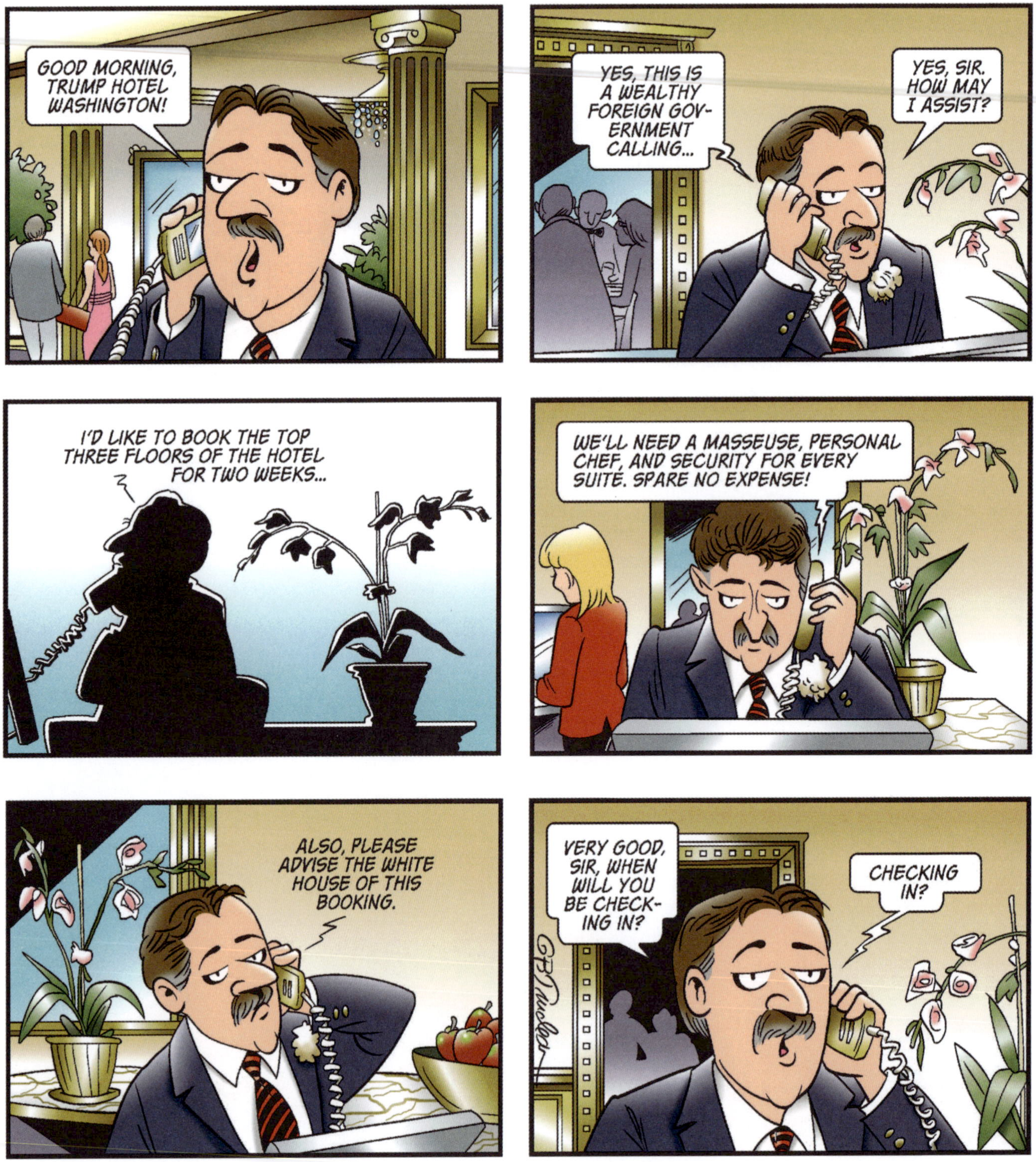
GOOD MORNING, TRUMP HOTEL WASHINGTON!
YES, THIS IS A WEALTHY FOREIGN GOVERNMENT CALLING...
YES, SIR. HOW MAY I ASSIST?
I'D LIKE TO BOOK THE TOP THREE FLOORS OF THE HOTEL FOR TWO WEEKS...
WE'LL NEED A MASSEUSE, PERSONAL CHEF, AND SECURITY FOR EVERY SUITE. SPARE NO EXPENSE!
ALSO, PLEASE ADVISE THE WHITE HOUSE OF THIS BOOKING.
VERY GOOD, SIR, WHEN WILL YOU BE CHECKING IN?
CHECKING IN?
GBTrudeau

August 13, 2017

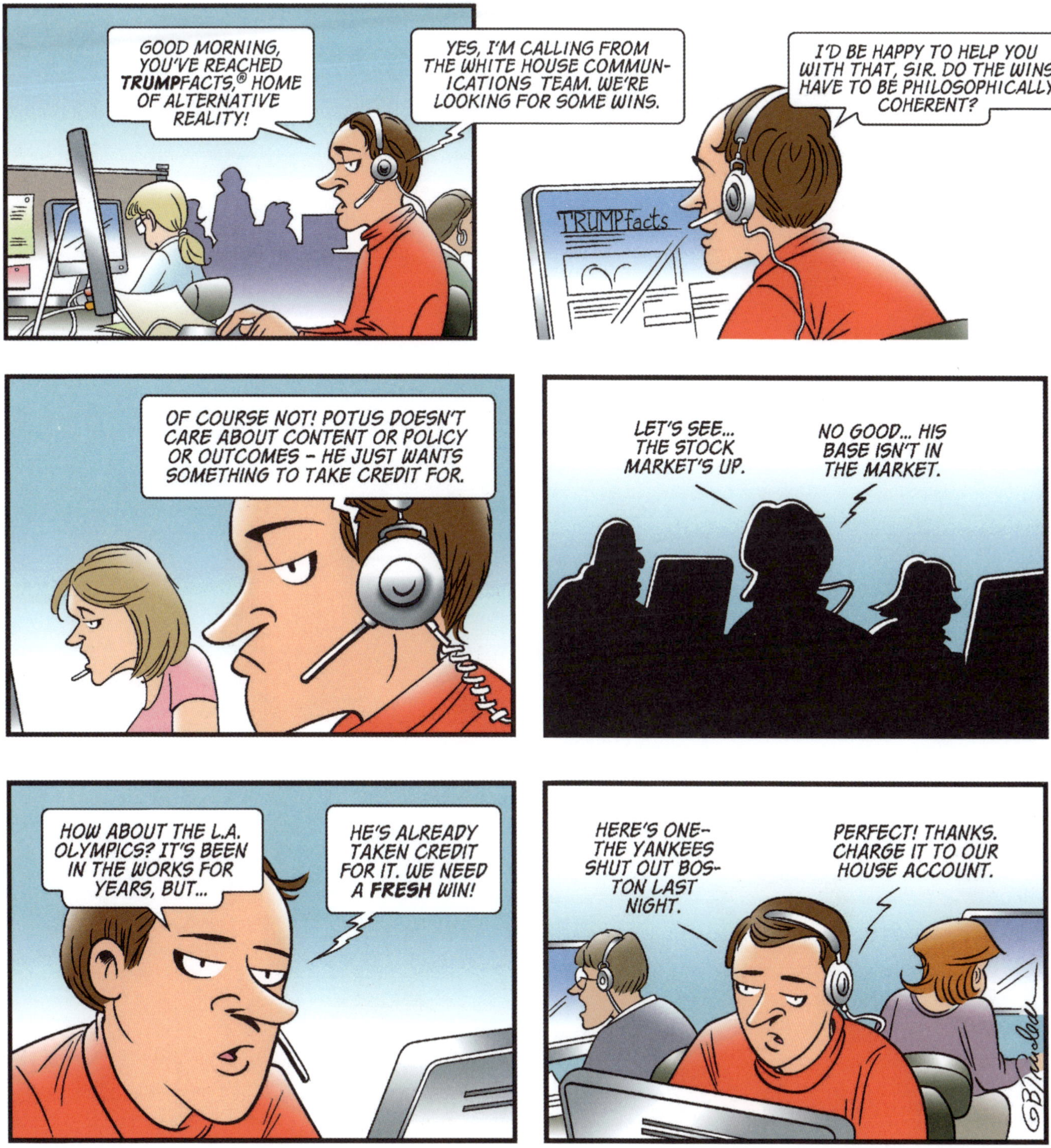
GOOD MORNING, YOU'VE REACHED **TRUMP**FACTS,® HOME OF ALTERNATIVE REALITY!
YES, I'M CALLING FROM THE WHITE HOUSE COMMUNICATIONS TEAM. WE'RE LOOKING FOR SOME WINS.
TRUMPfacts
I'D BE HAPPY TO HELP YOU WITH THAT, SIR. DO THE WINS HAVE TO BE PHILOSOPHICALLY COHERENT?
OF COURSE NOT! POTUS DOESN'T CARE ABOUT CONTENT OR POLICY OR OUTCOMES – HE JUST WANTS SOMETHING TO TAKE CREDIT FOR.
LET'S SEE... THE STOCK MARKET'S UP.
NO GOOD... HIS BASE ISN'T IN THE MARKET.
HOW ABOUT THE L.A. OLYMPICS? IT'S BEEN IN THE WORKS FOR YEARS, BUT...
HE'S ALREADY TAKEN CREDIT FOR IT. WE NEED A **FRESH** WIN!
HERE'S ONE– THE YANKEES SHUT OUT BOSTON LAST NIGHT.
PERFECT! THANKS. CHARGE IT TO OUR HOUSE ACCOUNT.
GBTrudeau

August 20, 2017

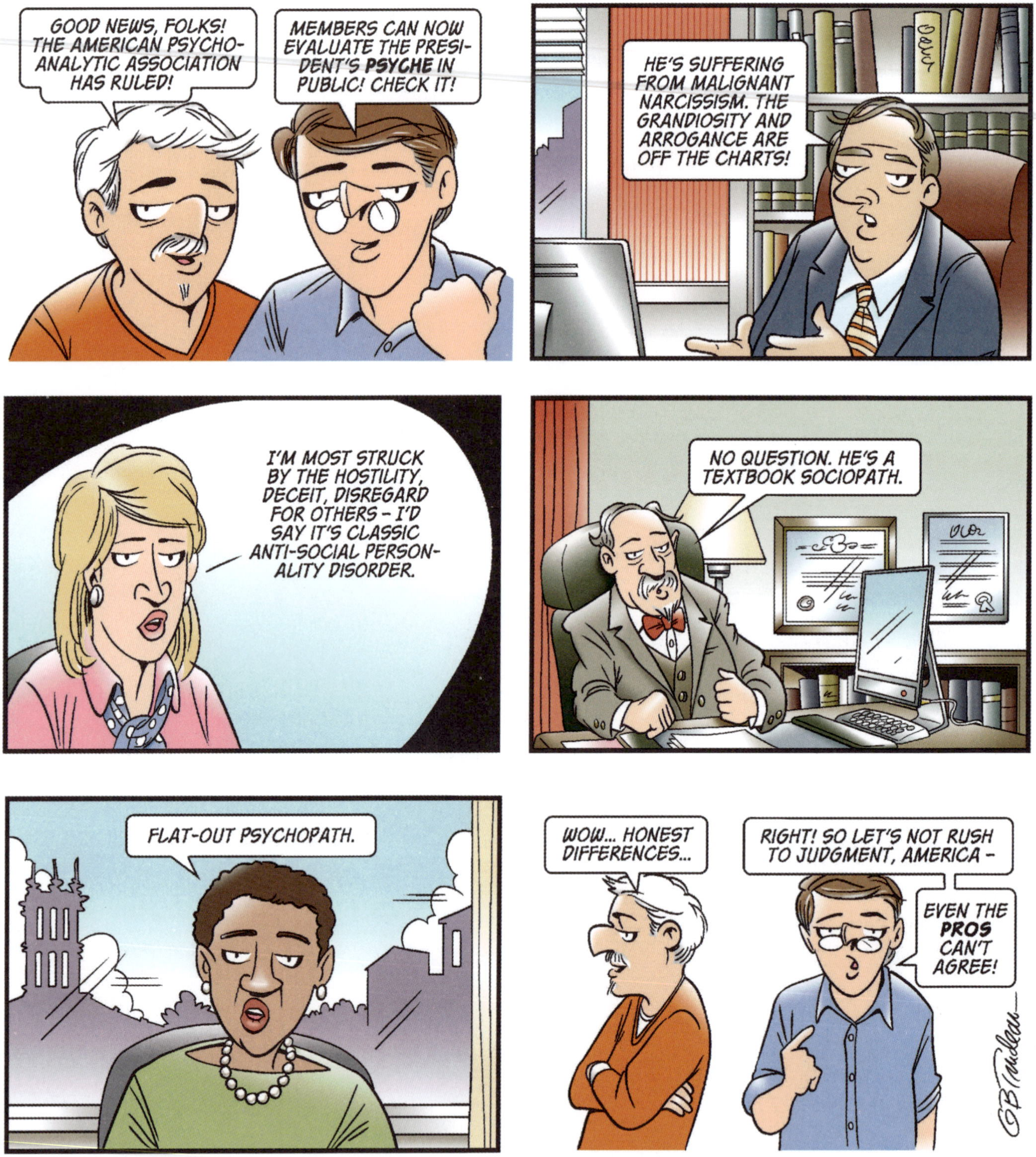
GOOD NEWS, FOLKS! THE AMERICAN PSYCHO-ANALYTIC ASSOCIATION HAS RULED!
MEMBERS CAN NOW EVALUATE THE PRESI-DENT'S **PSYCHE** IN PUBLIC! CHECK IT!
HE'S SUFFERING FROM MALIGNANT NARCISSISM. THE GRANDIOSITY AND ARROGANCE ARE OFF THE CHARTS!
I'M MOST STRUCK BY THE HOSTILITY, DECEIT, DISREGARD FOR OTHERS – I'D SAY IT'S CLASSIC ANTI-SOCIAL PERSON-ALITY DISORDER.
NO QUESTION. HE'S A TEXTBOOK SOCIOPATH.
FLAT-OUT PSYCHOPATH.
WOW... HONEST DIFFERENCES...
RIGHT! SO LET'S NOT RUSH TO JUDGMENT, AMERICA –
EVEN THE **PROS** CAN'T AGREE!
GBTrudeau

August 27, 2017

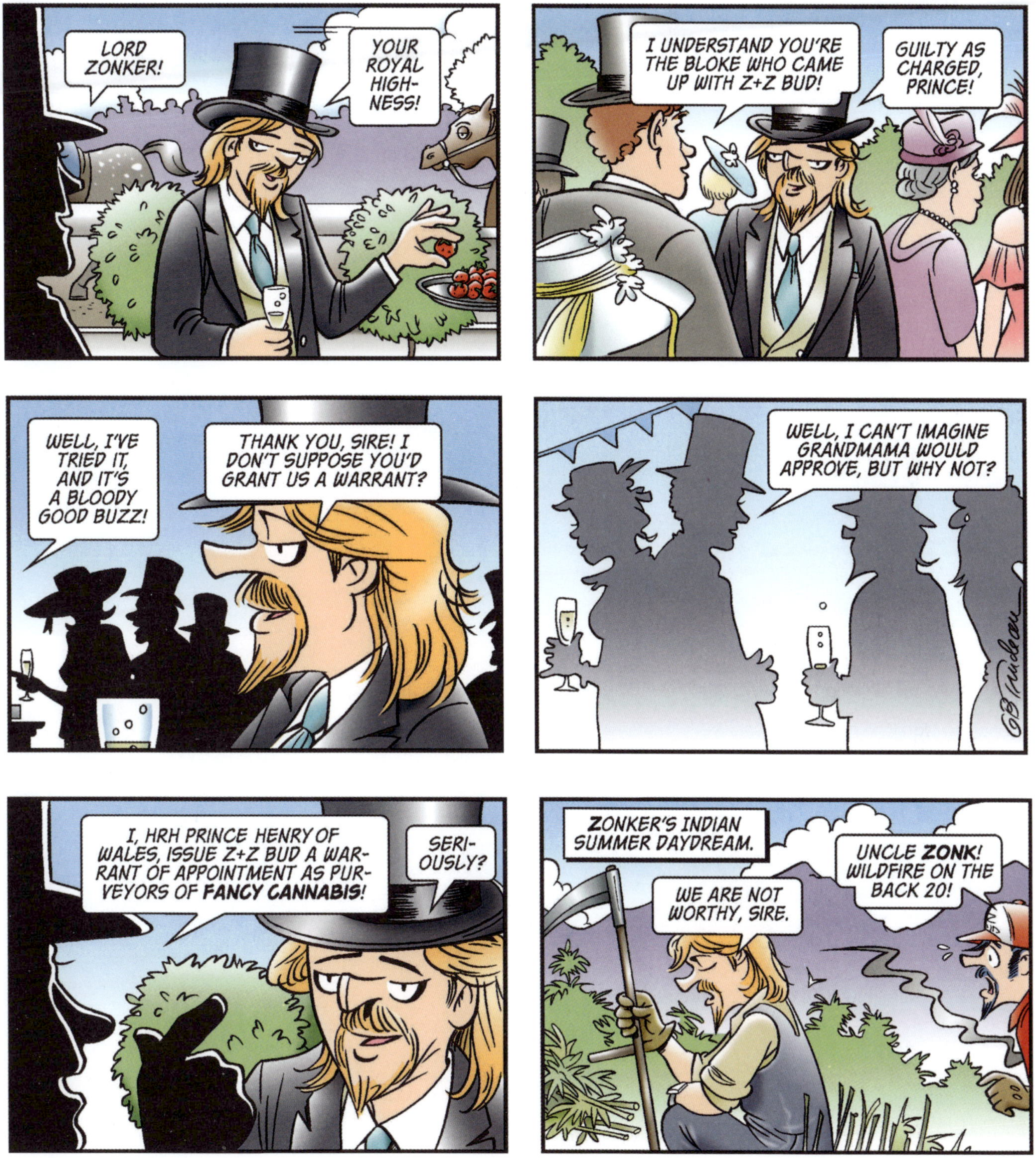
LORD ZONKER!
YOUR ROYAL HIGH-NESS!
I UNDERSTAND YOU'RE THE BLOKE WHO CAME UP WITH Z+Z BUD!
GUILTY AS CHARGED, PRINCE!
WELL, I'VE TRIED IT, AND IT'S A BLOODY GOOD BUZZ!
THANK YOU, SIRE! I DON'T SUPPOSE YOU'D GRANT US A WARRANT?
WELL, I CAN'T IMAGINE GRANDMAMA WOULD APPROVE, BUT WHY NOT?
I, HRH PRINCE HENRY OF WALES, ISSUE Z+Z BUD A WARRANT OF APPOINTMENT AS PURVEYORS OF **FANCY CANNABIS**!
SERIOUSLY?
ZONKER'S INDIAN SUMMER DAYDREAM.
WE ARE NOT WORTHY, SIRE.
UNCLE **ZONK**! WILDFIRE ON THE BACK 20!
GBTrudeau

October 11, 2015

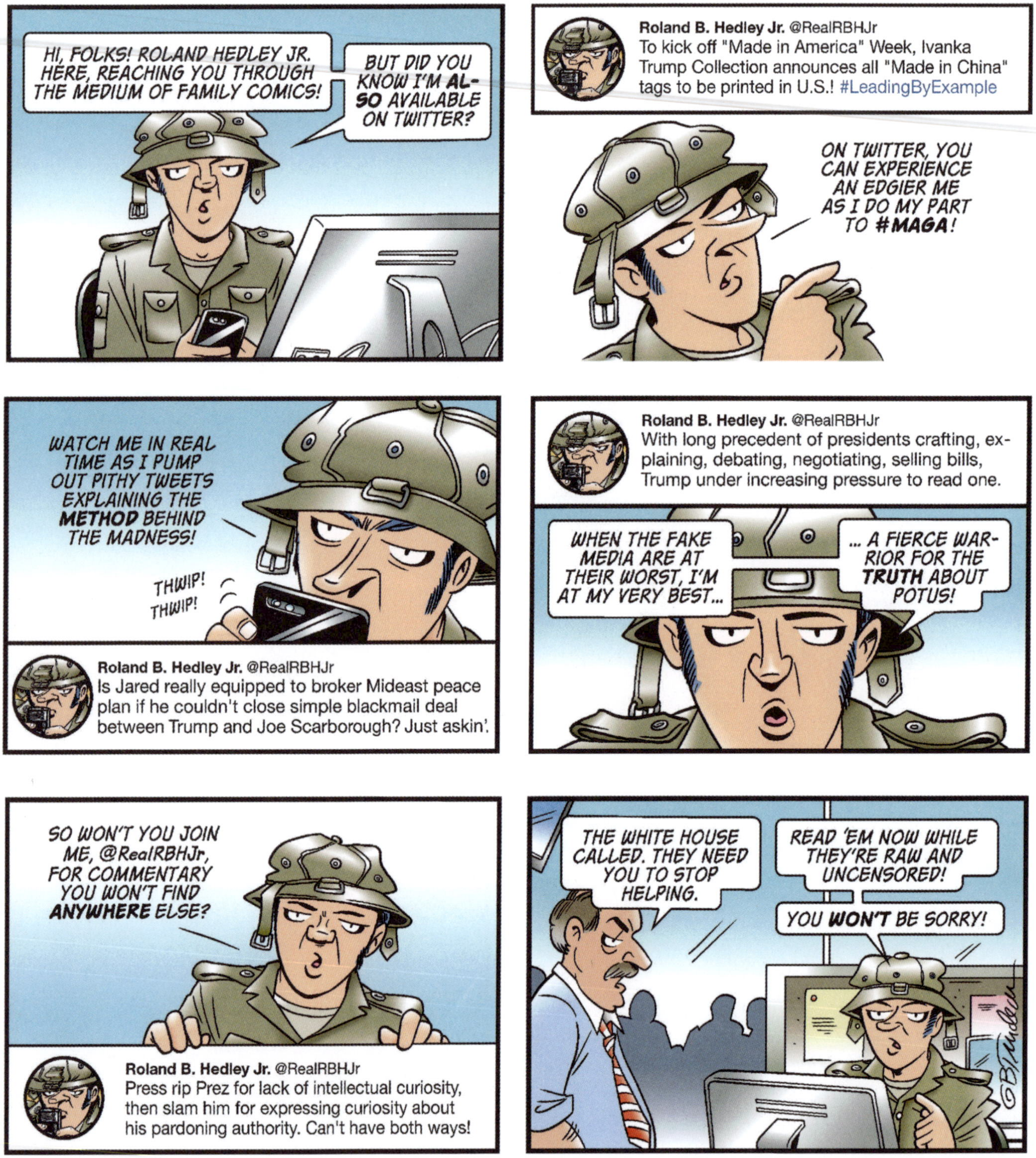

HI, FOLKS! ROLAND HEDLEY JR. HERE, REACHING YOU THROUGH THE MEDIUM OF FAMILY COMICS!
BUT DID YOU KNOW I'M ALSO AVAILABLE ON TWITTER?
Roland B. Hedley Jr. @RealRBHJr
To kick off "Made in America" Week, Ivanka Trump Collection announces all "Made in China" tags to be printed in U.S.! #LeadingByExample
ON TWITTER, YOU CAN EXPERIENCE AN EDGIER ME AS I DO MY PART TO #MAGA!
WATCH ME IN REAL TIME AS I PUMP OUT PITHY TWEETS EXPLAINING THE METHOD BEHIND THE MADNESS!
THWIP! THWIP!
Roland B. Hedley Jr. @RealRBHJr
Is Jared really equipped to broker Mideast peace plan if he couldn't close simple blackmail deal between Trump and Joe Scarborough? Just askin'.
Roland B. Hedley Jr. @RealRBHJr
With long precedent of presidents crafting, explaining, debating, negotiating, selling bills, Trump under increasing pressure to read one.
WHEN THE FAKE MEDIA ARE AT THEIR WORST, I'M AT MY VERY BEST...
... A FIERCE WARRIOR FOR THE TRUTH ABOUT POTUS!
SO WON'T YOU JOIN ME, @RealRBHJr, FOR COMMENTARY YOU WON'T FIND ANYWHERE ELSE?
Roland B. Hedley Jr. @RealRBHJr
Press rip Prez for lack of intellectual curiosity, then slam him for expressing curiosity about his pardoning authority. Can't have both ways!
THE WHITE HOUSE CALLED. THEY NEED YOU TO STOP HELPING.
READ 'EM NOW WHILE THEY'RE RAW AND UNCENSORED!
YOU WON'T BE SORRY!
©BTrudeau

September 3, 2017

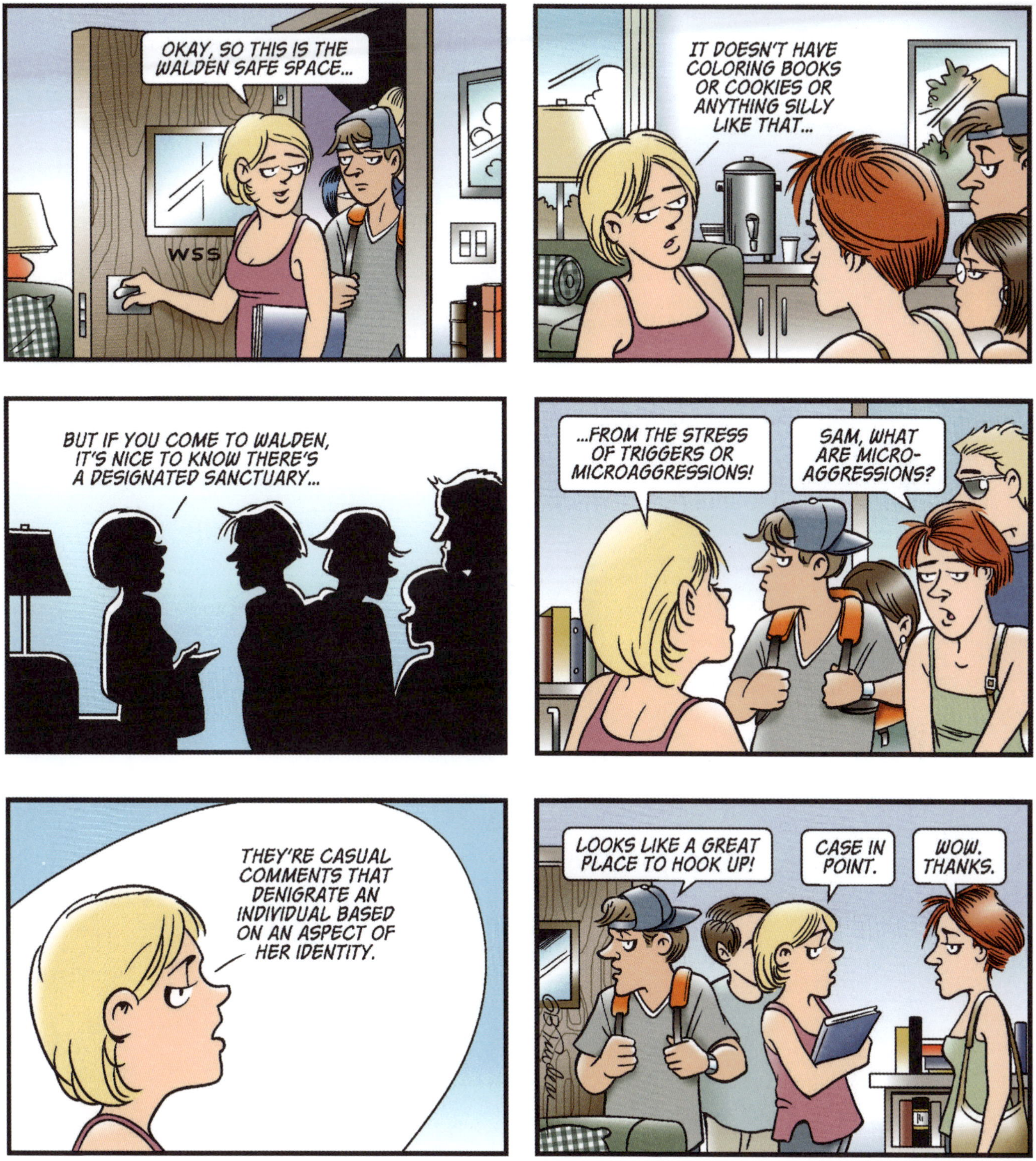
OKAY, SO THIS IS THE WALDEN SAFE SPACE...
WSS
IT DOESN'T HAVE COLORING BOOKS OR COOKIES OR ANYTHING SILLY LIKE THAT...
BUT IF YOU COME TO WALDEN, IT'S NICE TO KNOW THERE'S A DESIGNATED SANCTUARY...
...FROM THE STRESS OF TRIGGERS OR MICROAGGRESSIONS!
SAM, WHAT ARE MICRO-AGGRESSIONS?
THEY'RE CASUAL COMMENTS THAT DENIGRATE AN INDIVIDUAL BASED ON AN ASPECT OF HER IDENTITY.
LOOKS LIKE A GREAT PLACE TO HOOK UP!
CASE IN POINT.
WOW. THANKS.

October 16, 2016

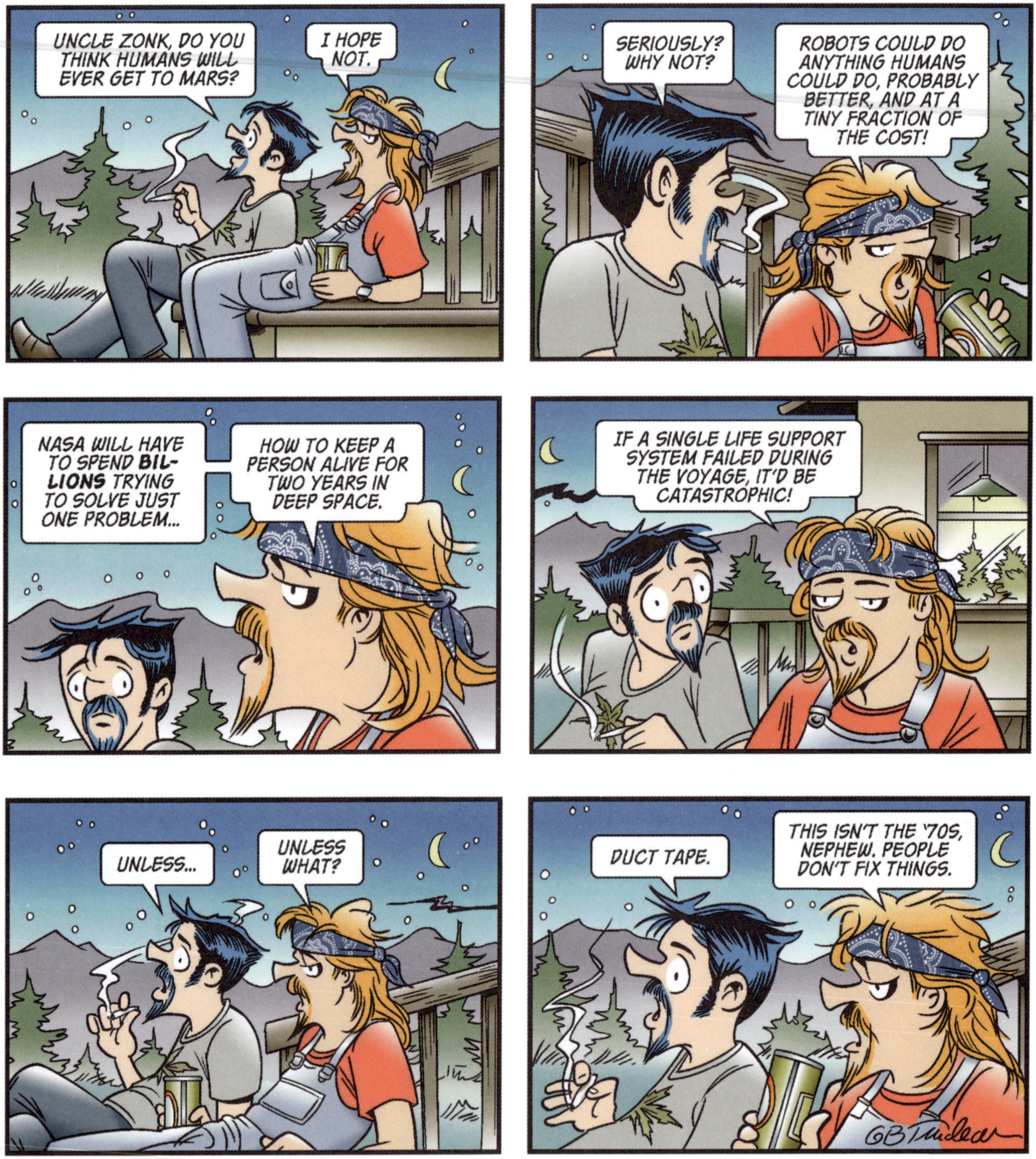
UNCLE ZONK, DO YOU THINK HUMANS WILL EVER GET TO MARS?
I HOPE NOT.
SERIOUSLY? WHY NOT?
ROBOTS COULD DO ANYTHING HUMANS COULD DO, PROBABLY BETTER, AND AT A TINY FRACTION OF THE COST!
NASA WILL HAVE TO SPEND **BILLIONS** TRYING TO SOLVE JUST ONE PROBLEM...
HOW TO KEEP A PERSON ALIVE FOR TWO YEARS IN DEEP SPACE.
IF A SINGLE LIFE SUPPORT SYSTEM FAILED DURING THE VOYAGE, IT'D BE CATASTROPHIC!
UNLESS...
UNLESS WHAT?
DUCT TAPE.
THIS ISN'T THE '70S, NEPHEW. PEOPLE DON'T FIX THINGS.
GBTrudeau

September 10, 2017

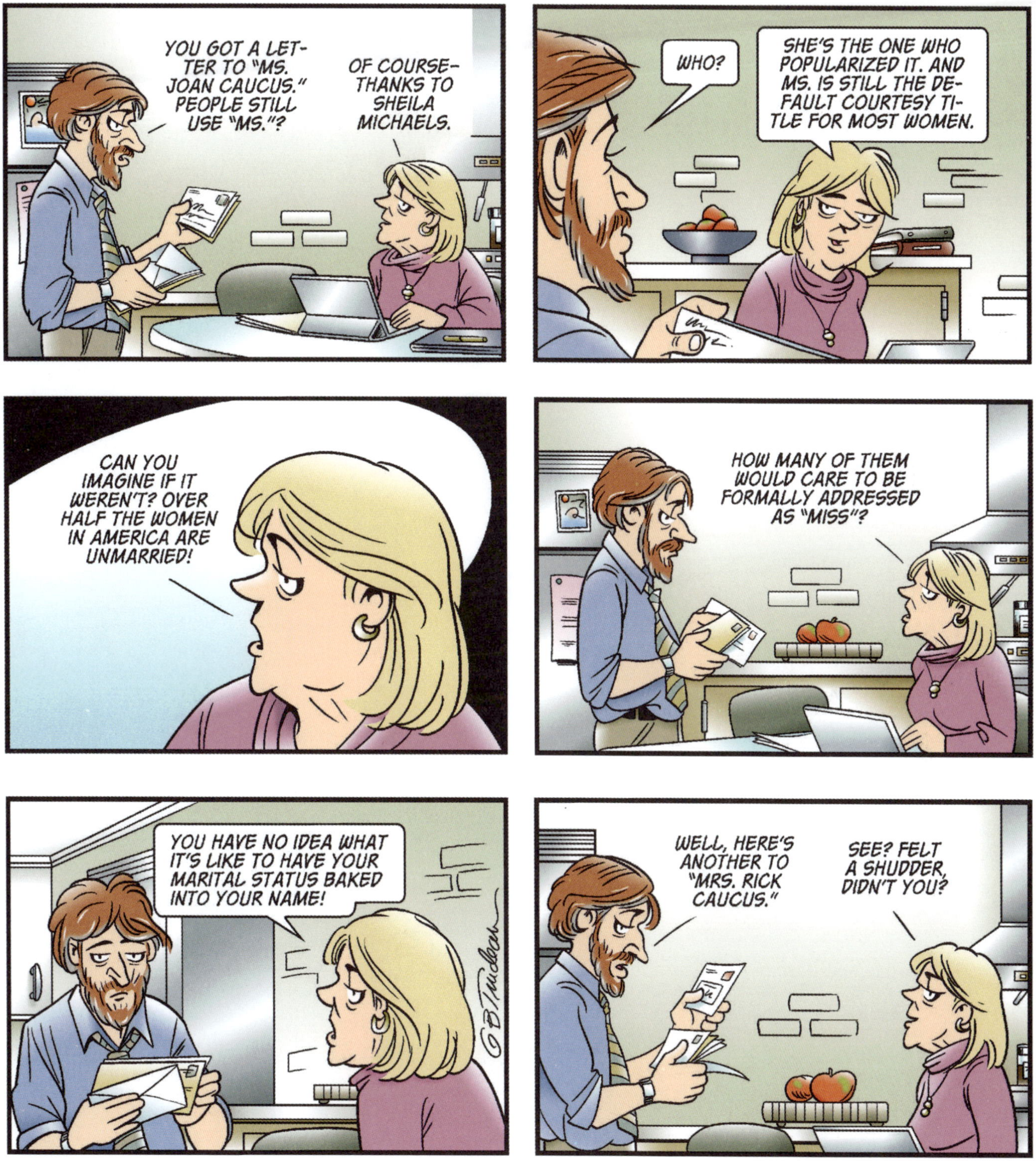
YOU GOT A LETTER TO "MS. JOAN CAUCUS." PEOPLE STILL USE "MS."?
OF COURSE–THANKS TO SHEILA MICHAELS.
WHO?
SHE'S THE ONE WHO POPULARIZED IT. AND MS. IS STILL THE DEFAULT COURTESY TITLE FOR MOST WOMEN.
CAN YOU IMAGINE IF IT WEREN'T? OVER HALF THE WOMEN IN AMERICA ARE UNMARRIED!
HOW MANY OF THEM WOULD CARE TO BE FORMALLY ADDRESSED AS "MISS"?
YOU HAVE NO IDEA WHAT IT'S LIKE TO HAVE YOUR MARITAL STATUS BAKED INTO YOUR NAME!
GBTrudeau
WELL, HERE'S ANOTHER TO "MRS. RICK CAUCUS."
SEE? FELT A SHUDDER, DIDN'T YOU?

September 17, 2017

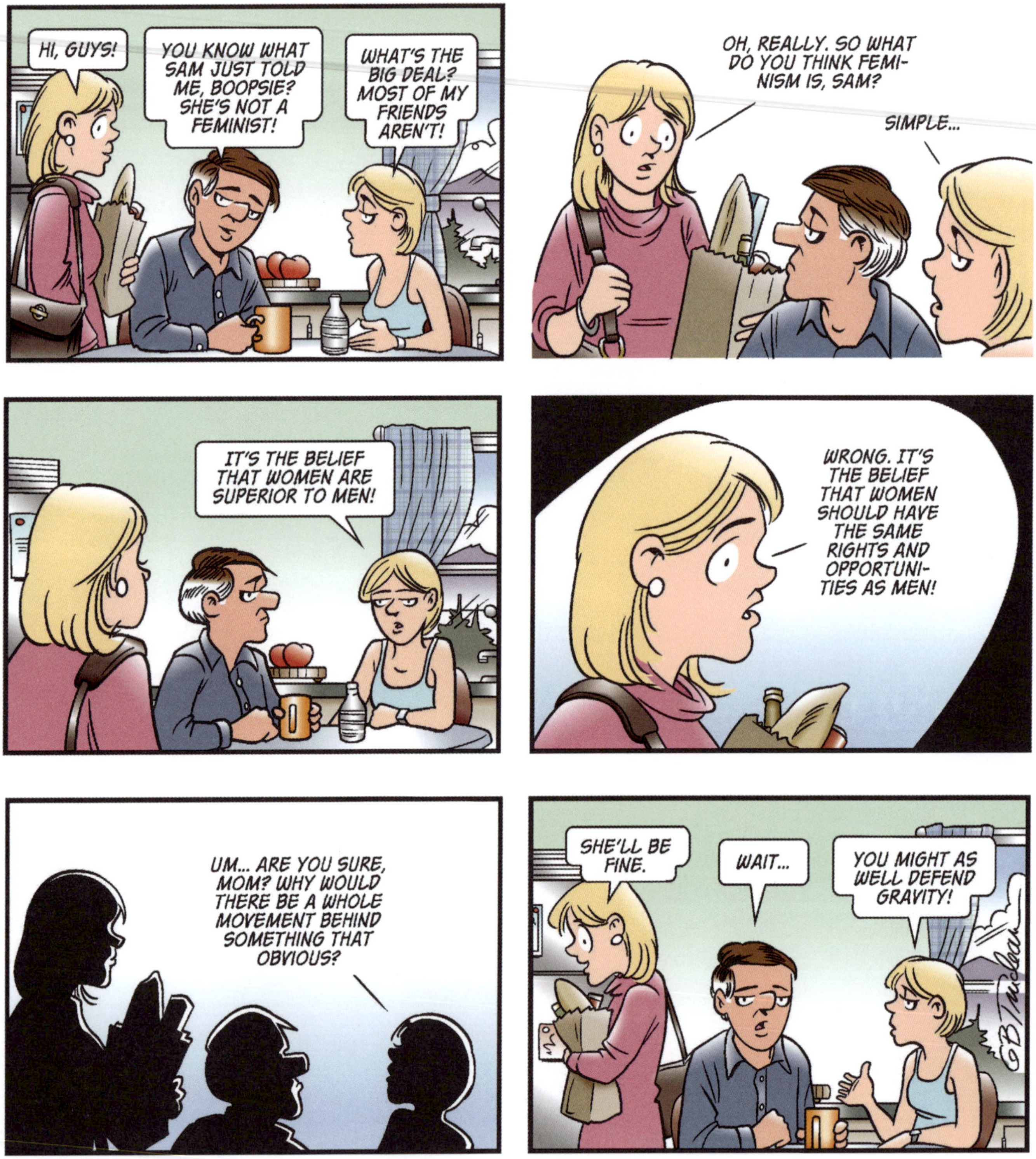
HI, GUYS!
YOU KNOW WHAT SAM JUST TOLD ME, BOOPSIE? SHE'S NOT A FEMINIST!
WHAT'S THE BIG DEAL? MOST OF MY FRIENDS AREN'T!
OH, REALLY. SO WHAT DO YOU THINK FEMINISM IS, SAM?
SIMPLE...
IT'S THE BELIEF THAT WOMEN ARE SUPERIOR TO MEN!
WRONG. IT'S THE BELIEF THAT WOMEN SHOULD HAVE THE SAME RIGHTS AND OPPORTUNITIES AS MEN!
UM... ARE YOU SURE, MOM? WHY WOULD THERE BE A WHOLE MOVEMENT BEHIND SOMETHING THAT OBVIOUS?
SHE'LL BE FINE.
WAIT...
YOU MIGHT AS WELL DEFEND GRAVITY!
GBTrudeau

September 24, 2017

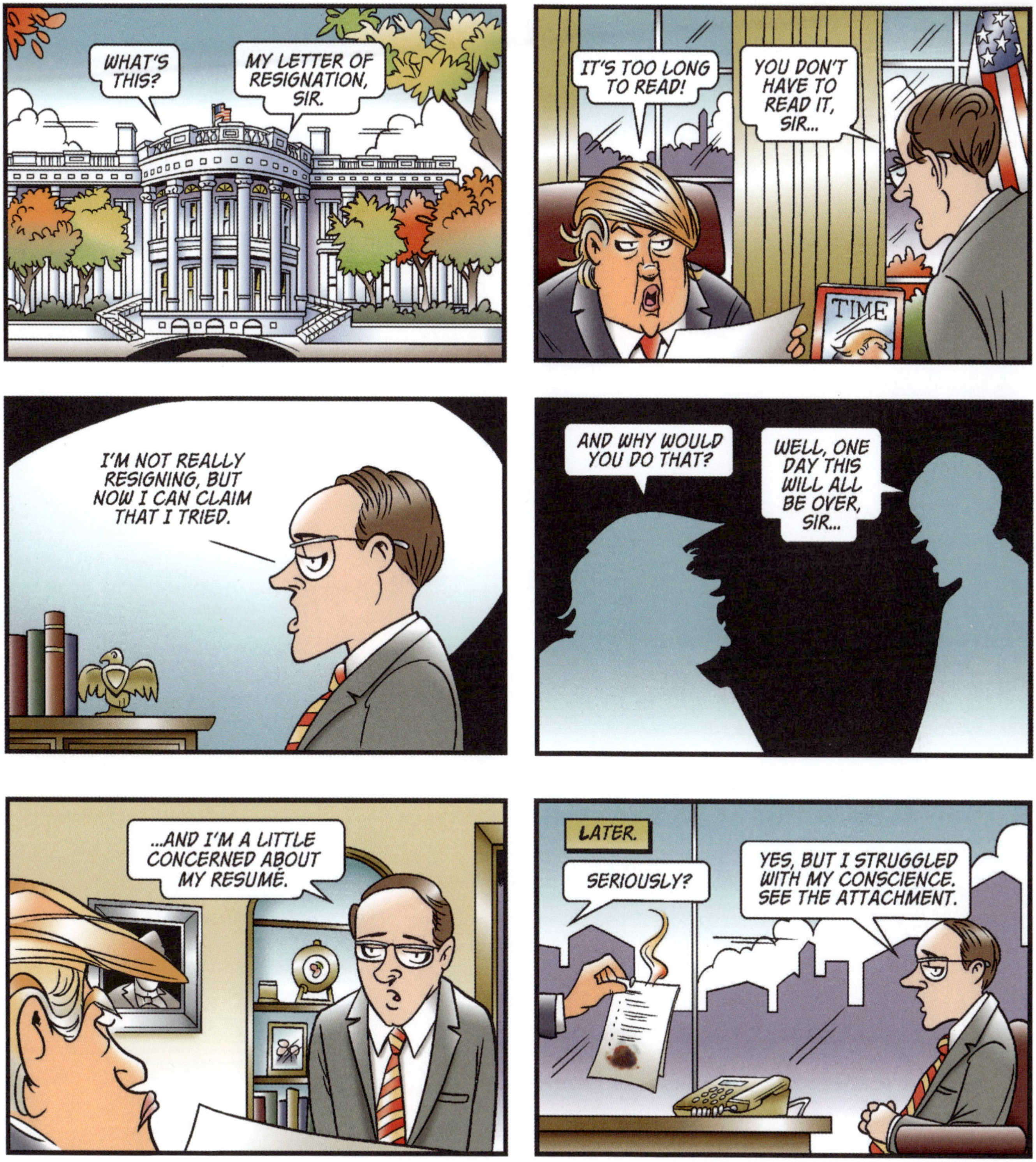
WHAT'S THIS?
MY LETTER OF RESIGNATION, SIR.
IT'S TOO LONG TO READ!
YOU DON'T HAVE TO READ IT, SIR...
TIME
I'M NOT REALLY RESIGNING, BUT NOW I CAN CLAIM THAT I TRIED.
AND WHY WOULD YOU DO THAT?
WELL, ONE DAY THIS WILL ALL BE OVER, SIR...
...AND I'M A LITTLE CONCERNED ABOUT MY RESUMÉ.
LATER.
SERIOUSLY?
YES, BUT I STRUGGLED WITH MY CONSCIENCE. SEE THE ATTACHMENT.

October 1, 2017

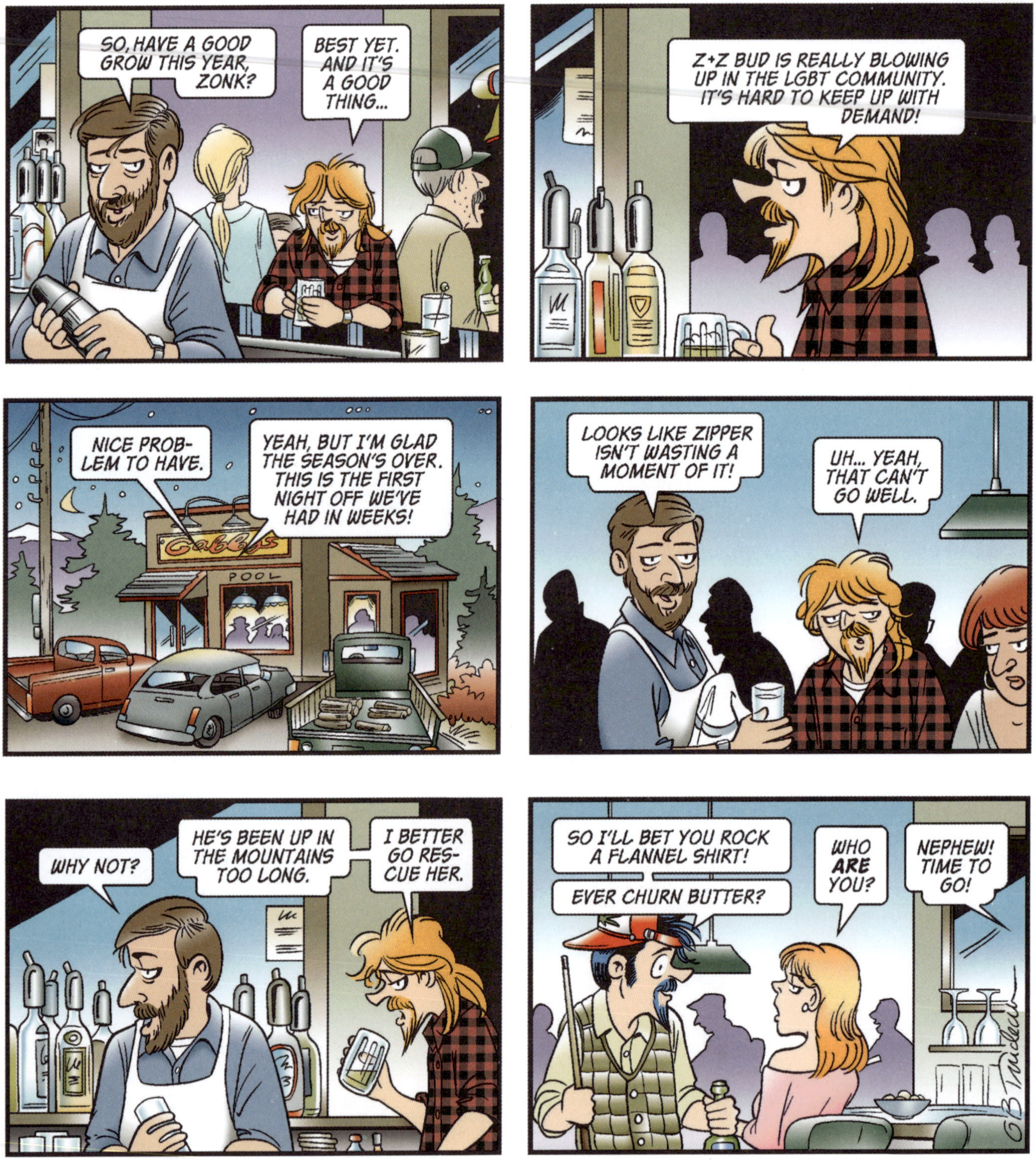
SO, HAVE A GOOD GROW THIS YEAR, ZONK?
BEST YET. AND IT'S A GOOD THING...
Z+Z BUD IS REALLY BLOWING UP IN THE LGBT COMMUNITY. IT'S HARD TO KEEP UP WITH DEMAND!
NICE PROB-LEM TO HAVE.
YEAH, BUT I'M GLAD THE SEASON'S OVER. THIS IS THE FIRST NIGHT OFF WE'VE HAD IN WEEKS!
Gabby's
POOL
LOOKS LIKE ZIPPER ISN'T WASTING A MOMENT OF IT!
UH... YEAH, THAT CAN'T GO WELL.
WHY NOT?
HE'S BEEN UP IN THE MOUNTAINS TOO LONG.
I BETTER GO RES-CUE HER.
SO I'LL BET YOU ROCK A FLANNEL SHIRT!
EVER CHURN BUTTER?
WHO **ARE** YOU?
NEPHEW! TIME TO GO!
GB Trudeau

October 8, 2017

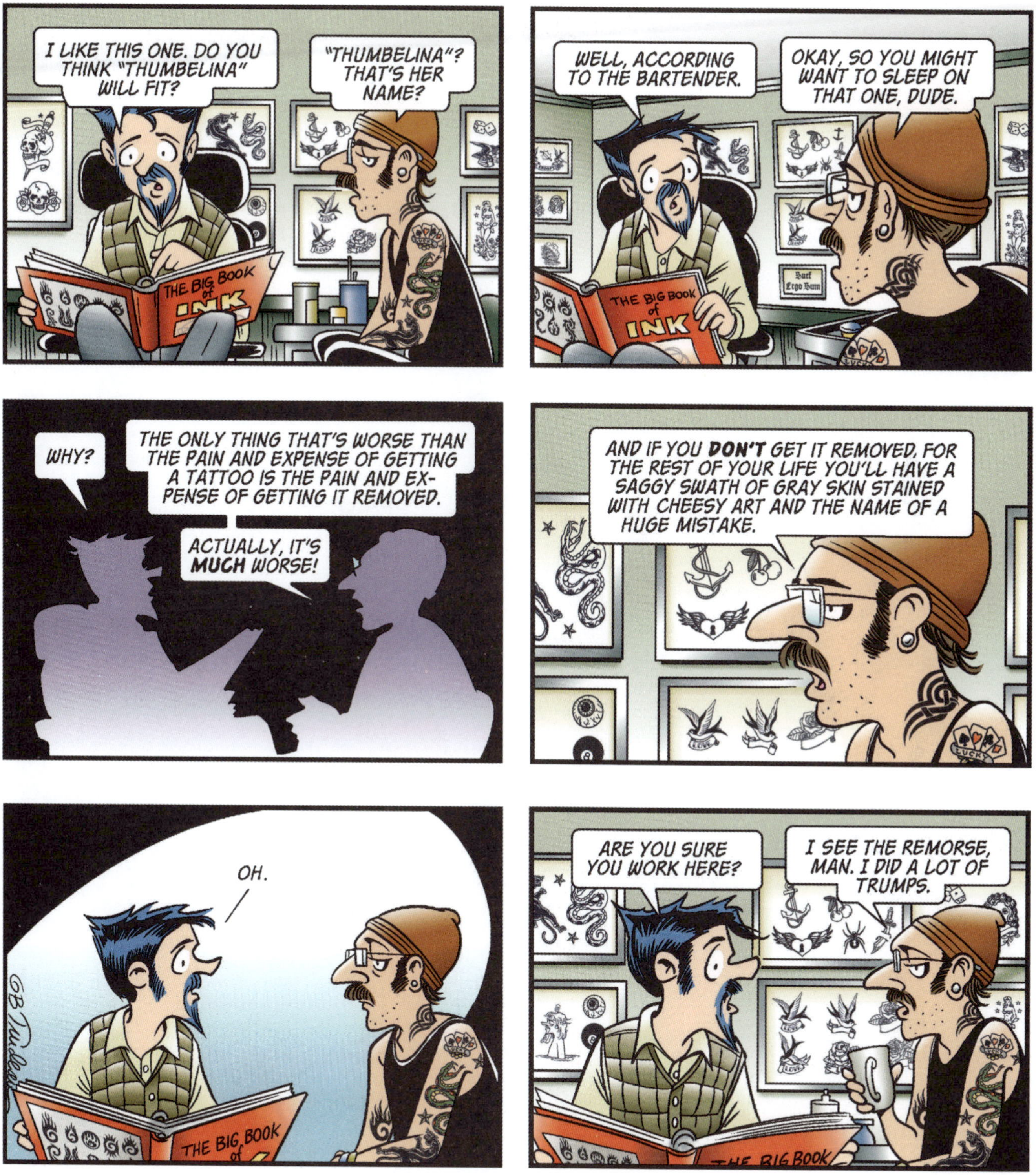
I LIKE THIS ONE. DO YOU THINK "THUMBELINA" WILL FIT?
"THUMBELINA"? THAT'S HER NAME?
THE BIG BOOK of INK
WELL, ACCORDING TO THE BARTENDER.
OKAY, SO YOU MIGHT WANT TO SLEEP ON THAT ONE, DUDE.
WHY?
THE ONLY THING THAT'S WORSE THAN THE PAIN AND EXPENSE OF GETTING A TATTOO IS THE PAIN AND EXPENSE OF GETTING IT REMOVED.
ACTUALLY, IT'S **MUCH** WORSE!
AND IF YOU **DON'T** GET IT REMOVED, FOR THE REST OF YOUR LIFE YOU'LL HAVE A SAGGY SWATH OF GRAY SKIN STAINED WITH CHEESY ART AND THE NAME OF A HUGE MISTAKE.
OH.
ARE YOU SURE YOU WORK HERE?
I SEE THE REMORSE, MAN. I DID A LOT OF TRUMPS.

October 15, 2017

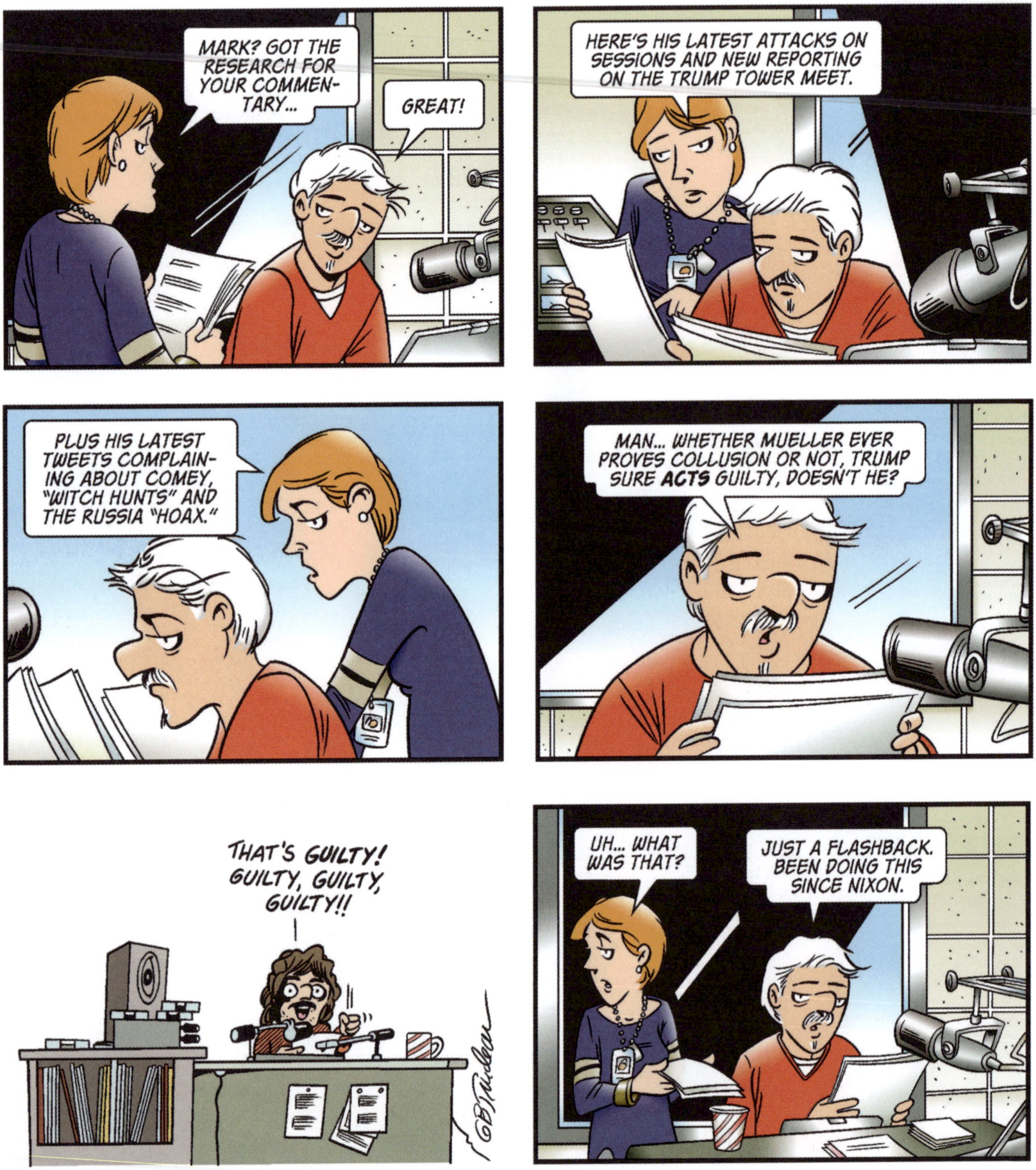
MARK? GOT THE RESEARCH FOR YOUR COMMENTARY...
GREAT!
HERE'S HIS LATEST ATTACKS ON SESSIONS AND NEW REPORTING ON THE TRUMP TOWER MEET.
PLUS HIS LATEST TWEETS COMPLAINING ABOUT COMEY, "WITCH HUNTS" AND THE RUSSIA "HOAX."
MAN... WHETHER MUELLER EVER PROVES COLLUSION OR NOT, TRUMP SURE **ACTS** GUILTY, DOESN'T HE?
THAT'S **GUILTY!** GUILTY, GUILTY, GUILTY!!
UH... WHAT WAS THAT?
JUST A FLASHBACK. BEEN DOING THIS SINCE NIXON.

October 22, 2017

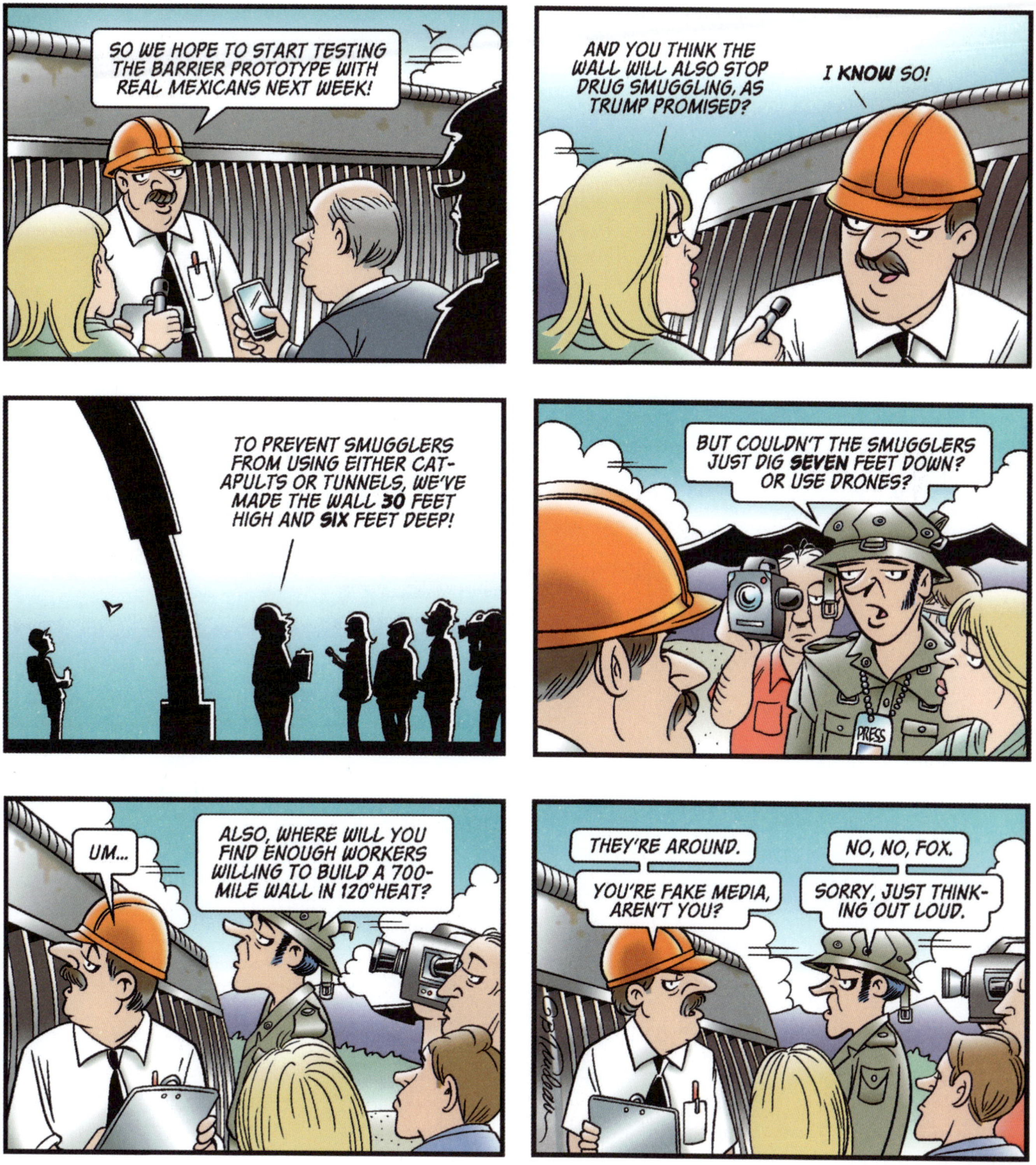
SO WE HOPE TO START TESTING THE BARRIER PROTOTYPE WITH REAL MEXICANS NEXT WEEK!
AND YOU THINK THE WALL WILL ALSO STOP DRUG SMUGGLING, AS TRUMP PROMISED?
I **KNOW** SO!
TO PREVENT SMUGGLERS FROM USING EITHER CAT-APULTS OR TUNNELS, WE'VE MADE THE WALL **30** FEET HIGH AND **SIX** FEET DEEP!
BUT COULDN'T THE SMUGGLERS JUST DIG **SEVEN** FEET DOWN? OR USE DRONES?
PRESS
UM...
ALSO, WHERE WILL YOU FIND ENOUGH WORKERS WILLING TO BUILD A 700-MILE WALL IN 120°HEAT?
THEY'RE AROUND.
YOU'RE FAKE MEDIA, AREN'T YOU?
NO, NO, FOX.
SORRY, JUST THINKING OUT LOUD.

October 29, 2017

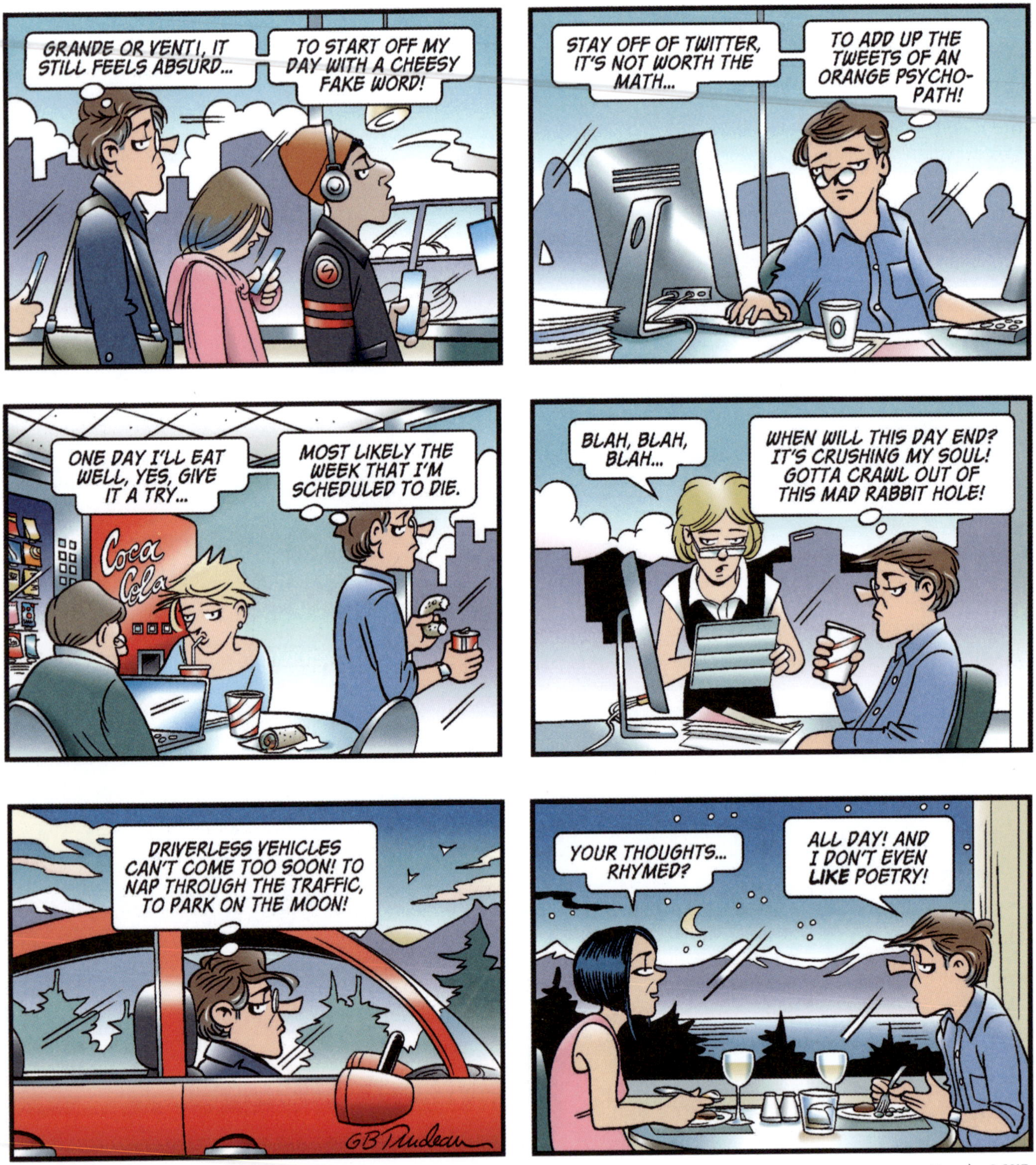
GRANDE OR VENTI, IT STILL FEELS ABSURD...
TO START OFF MY DAY WITH A CHEESY FAKE WORD!
STAY OFF OF TWITTER, IT'S NOT WORTH THE MATH...
TO ADD UP THE TWEETS OF AN ORANGE PSYCHO-PATH!
ONE DAY I'LL EAT WELL, YES, GIVE IT A TRY...
MOST LIKELY THE WEEK THAT I'M SCHEDULED TO DIE.
Coca Cola
BLAH, BLAH, BLAH...
WHEN WILL THIS DAY END? IT'S CRUSHING MY SOUL! GOTTA CRAWL OUT OF THIS MAD RABBIT HOLE!
DRIVERLESS VEHICLES CAN'T COME TOO SOON! TO NAP THROUGH THE TRAFFIC, TO PARK ON THE MOON!
GB Trudeau
YOUR THOUGHTS... RHYMED?
ALL DAY! AND I DON'T EVEN **LIKE** POETRY!

November 5, 2017

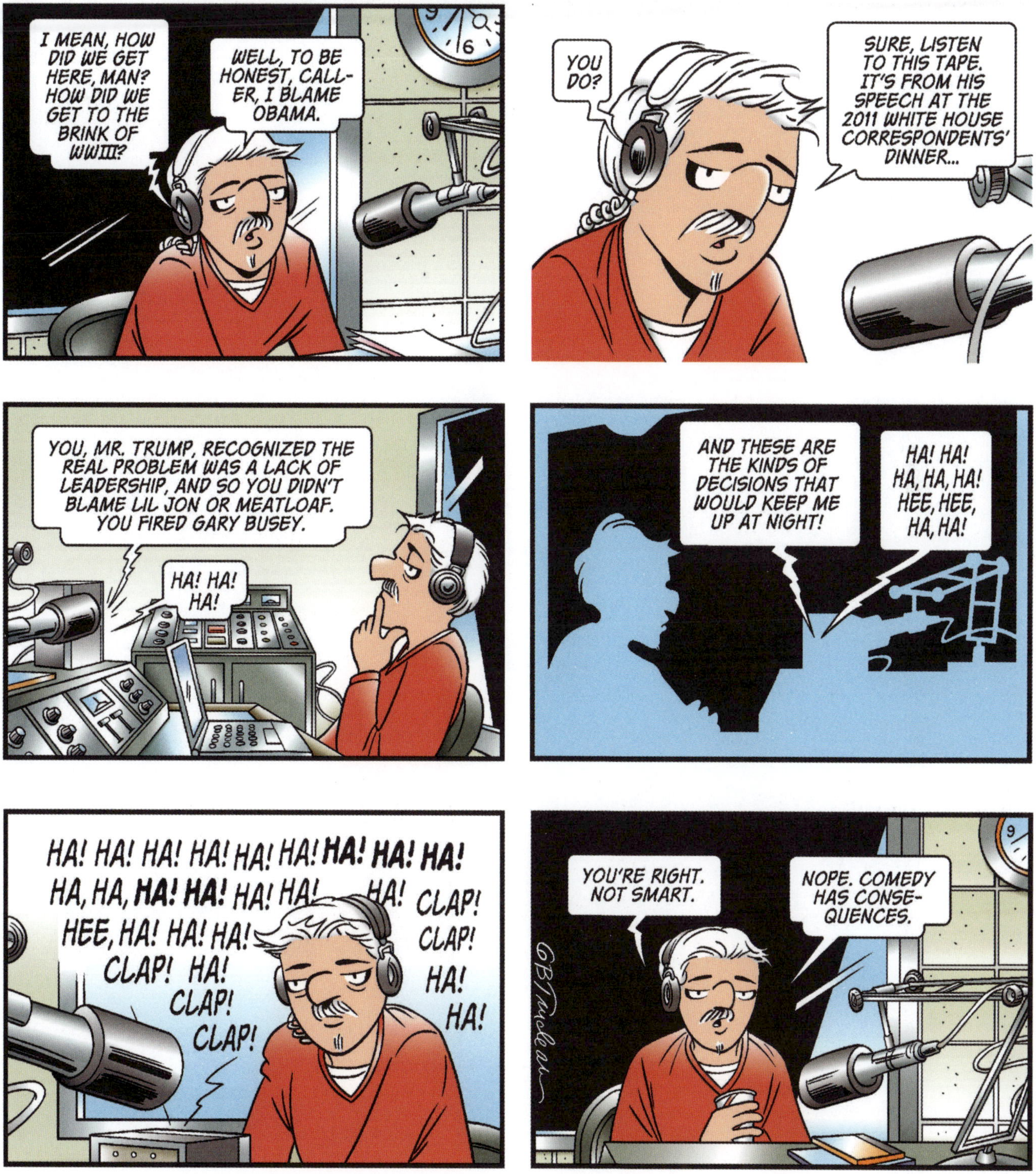
I MEAN, HOW DID WE GET HERE, MAN? HOW DID WE GET TO THE BRINK OF WWIII?
WELL, TO BE HONEST, CALLER, I BLAME OBAMA.
YOU DO?
SURE, LISTEN TO THIS TAPE. IT'S FROM HIS SPEECH AT THE 2011 WHITE HOUSE CORRESPONDENTS' DINNER...
YOU, MR. TRUMP, RECOGNIZED THE REAL PROBLEM WAS A LACK OF LEADERSHIP, AND SO YOU DIDN'T BLAME LIL JON OR MEATLOAF. YOU FIRED GARY BUSEY.
HA! HA! HA!
AND THESE ARE THE KINDS OF DECISIONS THAT WOULD KEEP ME UP AT NIGHT!
HA! HA! HA, HA, HA! HEE, HEE, HA, HA!
HA! HA! HA! HA! HA! HA! HA! HA! HA! HA, HA, HA! HA! HA! HA! HA! HEE, HA! HA! HA! CLAP! HA! CLAP! CLAP!
CLAP! CLAP! HA! HA!
YOU'RE RIGHT. NOT SMART.
NOPE. COMEDY HAS CONSEQUENCES.

November 12, 2017

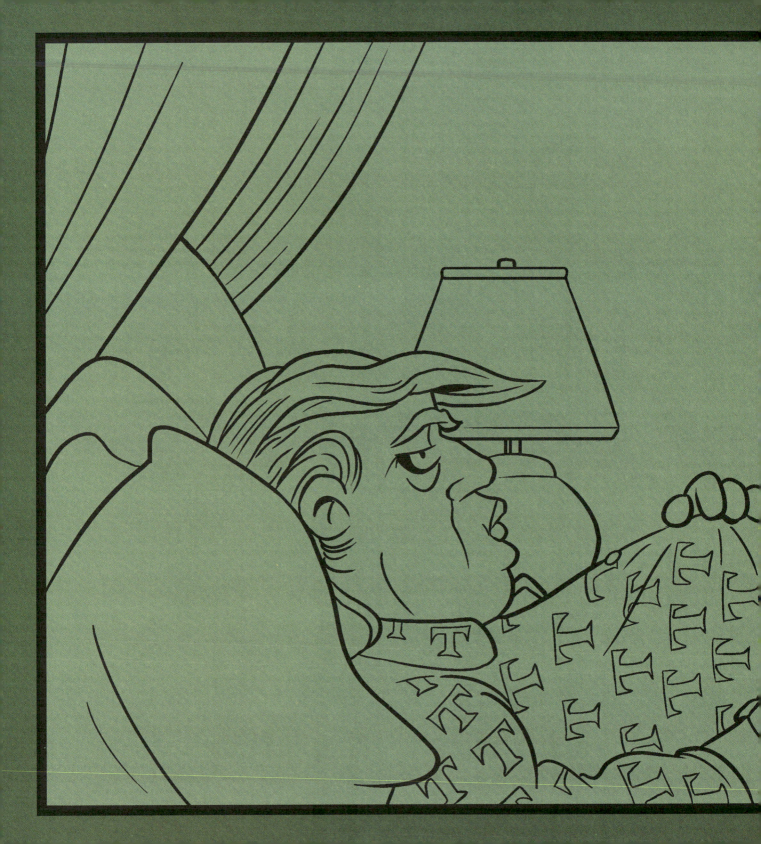

PART 4
Stormy Weather

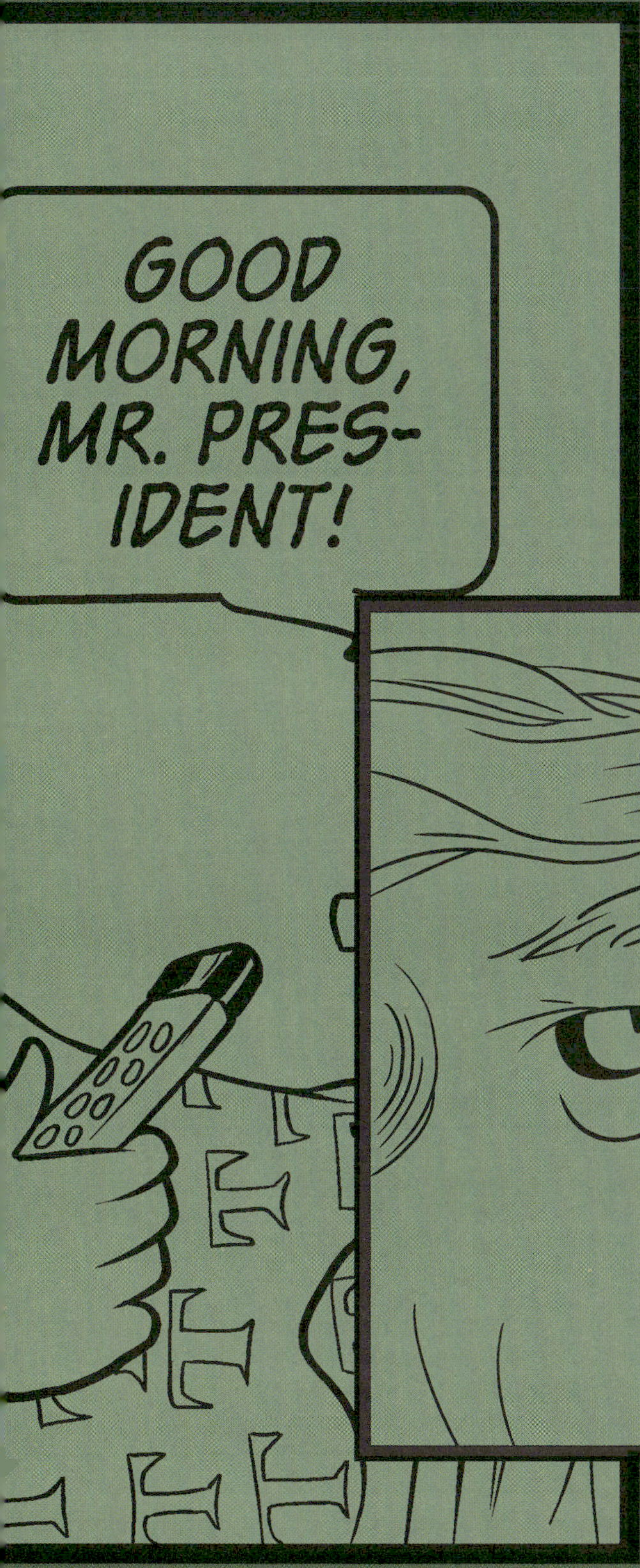
GOOD MORNING, MR. PRES-IDENT!

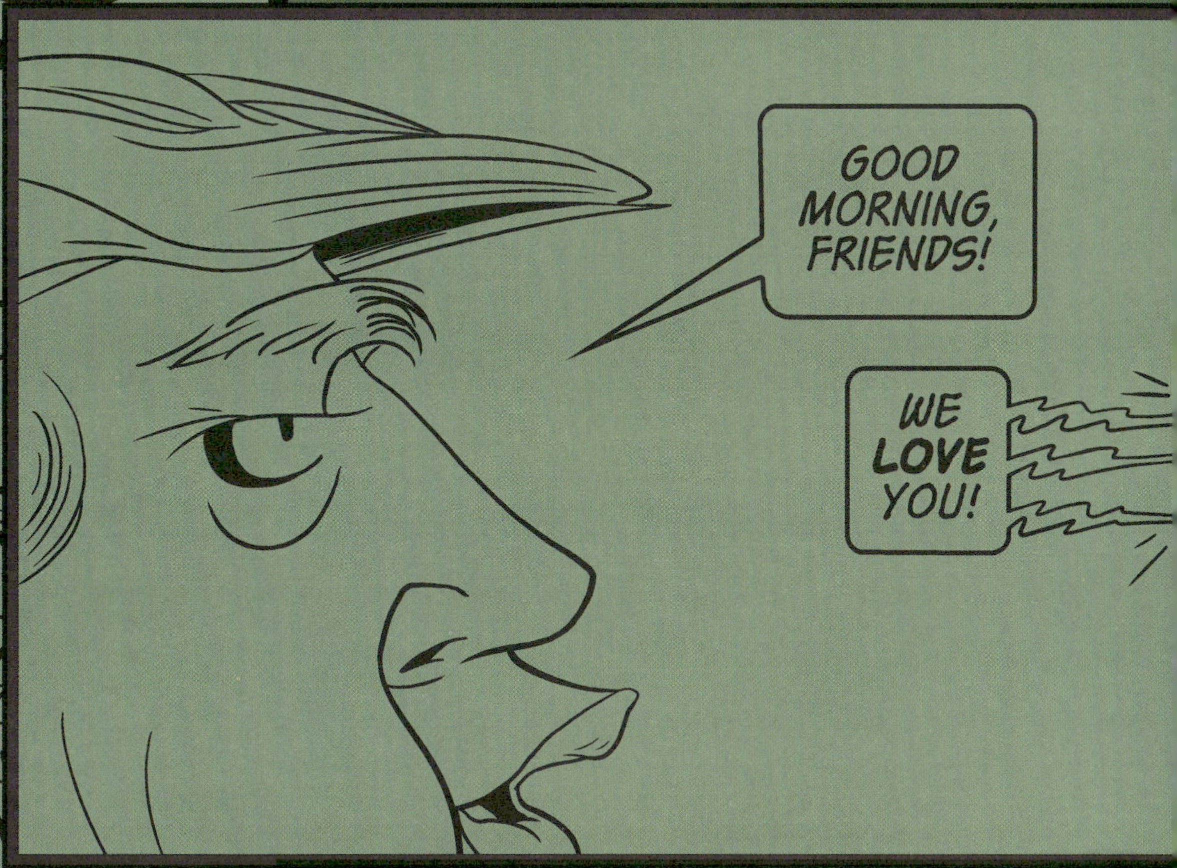
GOOD MORNING, FRIENDS!
WE LOVE YOU!

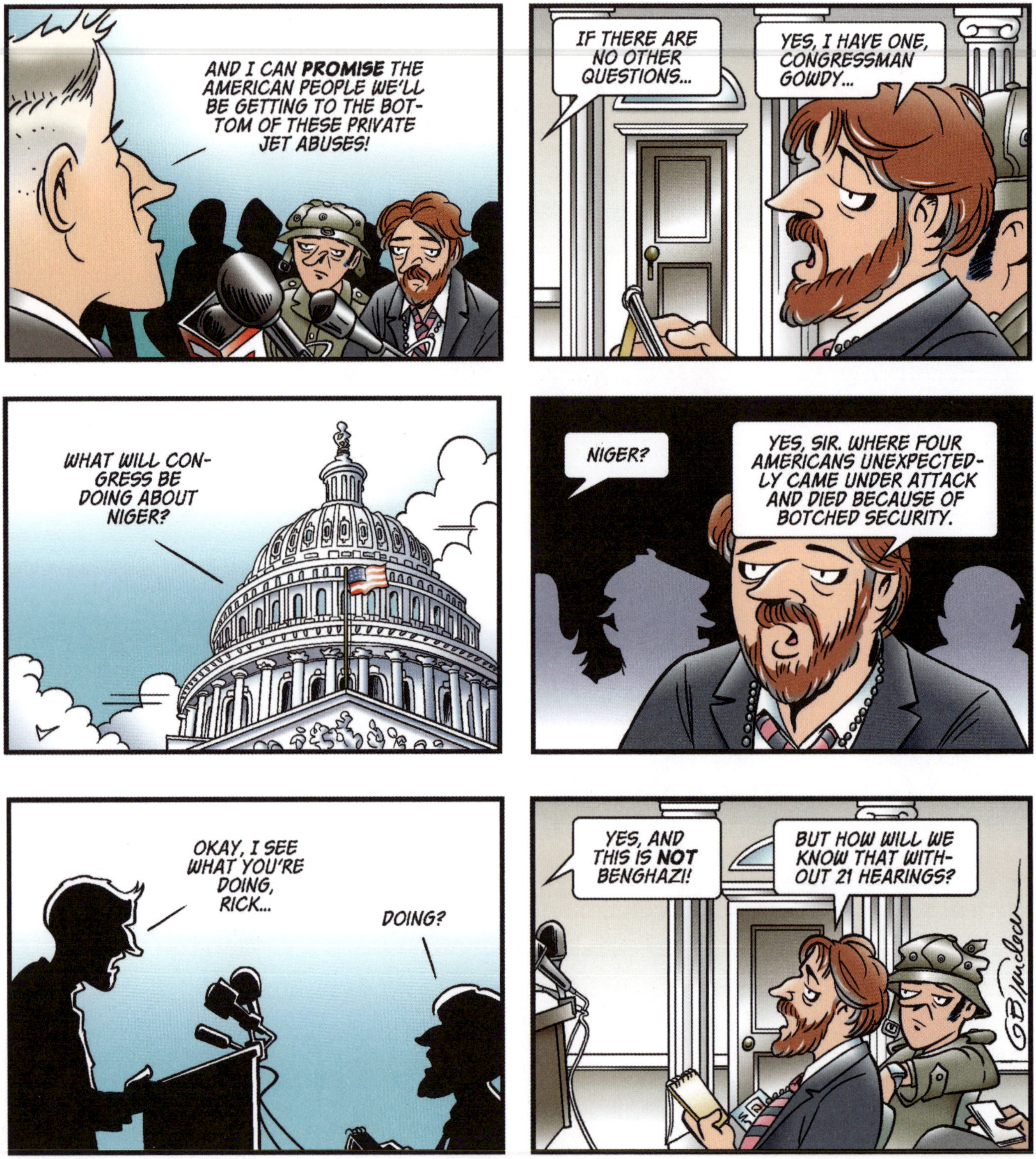
AND I CAN **PROMISE** THE AMERICAN PEOPLE WE'LL BE GETTING TO THE BOTTOM OF THESE PRIVATE JET ABUSES!
IF THERE ARE NO OTHER QUESTIONS...
YES, I HAVE ONE, CONGRESSMAN GOWDY...
WHAT WILL CONGRESS BE DOING ABOUT NIGER?
NIGER?
YES, SIR. WHERE FOUR AMERICANS UNEXPECTEDLY CAME UNDER ATTACK AND DIED BECAUSE OF BOTCHED SECURITY.
OKAY, I SEE WHAT YOU'RE DOING, RICK...
DOING?
YES, AND THIS IS **NOT** BENGHAZI!
BUT HOW WILL WE KNOW THAT WITHOUT 21 HEARINGS?
GBTrudeau

November 19, 2017

Roland B. Hedley Jr. @RealRBHJr
In address this morning, POTUS looked like a man playing a man playing a man playing a man who cares -- a huge improvement. Growing in job!

 **Roland B. Hedley Jr.** @RealRBHJr
POTUS says he met w. "president" of USVI. Actually, POTUS is president of USVI, but wanted to give best props to governor. All about #respect.

 Roland B. Hedley Jr. @RealRBHJr
Congress considering law to ban bump stocks but not military grade assault weapons. Like banning Madonna's cones but not her. #NotRightTime

 Roland B. Hedley Jr. @RealRBHJr
Been searching tax plan for POTUS's "middle class miracle." So far only see upper class miracle, but still have 3 pages to go. Pumped!

Roland B. Hedley Jr. @RealRBHJr
In speech, Zinke says always runs private jet travel by lawyer "to make sure I am above the law." Must be same lawyer who checks his speeches.

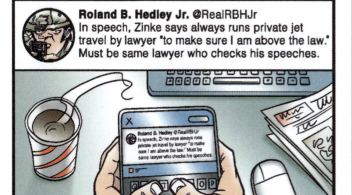

Roland B. Hedley Jr. @RealRBHJr
To reassure world, Tillerson corrects record, calls POTUS "smart." In US, "(bleeping) moron" just affectionate nickname for bosses, husbands.

FOLLOW ROLAND ON TWITTER @ RealRBHJr

November 26, 2017

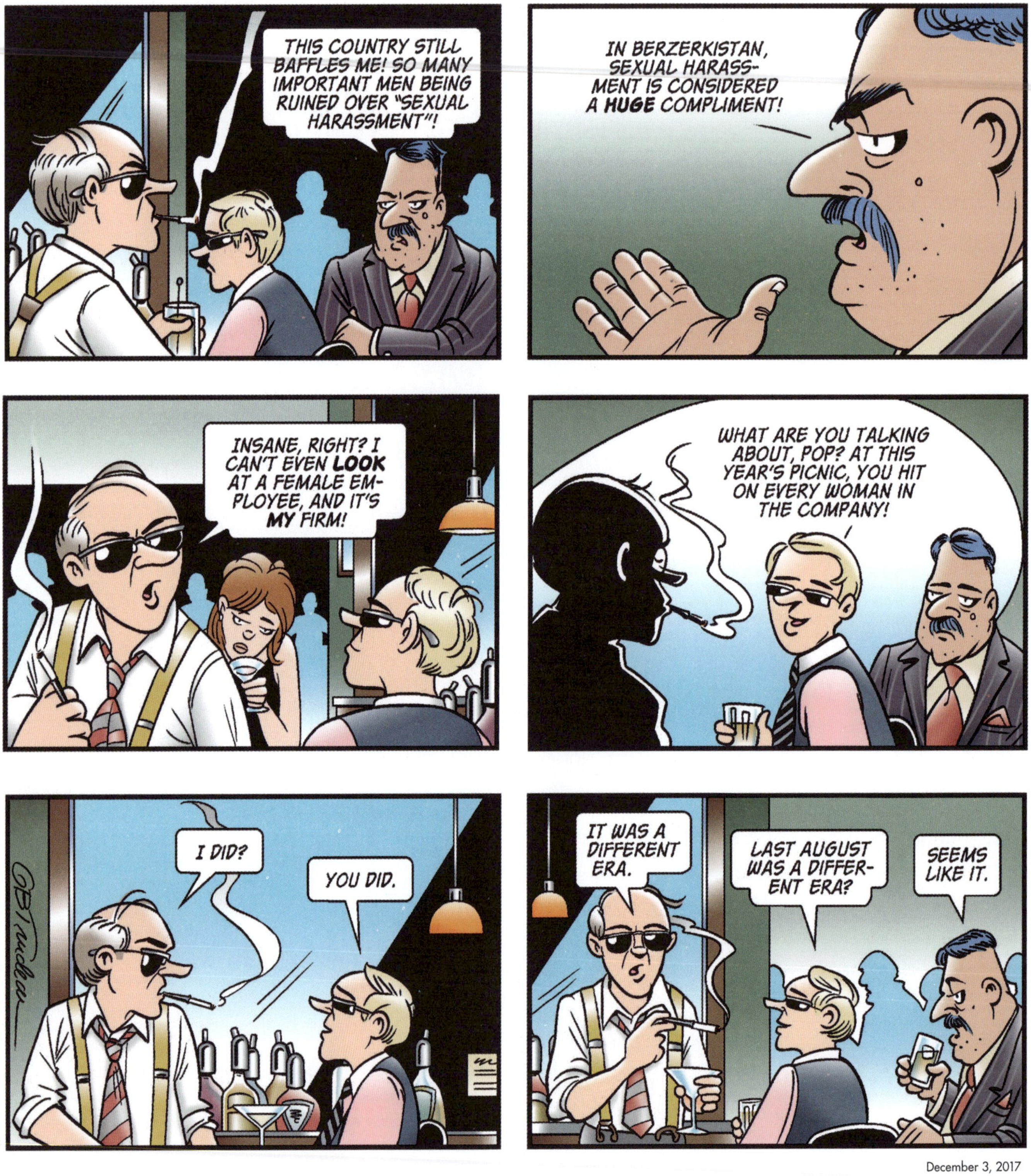
THIS COUNTRY STILL BAFFLES ME! SO MANY IMPORTANT MEN BEING RUINED OVER "SEXUAL HARASSMENT"!
IN BERZERKISTAN, SEXUAL HARASS-MENT IS CONSIDERED A **HUGE** COMPLIMENT!
INSANE, RIGHT? I CAN'T EVEN **LOOK** AT A FEMALE EM-PLOYEE, AND IT'S **MY** FIRM!
WHAT ARE YOU TALKING ABOUT, POP? AT THIS YEAR'S PICNIC, YOU HIT ON EVERY WOMAN IN THE COMPANY!
GBTrudeau
I DID?
YOU DID.
IT WAS A DIFFERENT ERA.
LAST AUGUST WAS A DIFFER-ENT ERA?
SEEMS LIKE IT.

December 3, 2017

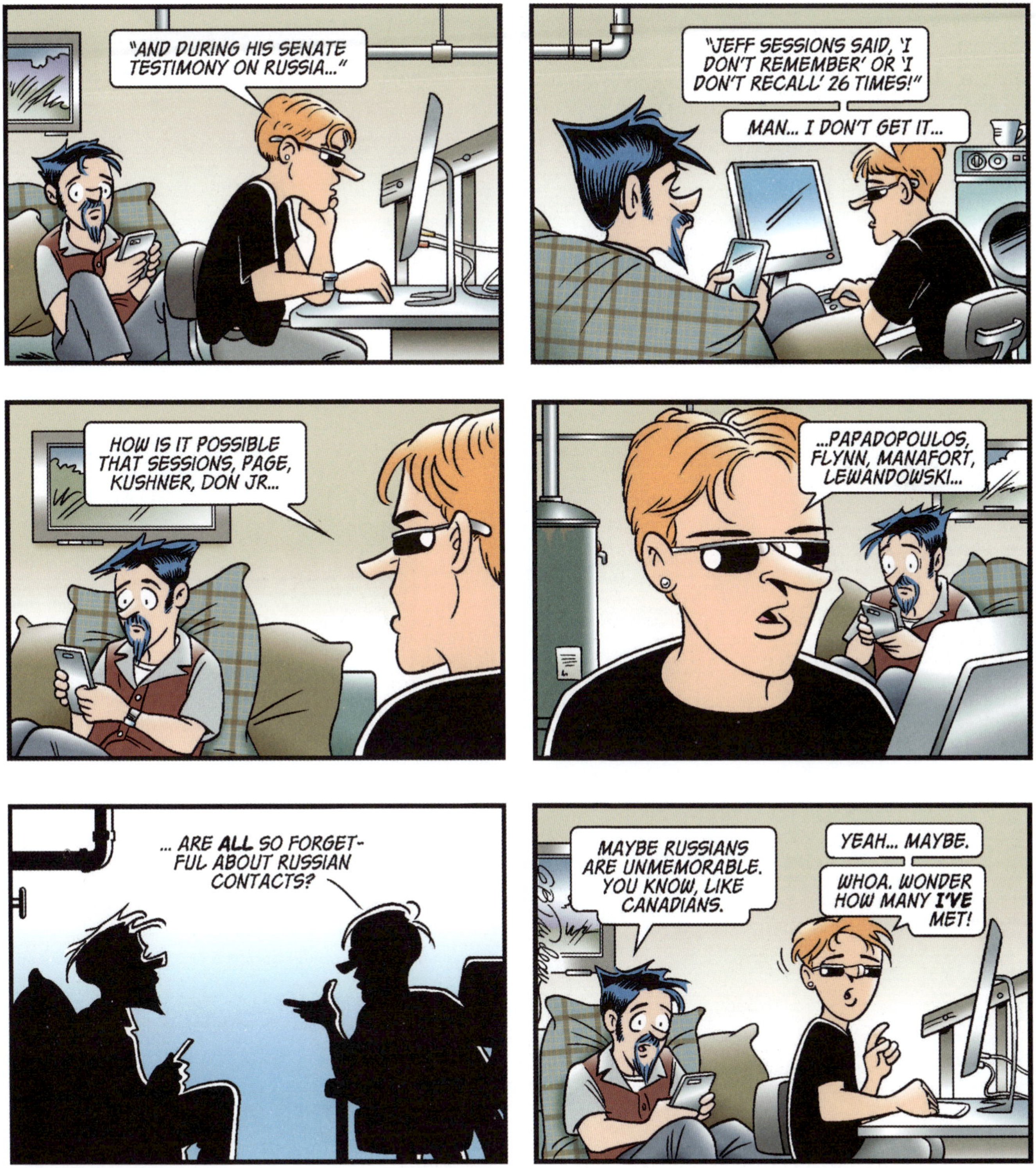
"AND DURING HIS SENATE TESTIMONY ON RUSSIA..."
"JEFF SESSIONS SAID, 'I DON'T REMEMBER' OR 'I DON'T RECALL' 26 TIMES!"
MAN... I DON'T GET IT...
HOW IS IT POSSIBLE THAT SESSIONS, PAGE, KUSHNER, DON JR...
...PAPADOPOULOS, FLYNN, MANAFORT, LEWANDOWSKI...
... ARE **ALL** SO FORGETFUL ABOUT RUSSIAN CONTACTS?
MAYBE RUSSIANS ARE UNMEMORABLE. YOU KNOW, LIKE CANADIANS.
YEAH... MAYBE.
WHOA. WONDER HOW MANY **I'VE** MET!

December 10, 2017

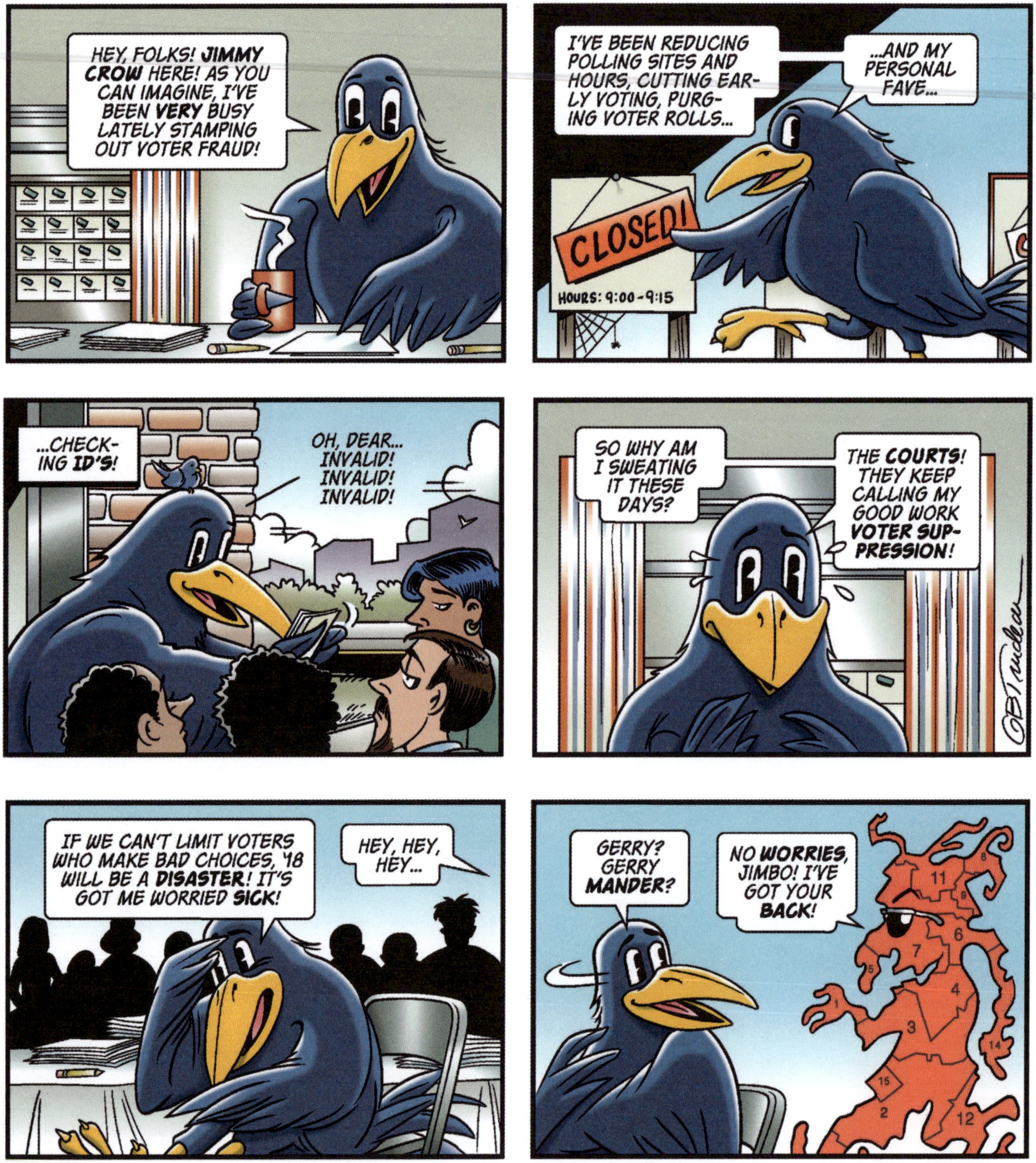
HEY, FOLKS! JIMMY CROW HERE! AS YOU CAN IMAGINE, I'VE BEEN VERY BUSY LATELY STAMPING OUT VOTER FRAUD!
I'VE BEEN REDUCING POLLING SITES AND HOURS, CUTTING EARLY VOTING, PURGING VOTER ROLLS...
...AND MY PERSONAL FAVE...
CLOSED!
HOURS: 9:00-9:15
...CHECKING ID'S!
OH, DEAR... INVALID! INVALID! INVALID!
SO WHY AM I SWEATING IT THESE DAYS?
THE COURTS! THEY KEEP CALLING MY GOOD WORK VOTER SUPPRESSION!
IF WE CAN'T LIMIT VOTERS WHO MAKE BAD CHOICES, '18 WILL BE A DISASTER! IT'S GOT ME WORRIED SICK!
HEY, HEY, HEY...
GERRY? GERRY MANDER?
NO WORRIES, JIMBO! I'VE GOT YOUR BACK!

December 17, 2017

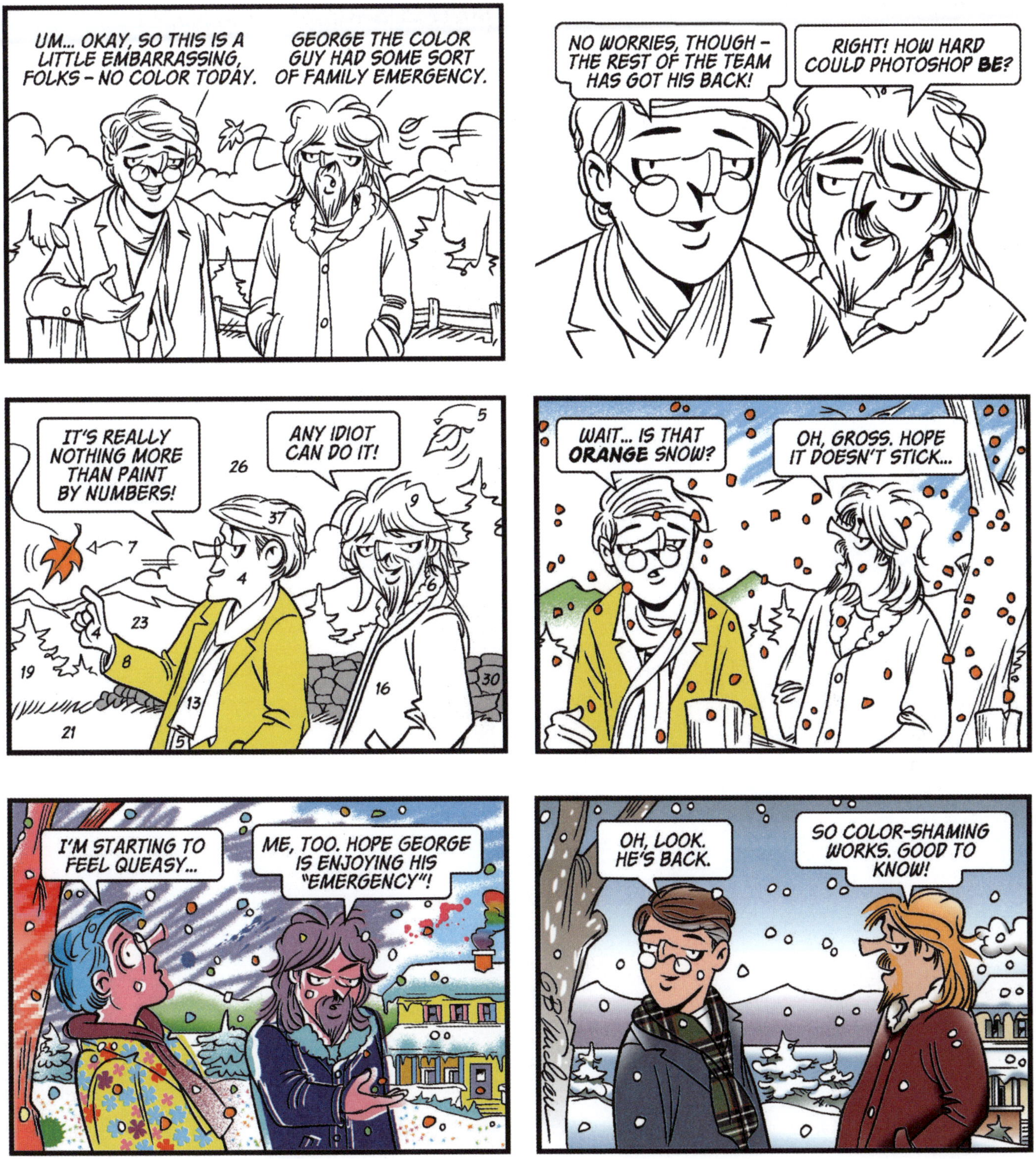
UM... OKAY, SO THIS IS A LITTLE EMBARRASSING, FOLKS – NO COLOR TODAY.
GEORGE THE COLOR GUY HAD SOME SORT OF FAMILY EMERGENCY.
NO WORRIES, THOUGH – THE REST OF THE TEAM HAS GOT HIS BACK!
RIGHT! HOW HARD COULD PHOTOSHOP **BE**?
IT'S REALLY NOTHING MORE THAN PAINT BY NUMBERS!
ANY IDIOT CAN DO IT!
WAIT... IS THAT **ORANGE** SNOW?
OH, GROSS. HOPE IT DOESN'T STICK...
I'M STARTING TO FEEL QUEASY...
ME, TOO. HOPE GEORGE IS ENJOYING HIS "EMERGENCY"!
OH, LOOK. HE'S BACK.
SO COLOR-SHAMING WORKS. GOOD TO KNOW!

December 4, 2016

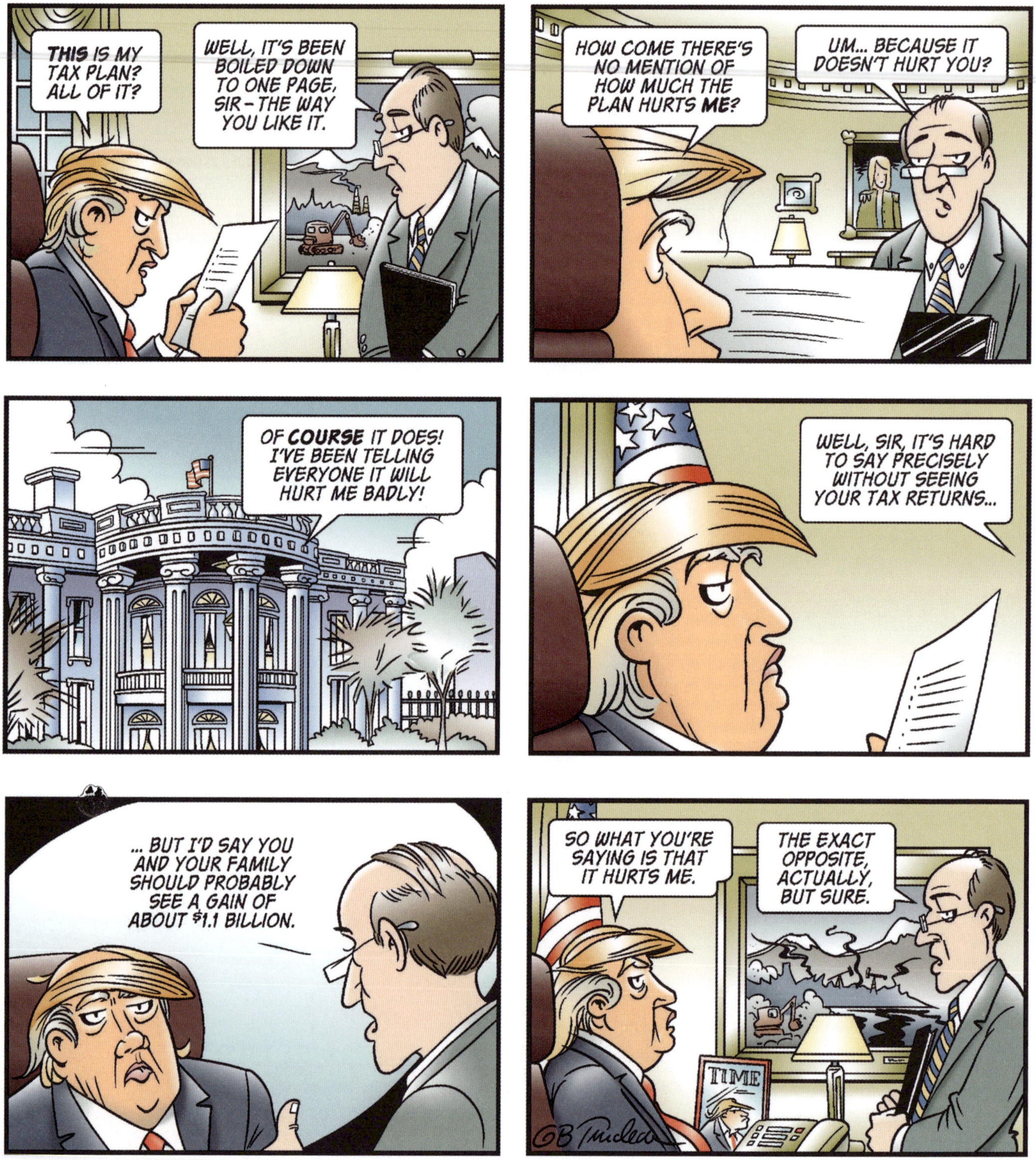

THIS IS MY TAX PLAN? ALL OF IT?
WELL, IT'S BEEN BOILED DOWN TO ONE PAGE, SIR – THE WAY YOU LIKE IT.
HOW COME THERE'S NO MENTION OF HOW MUCH THE PLAN HURTS **ME**?
UM... BECAUSE IT DOESN'T HURT YOU?
OF **COURSE** IT DOES! I'VE BEEN TELLING EVERYONE IT WILL HURT ME BADLY!
WELL, SIR, IT'S HARD TO SAY PRECISELY WITHOUT SEEING YOUR TAX RETURNS...
... BUT I'D SAY YOU AND YOUR FAMILY SHOULD PROBABLY SEE A GAIN OF ABOUT $1.1 BILLION.
SO WHAT YOU'RE SAYING IS THAT IT HURTS ME.
THE EXACT OPPOSITE, ACTUALLY, BUT SURE.
TIME
©B Trudeau

January 7, 2018

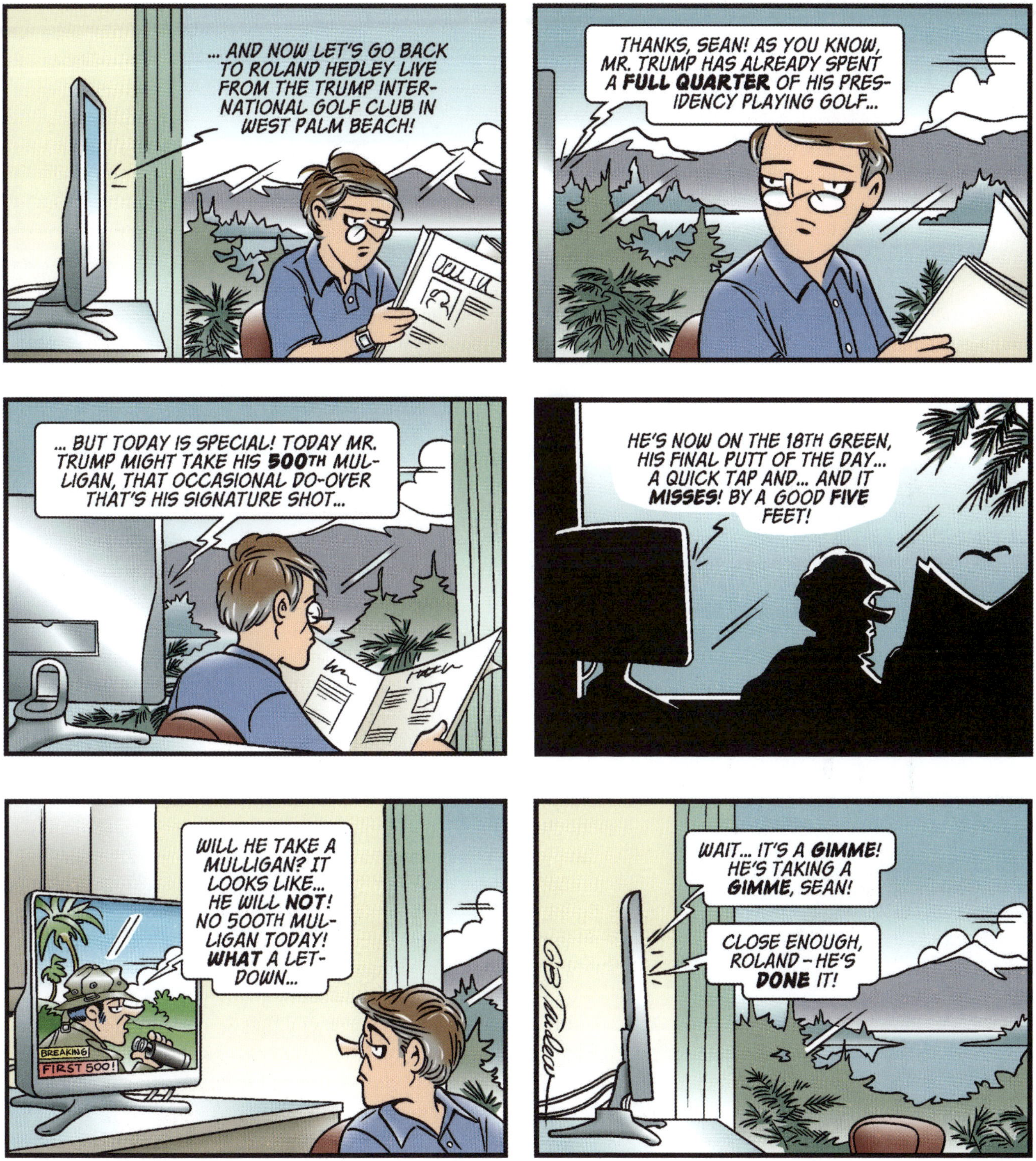
... AND NOW LET'S GO BACK TO ROLAND HEDLEY LIVE FROM THE TRUMP INTERNATIONAL GOLF CLUB IN WEST PALM BEACH!
THANKS, SEAN! AS YOU KNOW, MR. TRUMP HAS ALREADY SPENT A **FULL QUARTER** OF HIS PRESIDENCY PLAYING GOLF...
... BUT TODAY IS SPECIAL! TODAY MR. TRUMP MIGHT TAKE HIS **500TH** MULLIGAN, THAT OCCASIONAL DO-OVER THAT'S HIS SIGNATURE SHOT...
HE'S NOW ON THE 18TH GREEN, HIS FINAL PUTT OF THE DAY... A QUICK TAP AND... AND IT **MISSES**! BY A GOOD **FIVE** FEET!
WILL HE TAKE A MULLIGAN? IT LOOKS LIKE... HE WILL **NOT**! NO 500TH MULLIGAN TODAY! **WHAT** A LETDOWN...
BREAKING
FIRST 500!
WAIT... IT'S A **GIMME**! HE'S TAKING A **GIMME**, SEAN!
CLOSE ENOUGH, ROLAND – HE'S **DONE** IT!
GB Trudeau

January 21, 2018

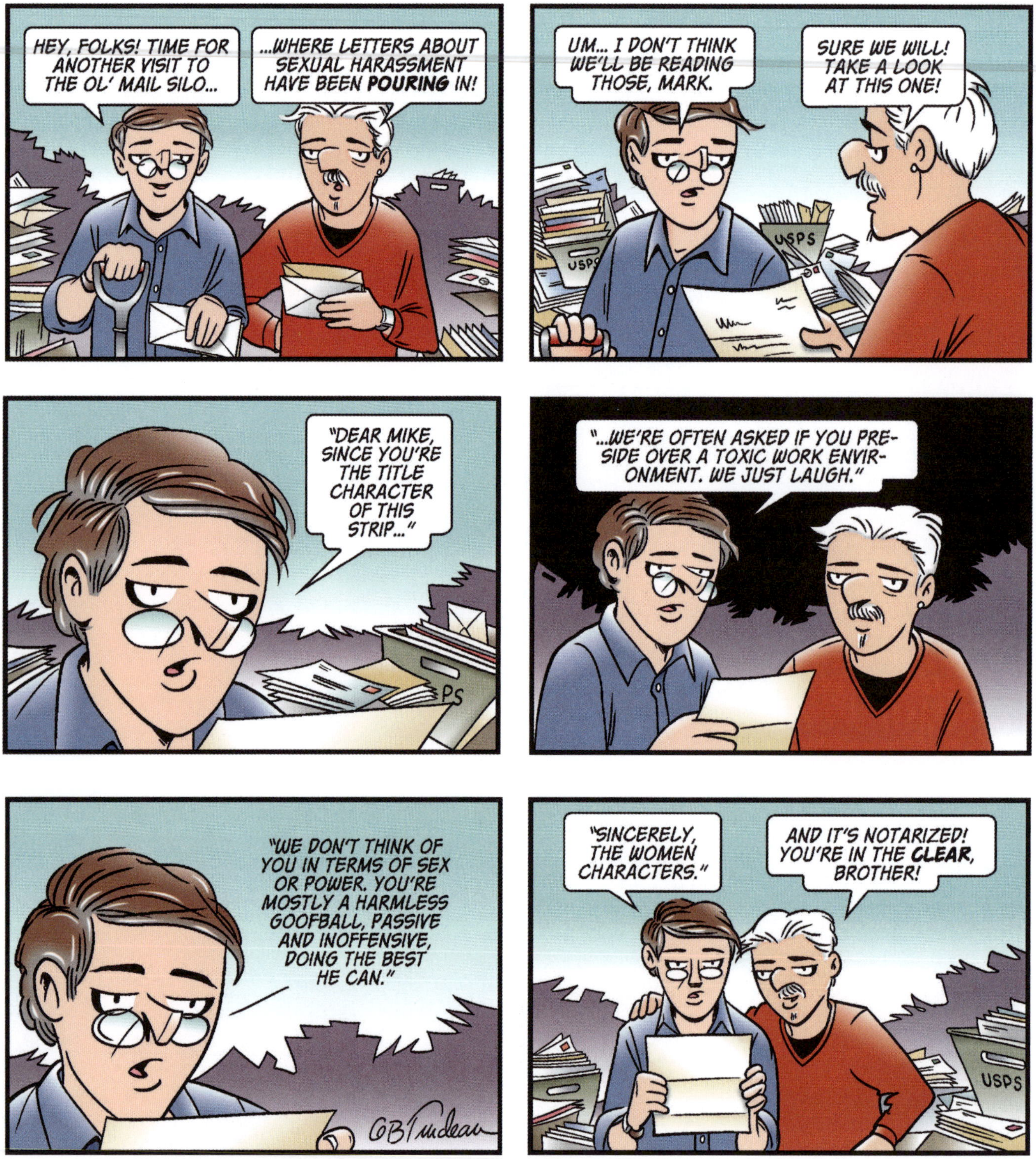
HEY, FOLKS! TIME FOR ANOTHER VISIT TO THE OL' MAIL SILO...
...WHERE LETTERS ABOUT SEXUAL HARASSMENT HAVE BEEN POURING IN!
UM... I DON'T THINK WE'LL BE READING THOSE, MARK.
SURE WE WILL! TAKE A LOOK AT THIS ONE!
USPS
"DEAR MIKE, SINCE YOU'RE THE TITLE CHARACTER OF THIS STRIP..."
"...WE'RE OFTEN ASKED IF YOU PRESIDE OVER A TOXIC WORK ENVIRONMENT. WE JUST LAUGH."
"WE DON'T THINK OF YOU IN TERMS OF SEX OR POWER. YOU'RE MOSTLY A HARMLESS GOOFBALL, PASSIVE AND INOFFENSIVE, DOING THE BEST HE CAN."
GBTrudeau
"SINCERELY, THE WOMEN CHARACTERS."
AND IT'S NOTARIZED! YOU'RE IN THE CLEAR, BROTHER!
USPS

January 14, 2018

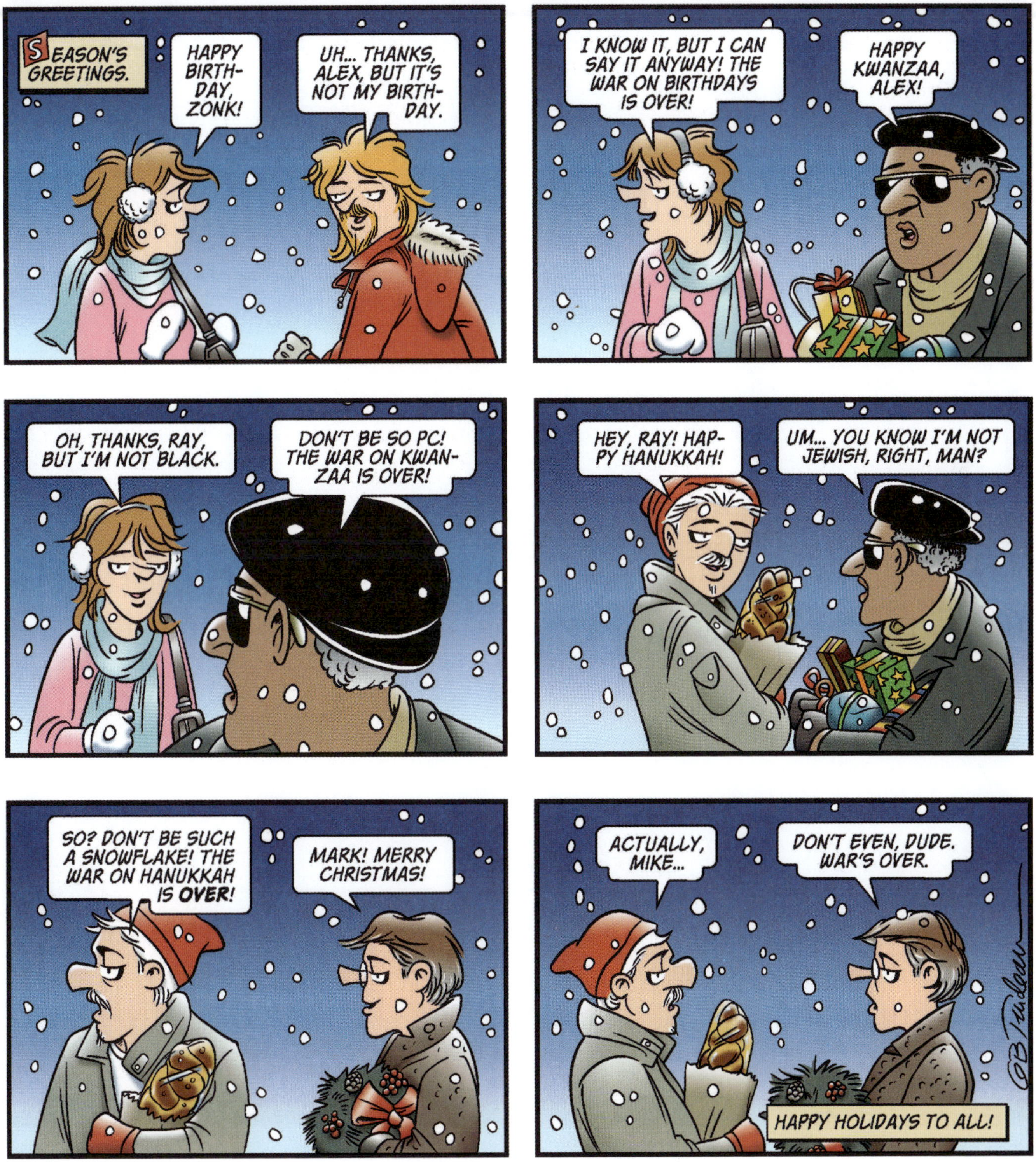
SEASON'S GREETINGS.
HAPPY BIRTH-DAY, ZONK!
UH... THANKS, ALEX, BUT IT'S NOT MY BIRTH-DAY.
I KNOW IT, BUT I CAN SAY IT ANYWAY! THE WAR ON BIRTHDAYS IS OVER!
HAPPY KWANZAA, ALEX!
OH, THANKS, RAY, BUT I'M NOT BLACK.
DON'T BE SO PC! THE WAR ON KWAN-ZAA IS OVER!
HEY, RAY! HAP-PY HANUKKAH!
UM... YOU KNOW I'M NOT JEWISH, RIGHT, MAN?
SO? DON'T BE SUCH A SNOWFLAKE! THE WAR ON HANUKKAH IS OVER!
MARK! MERRY CHRISTMAS!
ACTUALLY, MIKE...
DON'T EVEN, DUDE. WAR'S OVER.
HAPPY HOLIDAYS TO ALL!
GB Trudeau

December 24, 2017

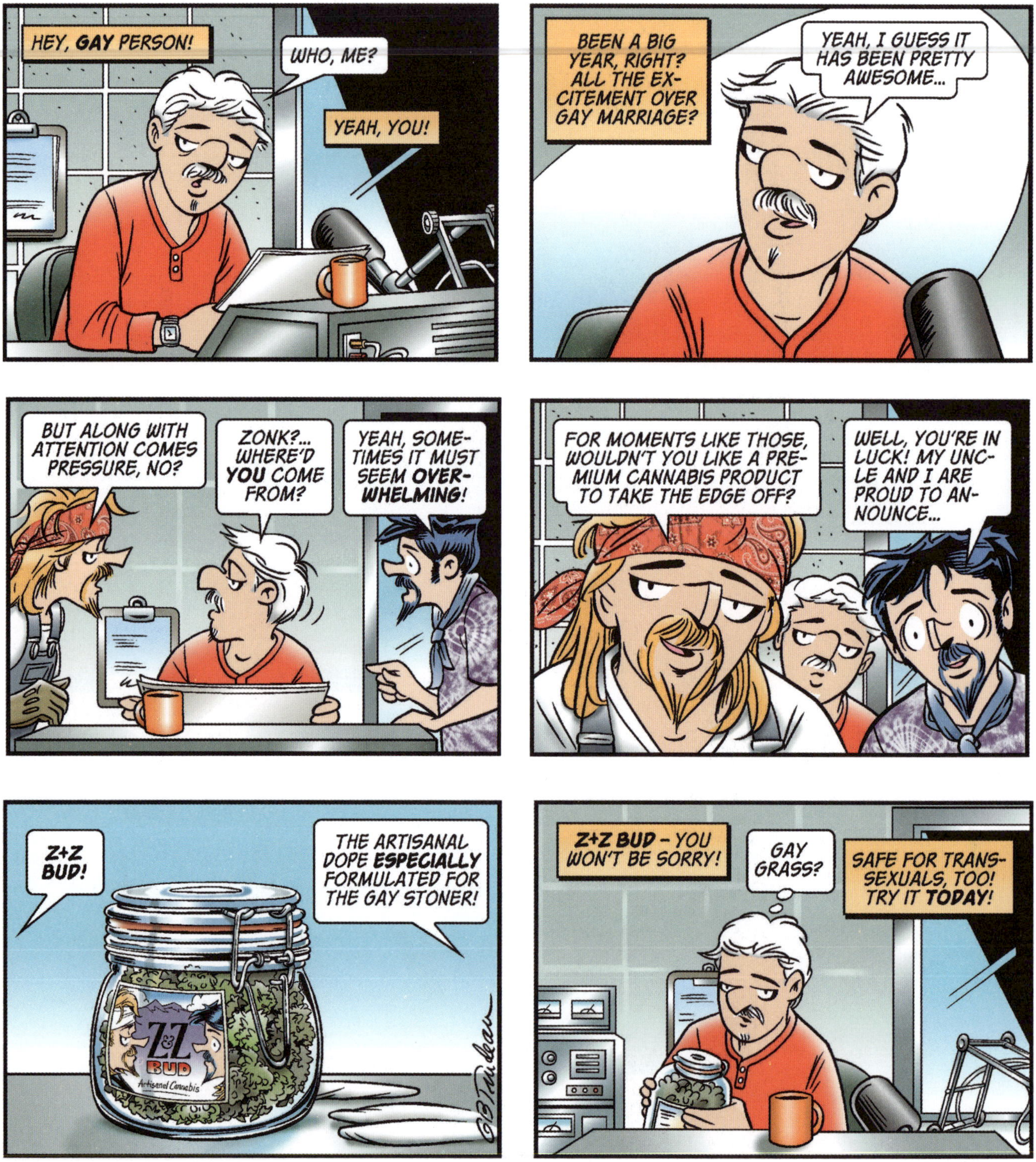
HEY, GAY PERSON!
WHO, ME?
YEAH, YOU!
BEEN A BIG YEAR, RIGHT? ALL THE EXCITEMENT OVER GAY MARRIAGE?
YEAH, I GUESS IT HAS BEEN PRETTY AWESOME...
BUT ALONG WITH ATTENTION COMES PRESSURE, NO?
ZONK?... WHERE'D YOU COME FROM?
YEAH, SOMETIMES IT MUST SEEM OVERWHELMING!
FOR MOMENTS LIKE THOSE, WOULDN'T YOU LIKE A PREMIUM CANNABIS PRODUCT TO TAKE THE EDGE OFF?
WELL, YOU'RE IN LUCK! MY UNCLE AND I ARE PROUD TO ANNOUNCE...
Z+Z BUD!
THE ARTISANAL DOPE ESPECIALLY FORMULATED FOR THE GAY STONER!
Z&Z BUD
Artisanal Cannabis
Z+Z BUD – YOU WON'T BE SORRY!
GAY GRASS?
SAFE FOR TRANSSEXUALS, TOO! TRY IT TODAY!

September 13, 2015

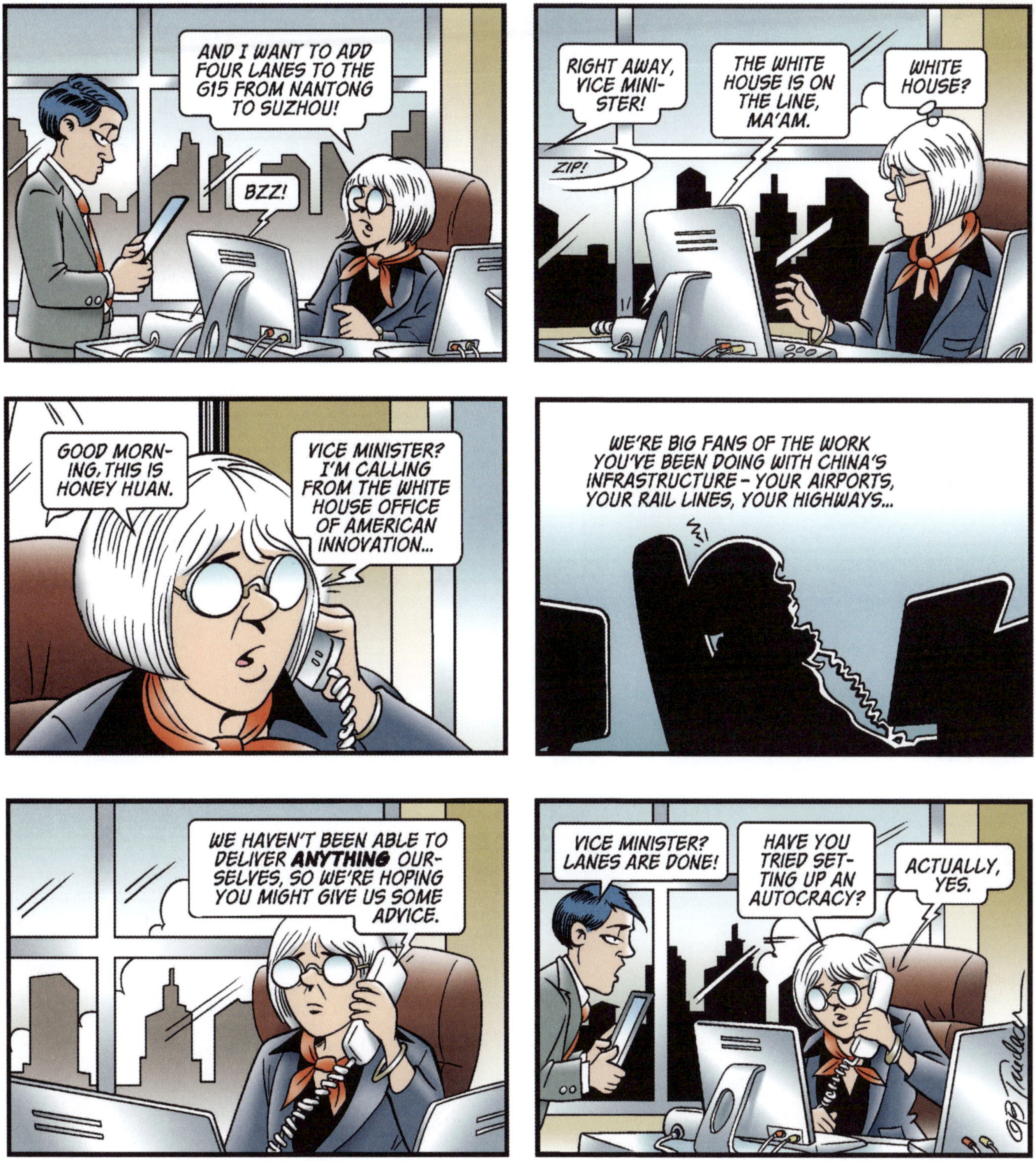
AND I WANT TO ADD FOUR LANES TO THE G15 FROM NANTONG TO SUZHOU!
BZZ!
RIGHT AWAY, VICE MINISTER!
ZIP!
THE WHITE HOUSE IS ON THE LINE, MA'AM.
WHITE HOUSE?
GOOD MORNING. THIS IS HONEY HUAN.
VICE MINISTER? I'M CALLING FROM THE WHITE HOUSE OFFICE OF AMERICAN INNOVATION...
WE'RE BIG FANS OF THE WORK YOU'VE BEEN DOING WITH CHINA'S INFRASTRUCTURE - YOUR AIRPORTS, YOUR RAIL LINES, YOUR HIGHWAYS...
WE HAVEN'T BEEN ABLE TO DELIVER **ANYTHING** OURSELVES, SO WE'RE HOPING YOU MIGHT GIVE US SOME ADVICE.
VICE MINISTER? LANES ARE DONE!
HAVE YOU TRIED SETTING UP AN AUTOCRACY?
ACTUALLY, YES.
GBTrudeau

January 28, 2018

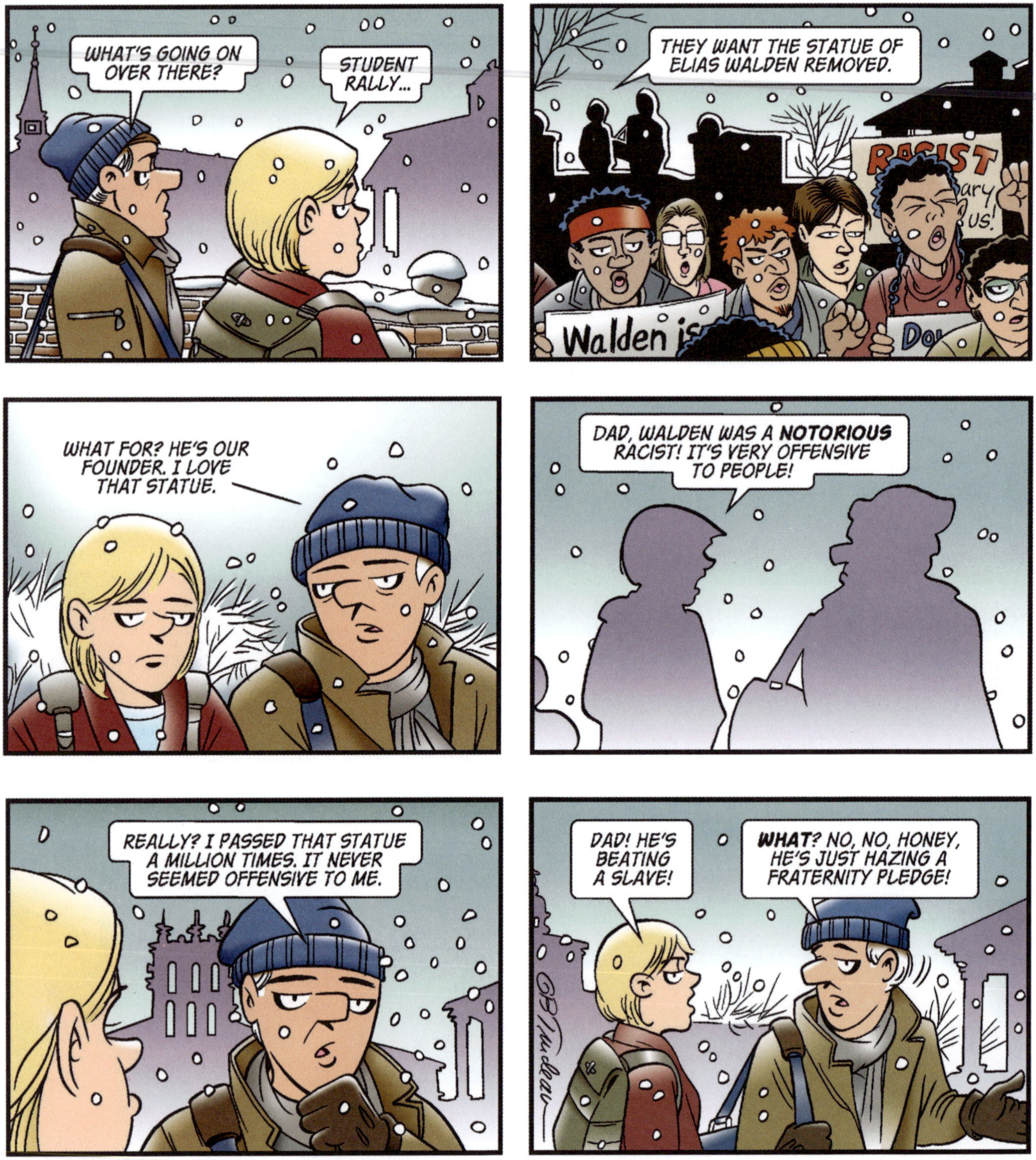
WHAT'S GOING ON OVER THERE?
STUDENT RALLY...
THEY WANT THE STATUE OF ELIAS WALDEN REMOVED.
RACIST
Walden is
WHAT FOR? HE'S OUR FOUNDER. I LOVE THAT STATUE.
DAD, WALDEN WAS A **NOTORIOUS** RACIST! IT'S VERY OFFENSIVE TO PEOPLE!
REALLY? I PASSED THAT STATUE A MILLION TIMES. IT NEVER SEEMED OFFENSIVE TO ME.
DAD! HE'S BEATING A SLAVE!
WHAT? NO, NO, HONEY, HE'S JUST HAZING A FRATERNITY PLEDGE!
©B Trudeau

January 17, 2016

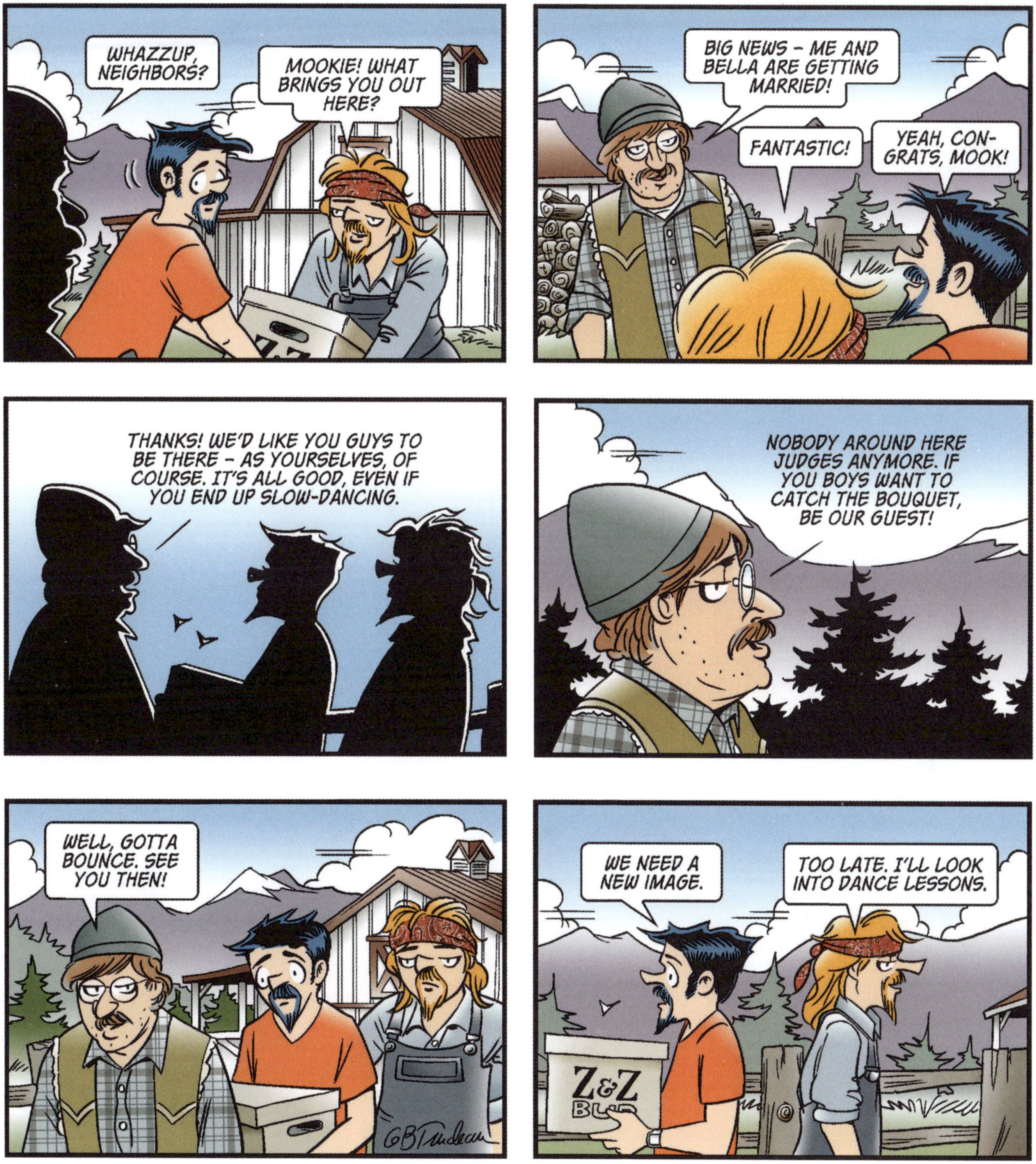
WHAZZUP, NEIGHBORS?
MOOKIE! WHAT BRINGS YOU OUT HERE?
BIG NEWS - ME AND BELLA ARE GETTING MARRIED!
FANTASTIC!
YEAH, CON-GRATS, MOOK!
THANKS! WE'D LIKE YOU GUYS TO BE THERE - AS YOURSELVES, OF COURSE. IT'S ALL GOOD, EVEN IF YOU END UP SLOW-DANCING.
NOBODY AROUND HERE JUDGES ANYMORE. IF YOU BOYS WANT TO CATCH THE BOUQUET, BE OUR GUEST!
WELL, GOTTA BOUNCE. SEE YOU THEN!
WE NEED A NEW IMAGE.
TOO LATE. I'LL LOOK INTO DANCE LESSONS.
Z&Z
GBTrudeau

May 15, 2016

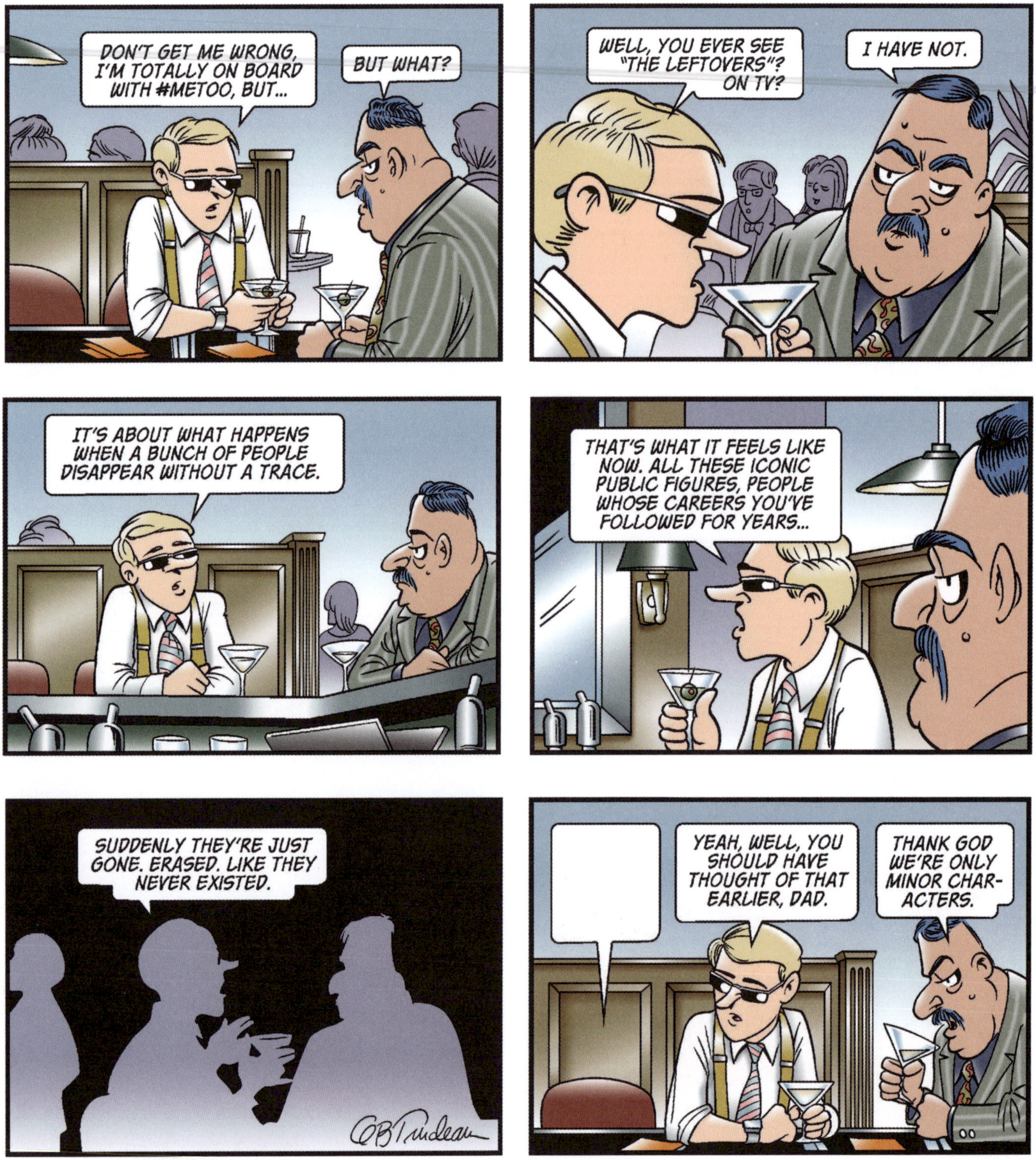
DON'T GET ME WRONG, I'M TOTALLY ON BOARD WITH #METOO, BUT...
BUT WHAT?
WELL, YOU EVER SEE "THE LEFTOVERS"? ON TV?
I HAVE NOT.
IT'S ABOUT WHAT HAPPENS WHEN A BUNCH OF PEOPLE DISAPPEAR WITHOUT A TRACE.
THAT'S WHAT IT FEELS LIKE NOW. ALL THESE ICONIC PUBLIC FIGURES, PEOPLE WHOSE CAREERS YOU'VE FOLLOWED FOR YEARS...
SUDDENLY THEY'RE JUST GONE. ERASED. LIKE THEY NEVER EXISTED.
GBTrudeau
YEAH, WELL, YOU SHOULD HAVE THOUGHT OF THAT EARLIER, DAD.
THANK GOD WE'RE ONLY MINOR CHAR-ACTERS.

February 25, 2018

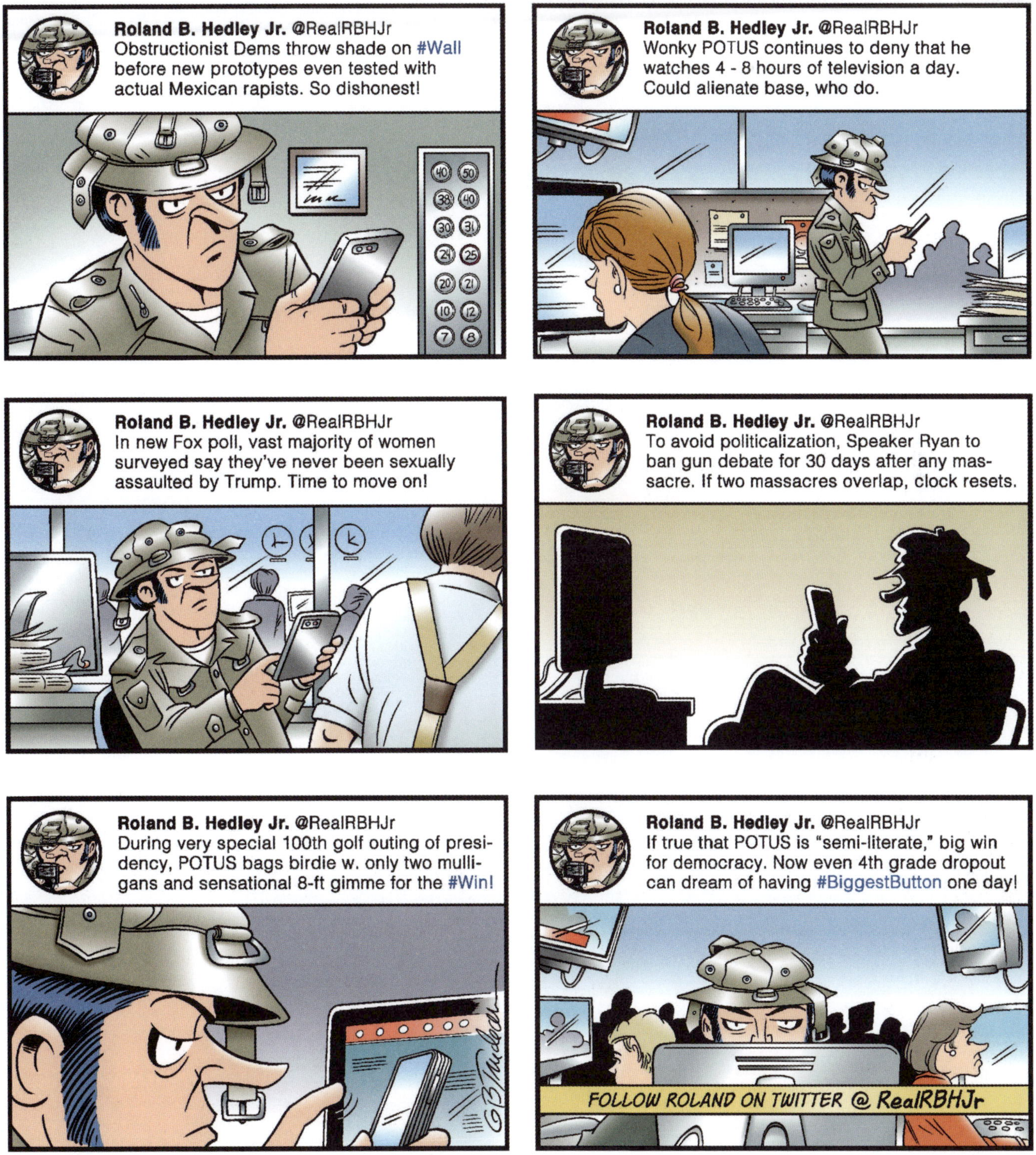
Roland B. Hedley Jr. @RealRBHJr
Obstructionist Dems throw shade on #Wall before new prototypes even tested with actual Mexican rapists. So dishonest!
Roland B. Hedley Jr. @RealRBHJr
Wonky POTUS continues to deny that he watches 4 - 8 hours of television a day. Could alienate base, who do.
Roland B. Hedley Jr. @RealRBHJr
In new Fox poll, vast majority of women surveyed say they've never been sexually assaulted by Trump. Time to move on!
Roland B. Hedley Jr. @RealRBHJr
To avoid politicalization, Speaker Ryan to ban gun debate for 30 days after any massacre. If two massacres overlap, clock resets.
Roland B. Hedley Jr. @RealRBHJr
During very special 100th golf outing of presidency, POTUS bags birdie w. only two mulligans and sensational 8-ft gimme for the #Win!
Roland B. Hedley Jr. @RealRBHJr
If true that POTUS is "semi-literate," big win for democracy. Now even 4th grade dropout can dream of having #BiggestButton one day!
FOLLOW ROLAND ON TWITTER @ RealRBHJr

February 18, 2018

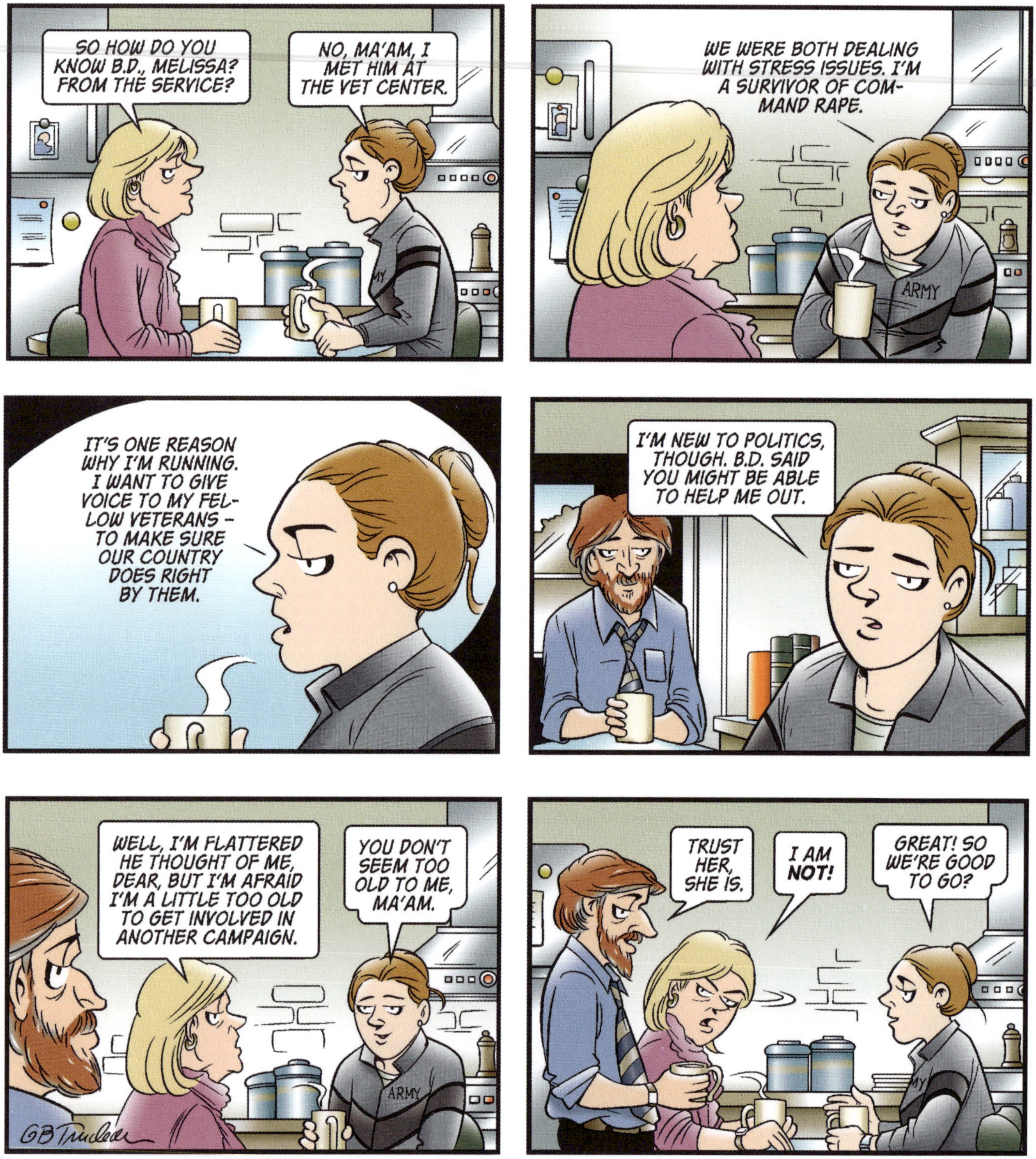
SO HOW DO YOU KNOW B.D., MELISSA? FROM THE SERVICE?
NO, MA'AM, I MET HIM AT THE VET CENTER.
WE WERE BOTH DEALING WITH STRESS ISSUES. I'M A SURVIVOR OF COM-MAND RAPE.
IT'S ONE REASON WHY I'M RUNNING. I WANT TO GIVE VOICE TO MY FEL-LOW VETERANS – TO MAKE SURE OUR COUNTRY DOES RIGHT BY THEM.
I'M NEW TO POLITICS, THOUGH. B.D. SAID YOU MIGHT BE ABLE TO HELP ME OUT.
WELL, I'M FLATTERED HE THOUGHT OF ME, DEAR, BUT I'M AFRAID I'M A LITTLE TOO OLD TO GET INVOLVED IN ANOTHER CAMPAIGN.
YOU DON'T SEEM TOO OLD TO ME, MA'AM.
TRUST HER, SHE IS.
I AM **NOT!**
GREAT! SO WE'RE GOOD TO GO?
ARMY
GB Trudeau

March 4, 2018

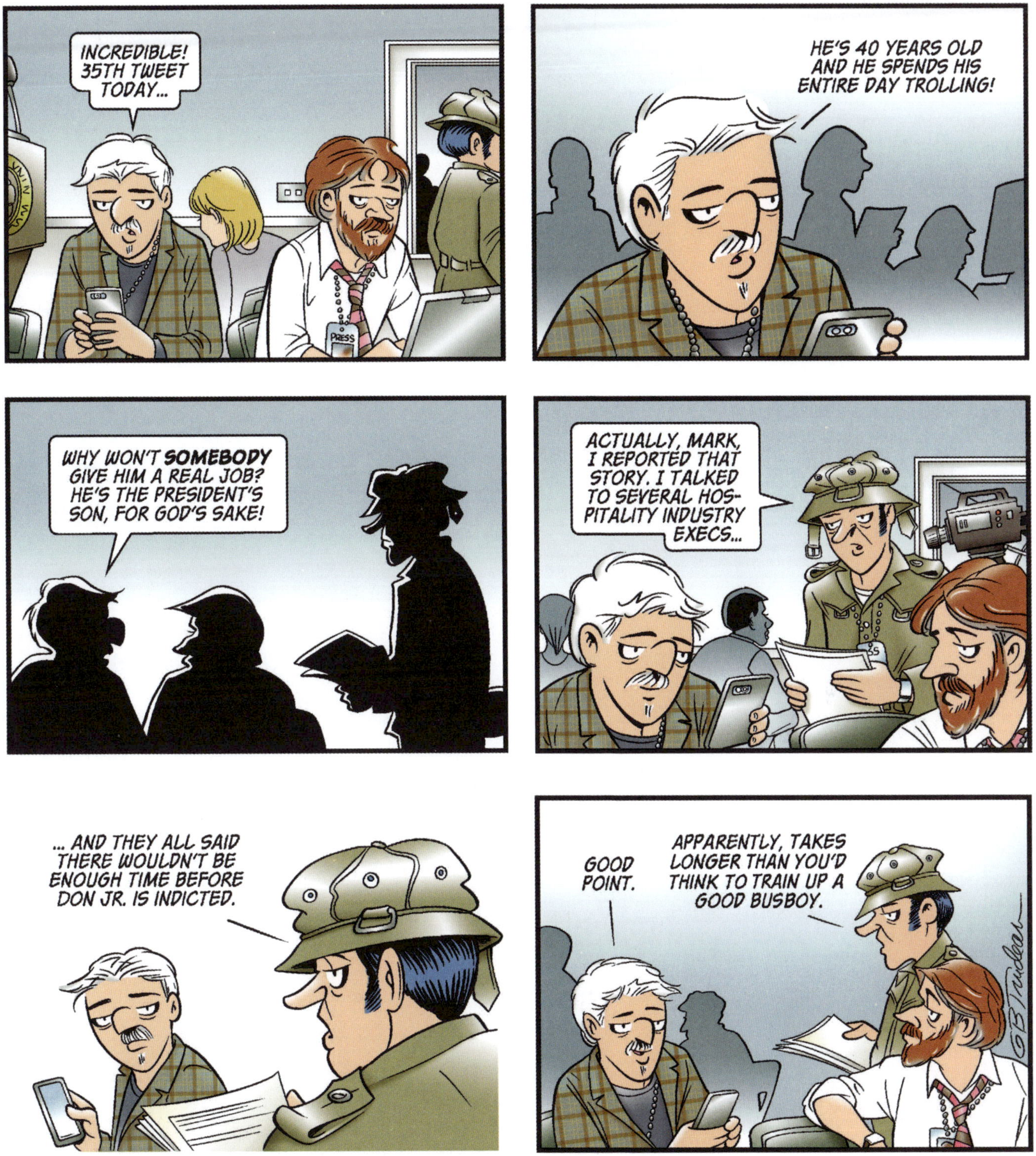
INCREDIBLE! 35TH TWEET TODAY...
PRESS
HE'S 40 YEARS OLD AND HE SPENDS HIS ENTIRE DAY TROLLING!
WHY WON'T **SOMEBODY** GIVE HIM A REAL JOB? HE'S THE PRESIDENT'S SON, FOR GOD'S SAKE!
ACTUALLY, MARK, I REPORTED THAT STORY. I TALKED TO SEVERAL HOS-PITALITY INDUSTRY EXECS...
... AND THEY ALL SAID THERE WOULDN'T BE ENOUGH TIME BEFORE DON JR. IS INDICTED.
GOOD POINT.
APPARENTLY, TAKES LONGER THAN YOU'D THINK TO TRAIN UP A GOOD BUSBOY.
GBTrudeau

March 11, 2018

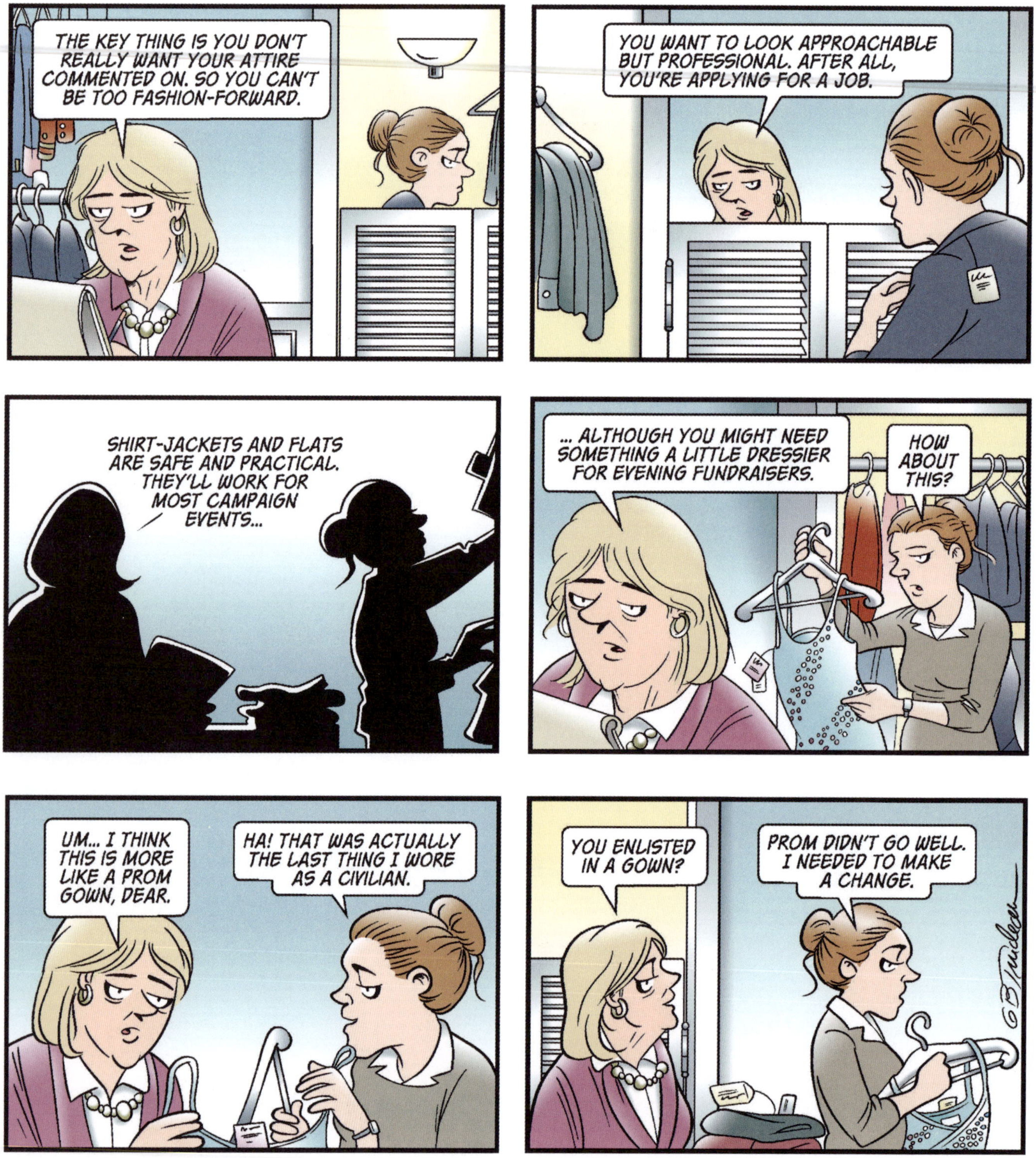
THE KEY THING IS YOU DON'T REALLY WANT YOUR ATTIRE COMMENTED ON. SO YOU CAN'T BE TOO FASHION-FORWARD.
YOU WANT TO LOOK APPROACHABLE BUT PROFESSIONAL. AFTER ALL, YOU'RE APPLYING FOR A JOB.
SHIRT-JACKETS AND FLATS ARE SAFE AND PRACTICAL. THEY'LL WORK FOR MOST CAMPAIGN EVENTS...
... ALTHOUGH YOU MIGHT NEED SOMETHING A LITTLE DRESSIER FOR EVENING FUNDRAISERS.
HOW ABOUT THIS?
UM... I THINK THIS IS MORE LIKE A PROM GOWN, DEAR.
HA! THAT WAS ACTUALLY THE LAST THING I WORE AS A CIVILIAN.
YOU ENLISTED IN A GOWN?
PROM DIDN'T GO WELL. I NEEDED TO MAKE A CHANGE.
GBTrudeau

March 18, 2018

CONTROL ROOM, "FOX AND FRIENDS."
YES, THIS IS JOHN KELLY AT THE WHITE HOUSE...
GENERAL! HOW MAY WE HELP YOU THIS MORNING?
WE'RE STILL HAVING TROUBLE WITH POTUS'S DAILY INTELLIGENCE BRIEFING...
HOW SO, SIR?
HE WON'T READ IT. NO MATTER HOW SIMPLE WE MAKE IT, HE CAN'T PROCESS IT.
IF I WERE TO SEND YOU TO-DAY'S PDB, COULD YOUR HOSTS BRIEF HIM WHILE HE'S STILL IN BED WATCH-ING TV?
IT'D BE AN HONOR, SIR!
GREAT! ALSO, COULD YOU GIVE HIM SOME LOVE FOR THIS MORNING'S TWEETS?
WE ALWAYS DO, SIR.
OH, AND REMIND HIM HE'S GOT A DENTIST APPOINTMENT.
WILL DO. WHAT TIME?
GBTrudeau

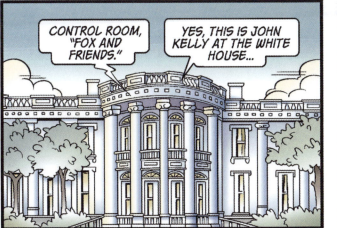

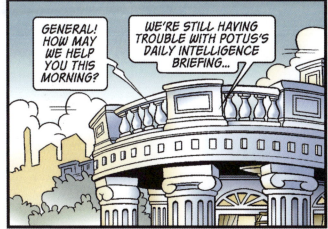

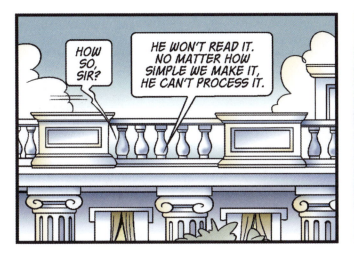

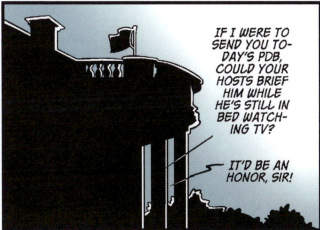

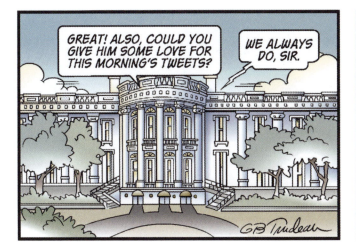

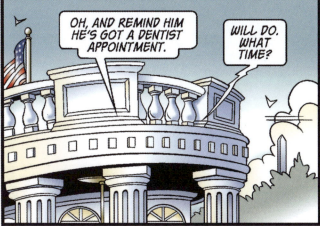

March 25, 2018

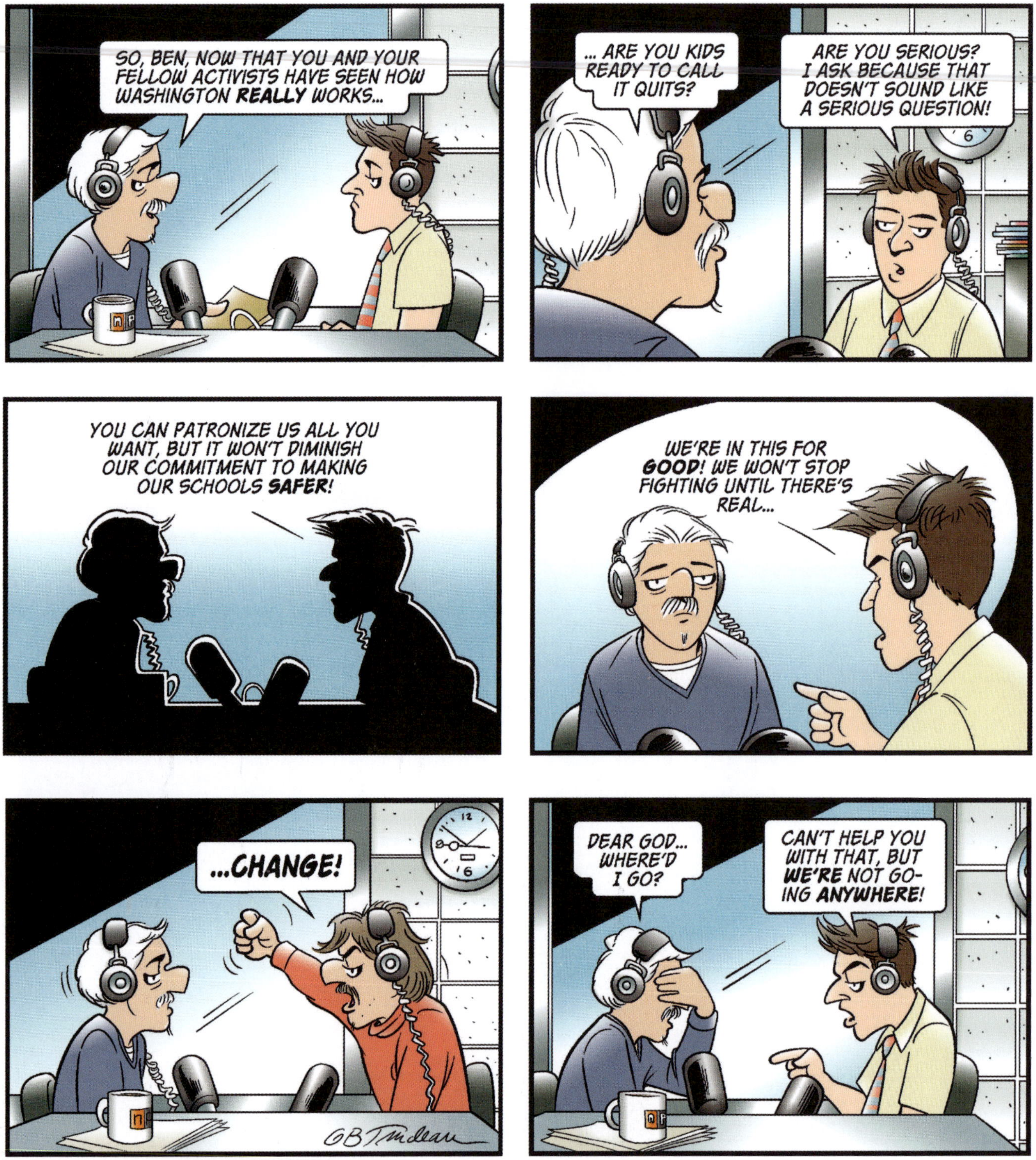
SO, BEN, NOW THAT YOU AND YOUR FELLOW ACTIVISTS HAVE SEEN HOW WASHINGTON **REALLY** WORKS...
... ARE YOU KIDS READY TO CALL IT QUITS?
ARE YOU SERIOUS? I ASK BECAUSE THAT DOESN'T SOUND LIKE A SERIOUS QUESTION!
YOU CAN PATRONIZE US ALL YOU WANT, BUT IT WON'T DIMINISH OUR COMMITMENT TO MAKING OUR SCHOOLS **SAFER**!
WE'RE IN THIS FOR **GOOD**! WE WON'T STOP FIGHTING UNTIL THERE'S REAL...
...CHANGE!
DEAR GOD... WHERE'D I GO?
CAN'T HELP YOU WITH THAT, BUT **WE'RE** NOT GOING **ANYWHERE**!
GB Trudeau

April 1, 2018

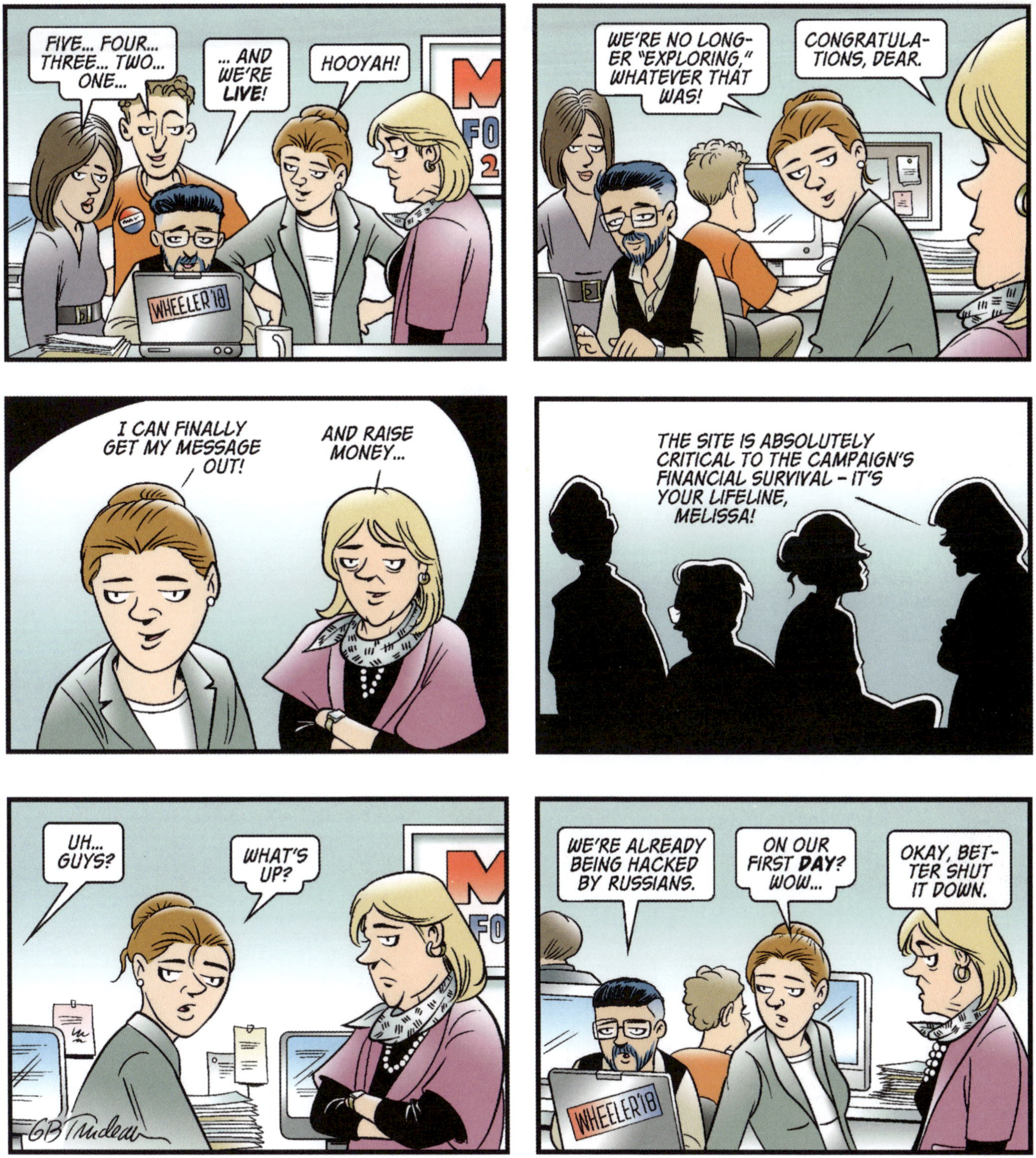
FIVE... FOUR... THREE... TWO... ONE...
... AND WE'RE **LIVE**!
HOOYAH!
WHEELER '18
WE'RE NO LONGER "EXPLORING," WHATEVER THAT WAS!
CONGRATULATIONS, DEAR.
I CAN FINALLY GET MY MESSAGE OUT!
AND RAISE MONEY...
THE SITE IS ABSOLUTELY CRITICAL TO THE CAMPAIGN'S FINANCIAL SURVIVAL – IT'S YOUR LIFELINE, MELISSA!
UH... GUYS?
WHAT'S UP?
GB Trudeau
WE'RE ALREADY BEING HACKED BY RUSSIANS.
ON OUR FIRST **DAY**? WOW...
OKAY, BETTER SHUT IT DOWN.
WHEELER '18

April 8, 2018

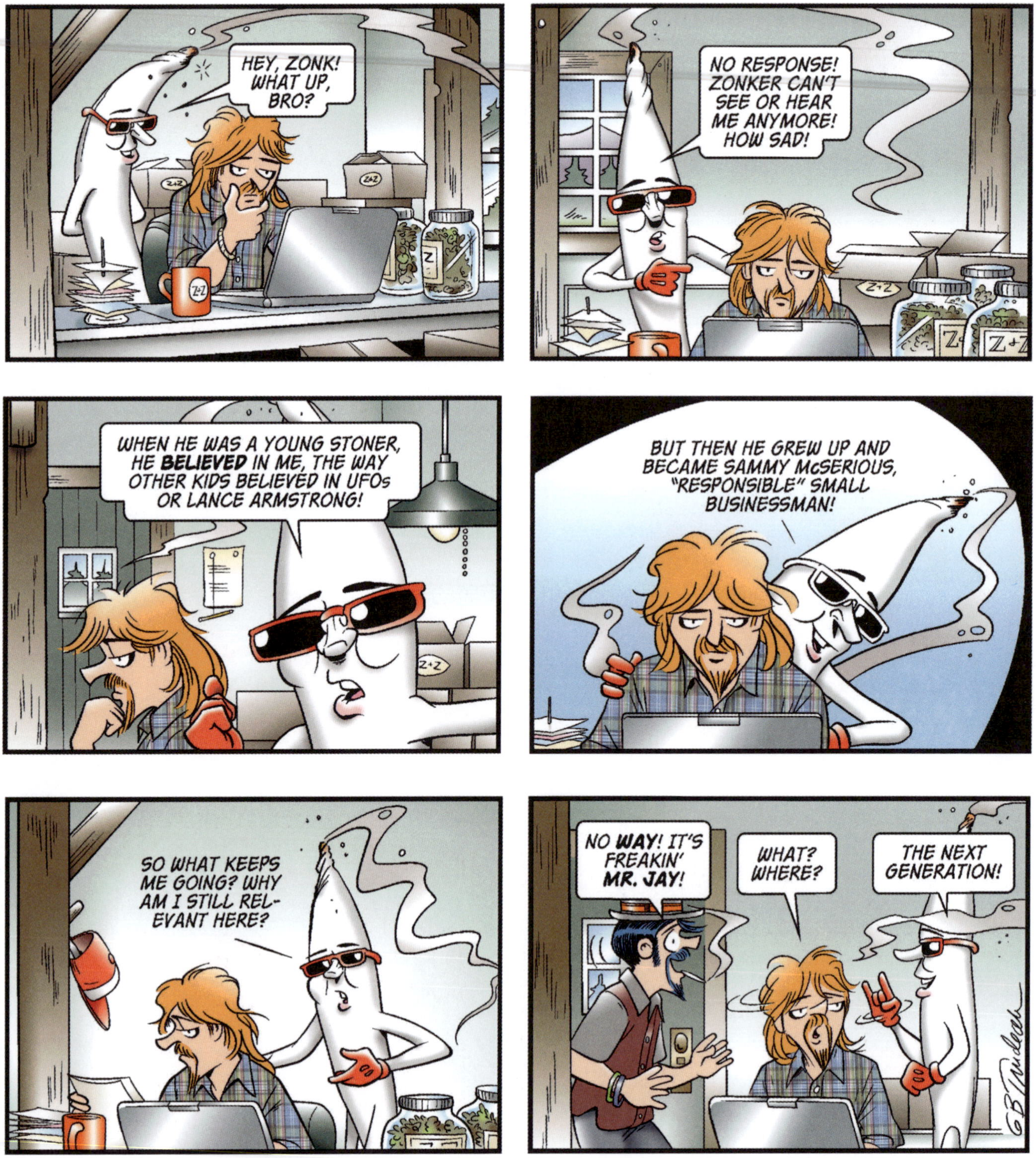
HEY, ZONK! WHAT UP, BRO?
NO RESPONSE! ZONKER CAN'T SEE OR HEAR ME ANYMORE! HOW SAD!
WHEN HE WAS A YOUNG STONER, HE **BELIEVED** IN ME, THE WAY OTHER KIDS BELIEVED IN UFOs OR LANCE ARMSTRONG!
BUT THEN HE GREW UP AND BECAME SAMMY McSERIOUS, "RESPONSIBLE" SMALL BUSINESSMAN!
SO WHAT KEEPS ME GOING? WHY AM I STILL REL-EVANT HERE?
NO **WAY**! IT'S FREAKIN' **MR. JAY**!
WHAT? WHERE?
THE NEXT GENERATION!
GBTrudeau

April 15, 2018

ONE FINAL ANNOUNCEMENT FROM THE BOARD OF ELDERS...

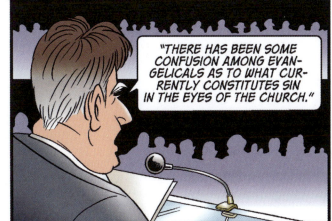

"THERE HAS BEEN SOME CONFUSION AMONG EVANGELICALS AS TO WHAT CURRENTLY CONSTITUTES SIN IN THE EYES OF THE CHURCH."

"SO TO CLARIFY, WE NOW CONDONE THE FOLLOWING CONDUCT: LEWDNESS, VULGARITY, PROFANITY, ADULTERY AND SEXUAL ASSAULT."

"EXEMPTIONS TO CHRISTIAN VALUES ALSO INCLUDE LYING, BULLYING, CHEATING, BOASTING, GREED, CRUELTY, WRATH, ENVY, SLOTH, GLUTTONY AND PRIDE. OTHERS TBA."

"LASTLY, WE'RE WILLING TO OVERLOOK BIBLICAL ILLITERACY, CHURCH NON-ATTENDANCE, AND NO CREDIBLE SIGN OF FAITH."

LOVIN' THE LOWER BAR, PASTOR!

ME, TOO. I FEEL LIKE A FREAKIN' SAINT NOW!

ENJOY.

April 22, 2018

125

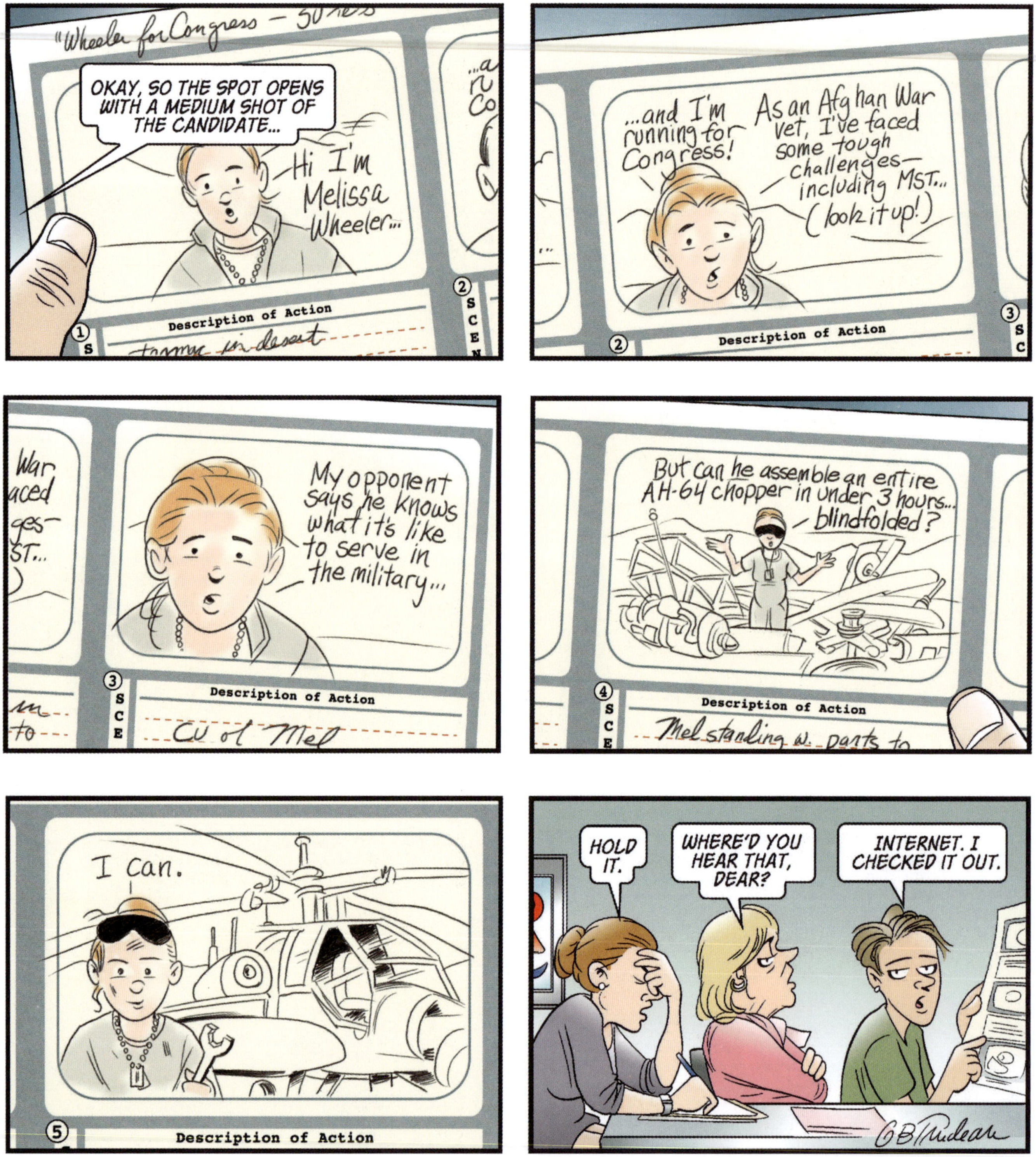
"Wheeler for Congress
OKAY, SO THE SPOT OPENS WITH A MEDIUM SHOT OF THE CANDIDATE...
Hi I'm Melissa Wheeler...
Description of Action
...and I'm running for Congress!
As an Afghan War vet, I've faced some tough challenges— including MST... (look it up!)
Description of Action
My opponent says he knows what it's like to serve in the military...
Description of Action
CU of Mel
But can he assemble an entire AH-64 chopper in under 3 hours... blindfolded?
Description of Action
I can.
Description of Action
HOLD IT.
WHERE'D YOU HEAR THAT, DEAR?
INTERNET. I CHECKED IT OUT.
GBTrudeau

April 29, 2018

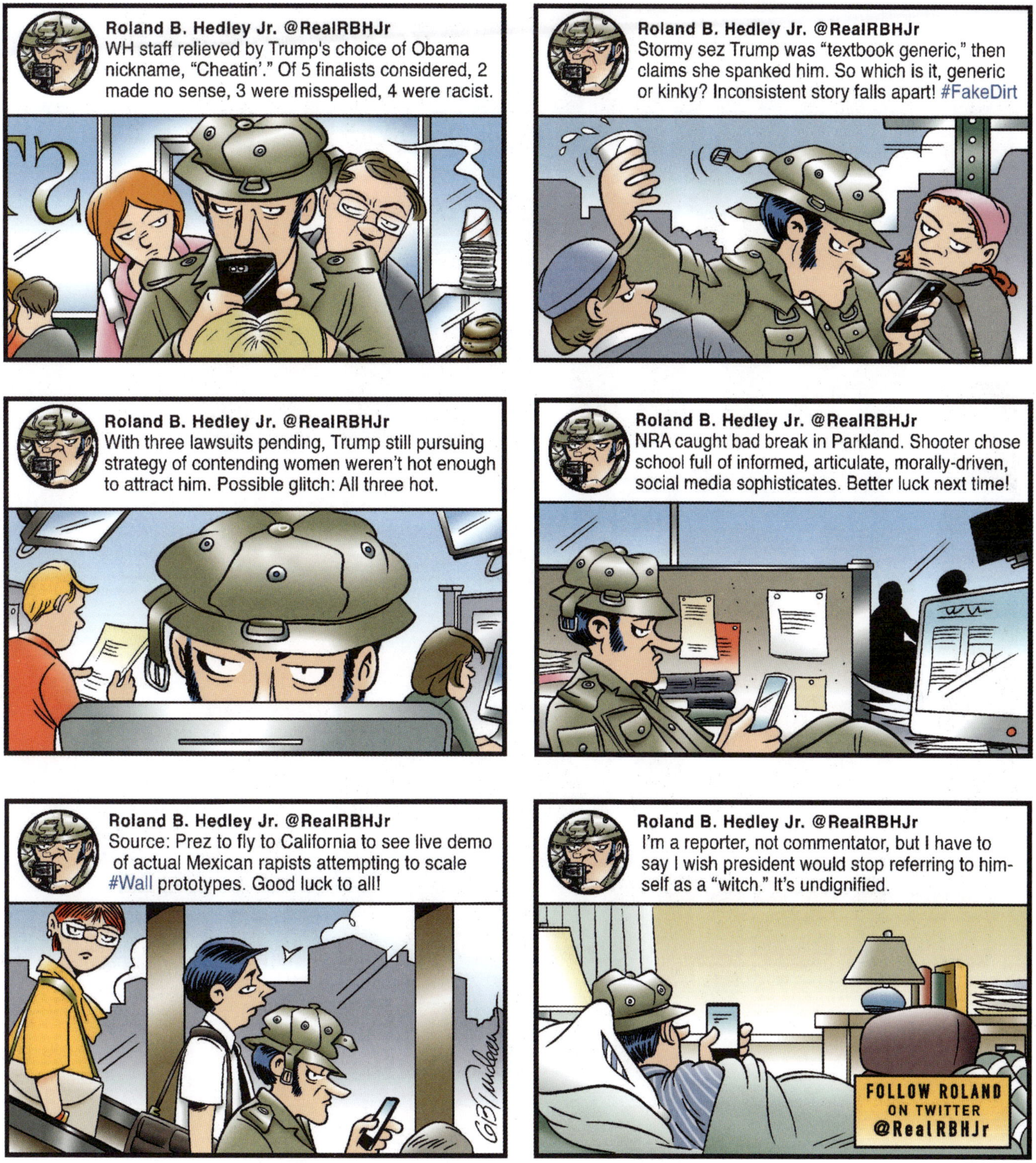
Roland B. Hedley Jr. @RealRBHJr
WH staff relieved by Trump's choice of Obama nickname, "Cheatin'." Of 5 finalists considered, 2 made no sense, 3 were misspelled, 4 were racist.
Roland B. Hedley Jr. @RealRBHJr
Stormy sez Trump was "textbook generic," then claims she spanked him. So which is it, generic or kinky? Inconsistent story falls apart! #FakeDirt
Roland B. Hedley Jr. @RealRBHJr
With three lawsuits pending, Trump still pursuing strategy of contending women weren't hot enough to attract him. Possible glitch: All three hot.
Roland B. Hedley Jr. @RealRBHJr
NRA caught bad break in Parkland. Shooter chose school full of informed, articulate, morally-driven, social media sophisticates. Better luck next time!
Roland B. Hedley Jr. @RealRBHJr
Source: Prez to fly to California to see live demo of actual Mexican rapists attempting to scale #Wall prototypes. Good luck to all!
Roland B. Hedley Jr. @RealRBHJr
I'm a reporter, not commentator, but I have to say I wish president would stop referring to himself as a "witch." It's undignified.
FOLLOW ROLAND
ON TWITTER
@RealRBHJr

May 6, 2018

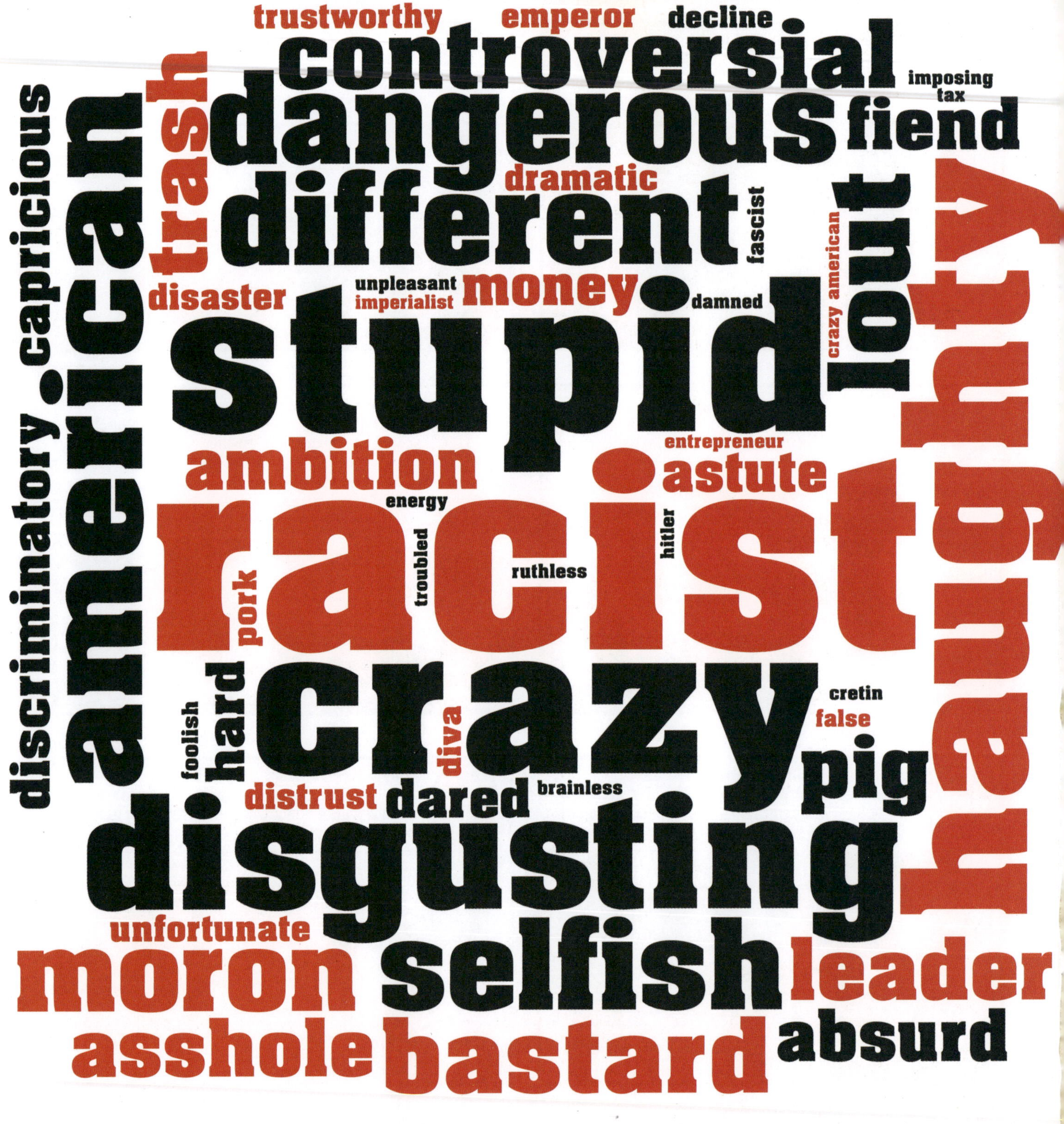
trustworthy
emperor
decline
controversial
imposing tax
trash
dangerous
fiend
capricious
amerirican
dramatic
different
fascist
lout
haughty
crazy american
unpleasant
imperialist
money
damned
disaster
stupid
discriminatory
entrepreneur
ambition
astute
energy
racist
hitler
troubled
ruthless
pork
crazy
hard
foolish
diva
cretin
false
pig
brainless
distrust
dared
disgusting
unfortunate
moron
selfish
leader
asshole
bastard
absurd

Poll (Mexico): "What is the one word you would use to describe President Trump?"